"In an era of mass incarceration, the American criminal justice system has become an unforgiving, heartbreaking place where optimism goes to die. *Redemption and Restoration* offers an inspiring alternative that focuses on restoring victims, protecting the community, and providing offenders with opportunity to change. This is a timely and important book that embraces the power of hope and allows for the possibility of reconciliation and justice. One finishes the book with a sense of urgency. We can't wait any longer to end this war against ourselves and restore trust and hope to our system of justice."

—Jim Wyda, Federal Public Defender for Maryland

"As a Catholic theologian with previous experience in law enforcement (corrections and policing) and youth ministry, I have seen first-hand how crime physically and emotionally harms persons, families, and communities. It also wounds, morally if not physically, the perpetrator and detrimentally impacts his or her family. Professionals working in the criminal justice system too— police, correctional officers, judges, and more—are deeply affected by what they do. Much of this is worsened when the focus of criminal justice is solely on retribution, with a state vs. offenders approach wherein authorities merely mete out punishment to criminals. The contributors to this much-needed volume propose that Catholics and others should both broaden and deepen our understanding of justice, integrating its varied forms (retributive justice, commutative justice, distributive justice, and social justice) so as to include and be reoriented toward restorative justice. Indeed, to borrow an adjective from recent popes, including Pope Francis, I would say this important endeavor exemplifies an *integral* justice that will help readers to promote and practice a just peace for all who are affected by crime in their communities."

—Tobias Winright
Maeder Endowed Chair of Health Care Ethics and Associate
Professor of Theological Ethics, Saint Louis University

"It is vitally important that we cultivate compassion and mercy in our relationships with one another and with those on the margins. We must stand with our brothers and sisters who know the deep wounds of crime and incarceration and who, too often, are disregarded and forgotten in our society. Restorative justice shows us a path toward true kinship, and this book offers great wisdom for how the Church can be a beacon for reconciliation, healing, and hope in a hurting world."

—Fr. Greg Boyle, SJ
Founder and Director of Homeboy Industries, author of *Tattoos on the Heart: The Power of Boundless Compassion* and *Barking to the Choir: The Power of Radical Kinship*

Redemption and Restoration

A Catholic Perspective on Restorative Justice

Edited by

Trudy D. Conway, David Matzko McCarthy,
and Vicki Schieber

LITURGICAL PRESS
Collegeville, Minnesota

www.litpress.org

1   2   3   4   5   6   7   8   9

Library of Congress Cataloging-in-Publication Data

Names: Conway, Trudy D., editor. | McCarthy, David Matzko, editor. | Schieber, Vicki, editor.
Title: Redemption and restoration : a Catholic perspective on restorative justice / edited by Trudy D. Conway, David Matzko McCarthy, and Vicki Schieber.
Description: Collegeville, Minnesota : Liturgical Press, [2017]
Identifiers: LCCN 2017037651 (print) | LCCN 2017020279 (ebook) | ISBN 9780814645864 (ebook) | ISBN 9780814645611
Subjects: LCSH: Christianity and justice. | Restorative justice—Religious aspects—Christianity. | Catholic Church—Doctrines.
Classification: LCC BR115.J8 (print) | LCC BR115.J8 R43 2017 (ebook) | DDC 241/.622—dc23
LC record available at https://lccn.loc.gov/2017037651

This book is dedicated to Shannon Schieber, Ruth Pelke, Susie Jaeger, Julie Welch, and all other crime victims whose goodness motivated others to do good in their names. May they continue to inspire us to promote restorative justice in our local communities and society.

Contents

Foreword

The Catholic Church has a long history of engagement with restorative justice. In fact, in the early 1980s, the first group to which I (Howard) presented the overall concept was a national gathering of Catholic clergy engaged in prison ministry. Their deep engagement with the idea encouraged me to continue developing it, leading eventually to my book, *Changing Lenses: A New Focus for Crime and Justice.* In the following years, the Catholic community continued to be engaged through individual encounter and intentional ministry. This text highlights such transformational stories as testament to theological interpretation and a call for new engagement of the church at large.

I (Caitlin) was involved in poverty-related service work through the church from an early age. Over time, I grew increasingly concerned about the role that crime and incarceration played in perpetuating cycles of poverty. Restorative justice offered not only an alternative method of responding to violence but also a new lens for addressing instances of harm and conflict in the communities I served. Both the theories and applications provided me with concrete ways to live the tenets of Catholic social teaching and engage in intentional Christian relationship.

Early on, restorative justice was conceived as an alternative response to punitive punishment in the US criminal legal system. It calls for a new paradigm of viewing crime, not as laws broken, but as harm to human dignity and relationship. This harm creates needs and obligations for all those impacted. Today, restorative justice is a vibrant and growing movement that also seeks to transform systems of harm and conflict to include truth and reconciliation in postwar scenarios and nationwide racial healing efforts. Educational systems are increasingly adopting forms of restorative justice to address conflicts and wrongdoing.

The concept of justice underlying the criminal justice system is essentially individualistic and rights-based. Restorative justice, on the other hand, is an interrelational understanding of wrongdoing and justice that emphasizes the responsibilities inherent in relationships. Thus the principles of restorative justice call us to examine interpersonal relationships and hold ourselves and one another to a higher standard of accountability and reconciliation. The intentional engagement of restorative approaches within familiar, supportive settings such as parishes and schools provide us with spaces to rehearse this way of life so that we may better live it out in our families, friendships, workplaces, and communities.

Much of this book is directly applicable to those connected to the criminal legal system by profession, ministry, or personal experience. Its themes will also resonate with Catholics who are concerned about timely issues of mass incarceration, community violence, and racial justice in America. For readers who are new to restorative justice, this text offers a broad overview of its history, theology, and applications. For those who are already familiar, here you will find a nuanced interpretation from the Catholic perspective.

Violence and harm, of course, do not happen in a vacuum. The field of neuroscience is telling us more and more about the physiological and psychosocial impacts of trauma. In its cyclical nature, those impacted by violence (victim, offender, or community) are at higher risk of acting in ways that harm themselves or others. Restorative practices interrupt these cycles, allowing individuals to find healing and live more fully as God calls us to be in loving relationship with him, ourselves, and one another. May the wisdom offered in this book compel the Catholic community to live this sacred way of love in the world.

Caitlin Morneau
Howard Zehr

Acknowledgments

Restorative justice views persons as existing in a network of relationships. This book is a testament to the belief that we exist in such networks and thrive when we appreciate and foster supportive relationships. We three editors appreciate that Mount St. Mary's University (in Emmitsburg, Maryland) values community and fosters collaborative initiatives. When we were approached by the Catholic Mobilizing Network (CMN) about the possibility of working on a book about Catholic teaching on the death penalty, our response was enthusiastic. First of all, how could anyone be anything but enthusiastic about supporting the work of an organization initiated by Sr. Helen Prejean? Secondly, we knew this would give us an opportunity to draw faculty from a range of disciplines into dialogue about an important social justice issue. Our campus had been sponsoring lectures, conferences, projects, and courses on the death penalty for over a decade. We knew that in working together on a book about the death penalty, we would learn much from each other. We also welcomed the opportunity to contribute to the national discussion of the death penalty. CMN was very pleased when our book, *Where Justice and Mercy Meet*, won two national awards. They also appreciated how much we enjoyed working together on a collaborative book project. We were not surprised when Karen Clifton, the CMN director, asked us to work on a second book about restorative justice.

This second project brought us to focus on our own disciplinary research and to gather to discuss readings on restorative justice. We also invited to campus a number of speakers who were restorative justice practitioners, drawing into our discussions other faculty, students, and administrators. In 2014 CMN sponsored a conference on restorative justice at Catholic University at which the chapter authors from our campus presented and attended keynote and workshop sessions with off-campus chapter authors and prominent practitioners of restorative justice. We also met with persons whose lives had been positively affected by the restorative justice programs described in this book. Our commitment to working to promote restorative justice in our communities and society has been deepened by exposure to so many persons whose lives are a testimony to the transformative power of restorative justice.

We are grateful for what we learned while working on this project. During this time, we have witnessed our country grappling with many issues centered on justice. Discussions about the need for criminal justice and prison reforms finally drew the attention of members of Congress and built support for reform efforts across political parties. Justice concerns, long present beneath the surface, boiled up into passionate expression in national and local discussions. Our nation witnessed protests, marches, and even riots focused on criminal justice concerns and a range of related justice issues tied to social and economic conditions, especially as they bear upon our inner cities. Our local communities and nation as a whole have been drawn into important discussions of justice. We welcomed the opportunity to reflect on justice at this time in our nation. We hope that our book's consideration of restorative justice contributes to the discussions of justice that will continue in our society in the future.

This book, as was the case with the death penalty book, was made possible through the collaborative work of a theologian, a philosopher, and a death penalty activist who was a sociology professor and business professional. As we worked on the book, our journeys headed in new, at times uncertain, directions. One of us retired and began an entirely new kind of service commitment. Another became an associate provost, assuming added responsibilities and leadership opportunities. The third extended a deeply personal restorative justice journey, as she commenced a murder victim family member-offender dialogue with the man who had murdered her daughter. We worked on this project as we jostled the responsibilities of busy and full lives devoted to our families and our Mount community. It was a pleasure to work with our colleagues, two former students, and invited external authors on these chapters. We valued the enthusiasm, guidance, and creative suggestions of the CMN staff. As always, we appreciated the support of our departments and their two excellent secretaries, Katie Soter and Gloria Balsley.

The virtue of hope surfaces frequently in the following chapters. Dorothy Day's emphasis on "hopeful perseverance" and the patience of laying one brick at a time defines the commitment of persons involved in restorative justice initiatives. Working on this book made us all too aware of all the work that needs to be done. The witness of so many individuals, families, community organizers and ministers, and professionals in our justice system—who sustain their commitment to restorative justice in the most difficult circumstances—has inspired us to seek out ways that we can join their efforts. We have seen the creative efforts of CMN in educating Catholic communities across our country about the church's commitment to restorative justice. At our university, we now look forward to creatively designing restorative justice programming for aspects of our campus life. We hope for the same regarding our readers—that each of you will consider how you can incorporate what you read in these chapters into your own local communities. Much work remains to be done. May we each have the "hopeful perseverance" that is so needed.

Vicki Schieber, Trudy D. Conway,
and David Matzko McCarthy
Editors

Catholic Mobilizing Network (CMN) is the national, Catholic organization working to end the death penalty and promote restorative justice. Working in close collaboration with the United States Conference of Catholic Bishops (USCCB) and living the mission of the Congregation of St. Joseph, CMN proclaims the Church's pro-life teaching and prepares Catholics through education, advocacy, and prayer. The organization seeks to advance the Church's prophetic message of responsibility, rehabilitation, and restoration in criminal justice and other incidents of harm. Education and advocacy materials such as presentations, short videos, workshop facilitator guides, state-specific fact sheets, prayer cards, parish bulletin inserts, and more are available at www.catholicsmobilizing.org.

Contributors

Friends of Mount St. Mary's University

Kirk Blackard is a retired lawyer and business executive. He is the chairman of the board of Bridges To Life, a Texas-based restorative justice prison ministry that has graduated over thirty-three thousand incarcerated individuals in over eighty facilities in Texas and other states. Kirk is author of *Restoring Peace*, the centerpiece of the BTL curriculum, as well as several other books relating to restorative justice in prisons.

Karen Clifton is the executive director of Catholic Mobilizing Network (CMN), whose mission is to educate and prepare Catholics for informed involvement in the public debate to end the death penalty and promote restorative justice. She has worked with and coordinated restorative programs within the framework of the church for several decades.

Lydia Cocom, at the time of writing her chapter, was the director of programs for Catholic Mobilizing Network (CMN) and currently is senior program assistant at the Fund for Global Human Rights.

Janine Geske is a retired Milwaukee Circuit Court judge, Wisconsin Supreme Court justice, and distinguished professor at Marquette University Law School, where she founded its Restorative Justice Initiative, providing restorative processes and training law students. She also lectures internationally.

Mount St. Mary's University

Richard Buck is a professor of philosophy. His research and writing are in the areas of ethics, political philosophy, philosophy of law, and Jewish philosophy. He regularly teaches courses in political philosophy, philosophy of law, and the core curriculum.

Sr. Mary Katherine Birge, SSJ, is a sister of St. Joseph of Springfield, Massachusetts, and a professor of theology. Her areas of research include the Synoptic Gospels, Pauline literature, and the Catholic epistles. She teaches in the Mount's core curriculum and a sequence of Scripture courses for theology majors.

Alejandro Cañadas is a professor of economics. He teaches courses in corporate finance, financial analysis, applied economic analysis, and ethics in business on the undergraduate and graduate levels. His research and writing are in the areas of economic theology, behavioral finance, inequality and economic growth, and the moral dimensions of financial markets.

David Cloutier, at the time of writing his chapter, was a professor of theology at Mount St. Mary's University and currently is a professor of theology at The Catholic University of America in Washington, DC. He is the author of *Walking God's Earth: The Environment and Catholic Faith* (Liturgical Press).

William J. Collinge is professor emeritus of theology and philosophy at Mount St. Mary's. Now semiretired, he has taught a broad range of courses in theology, philosophy, and religious studies, with a recent focus on Catholic social teaching. He is the author of *Historical Dictionary of Catholicism*, the director of research and publications of the College Theology Society, and the secretary of the Interfaith Center for Peace and Justice, Gettysburg, Pennsylvania.

Trudy D. Conway is professor emerita of philosophy. Before retiring, she taught courses in the core curriculum, and on contemporary philosophy, virtue ethics, the death penalty, and intercultural dialogue. Her areas of research and writing are contemporary philosophy, ethics, intercultural dialogue, and the death penalty. She is currently involved in service at *Manos Unidas*, a Hispanic outreach program in Gettysburg, Pennsylvania.

Rev. James M. Donohue, CR, is a Resurrectionist priest and a professor of theology. He is the vicar provincial of his Resurrectionist community that is based in Ontario, Canada. His research and writing focuses on the rites for the sick, the dying, and the deceased. He teaches ministry and pastoral education courses, as well as courses in the core curriculum. Father Jim presides and preaches at St. Bernadette Parish in Severn, Maryland.

Kelsey Kierce is a Mount graduate of the class of 2016 and is currently working as a fourth-grade teacher in York, Pennsylvania.

David Matzko McCarthy is the associate provost and former Fr. James M. Forker Professor of Catholic Social Teaching. He writes in the areas of moral theology and Catholic social ethics.

Vicki Schieber has cotaught courses on the death penalty at the Mount. She has been actively involved in the death penalty abolition movement since the murder of her daughter Shannon in 1998. In the last nineteen years she has worked in her daughter's honor in six states to pass repeal bills in their state legislatures, and hopes to continue her efforts until the death penalty is finally repealed in the United States.

Teressa Schuetz is a Mount graduate of the class of 2016 and is currently working as a third-grade teacher in Frederick County, Maryland.

Timothy W. Wolfe is a professor of sociology and criminal justice. He teaches a wide variety of sociology, criminal justice, and human services courses. His research and writing focuses on race and the criminal justice system, as well as the sociology of black music. He is an activist and professional musician.

Part I

Our Criminal Justice System

Chapter 1

Justice

Editors

Jane came home one day after work to find that her kitchen window had been broken. A burglar had come through the window, rummaged through the house, and been especially destructive to Jane's bedroom. She found that her jewelry had been stolen; particularly painful was the loss of her grandmother's wedding ring. Jane had a dog camera in the house, and, by using the playback feature, she was able to identify her nineteen-year-old neighbor. The young woman was arrested, and the stolen property recovered. The teenager pleaded guilty, received two years' probation, was obliged to enter a residential drug treatment, and, once released, was required to stay drug free and employed. Still, some matters were unresolved for Jane: the damage to her house, the personal violation and desecration of her home, and the rupture in her relationship with her long-time neighbors.[1]

Jane, the offender, and her parents participated in a restorative justice program. During a lengthy meeting, Jane explained that she felt "trampled on and violated," and to make matters worse, by "someone who I babysat for and sang happy birthday to for the last 15 years," someone she thought

---

[1] Lorenn Walker, "Restorative Justice: Definition and Purpose," in *Restorative Justice Today: Practical Applications*, ed. Katherine S. van Wormer and Lorenn Walker, 3–4 (Los Angeles: Sage Publications, 2013). Walker notes that Jane's story is "loosely based on real incidents" (4).

"would protect my house."[2] The young woman expressed her feelings of guilt, shame, and remorse. Her parents conveyed their own sense of guilt and regret—that Jane had been betrayed, that through their failures as parents they had contributed to their daughter's drug addiction and personal decline. The young woman pledged to pay for the cost of damages to Jane's house and to set out on a better, drug-free path. The effects of the meeting were salutary. But Jane's anxiety would still linger. The process of restorative justice, however, did open a route to personal restoration and a renewal of her relationship with the young woman and her parents.

Jane's story, the crime of neighbor against neighbor, is a common one; becoming more and more frequent is the turn to restorative justice for a real resolution to the suffering and harm caused by crime. As you will find throughout this book, restorative justice attends first of all to the injuries experienced by victims and the fractures created within communities. In this chapter on justice as a general term, however, we will focus specifically on the difference it makes that Jane knows well the person who has harmed her and violated her home. Because Jane knows the offender, her suffering is, in a sense, increased. She has been betrayed. Taken from her has been not only her property but also relationships she thought that she could trust and depend on as well as a sense of home and neighborhood as a safe place—as her place. The personal nature of the crime increases the pain of loss, but it seems that interpersonal loss also encourages a desire for restoration with the young woman and her family. Jane sees the young woman not only as a drug-addicted thief but also as a teenager who has lost her way, as a neighbor whom she has learned to love.

Jane's story introduces important questions for this chapter on justice. Jane has a relationship with the young woman and her family. Does this relationship make the process subsequent to the crime and its outcome more or less just? Do relationships cloud justice or clarify it? Is justice fundamentally impersonal or personal? Restorative justice is based on the belief that justice depends upon roles and relationships within community. Indeed, the process of restorative justice is directed to restoring persons, calling offenders to responsibility to others and community, and bringing together people who have been estranged. In this chapter, we will consider this question: Is such a person-centered and relationship-based process justice at all?

---

[2] Walker, "Restorative Justice," 4.

The Fabric of Human Life

David Cloutier

Justice is like oxygen: we might not be able to see it, but in fact we rely on it at every moment for our survival. More precisely, justice is like the oxygen needed for community life, and without community life, we would not only be unhappy (who wants to be lonely or constantly suspicious of others?) but we would also quickly face threats to our survival, from other humans, from nature, or from our sheer weakness in being able to provide basic material needs for ourselves. In short, it would be almost unthinkable to imagine human communities without an idea of justice.

But what exactly is justice? Where does it come from? And how do we get it wrong? Even if we see that justice is necessary for life, we are also likely to see that people are constantly disagreeing about it. And this disagreement is not new: Great thinkers in Western civilization have carried on competing arguments about justice for thousands of years, and some have even contended that all these disagreements show that justice is really an illusion, a cover-up, a verbal manipulation of others to get them to behave the way we want them to behave. There is no real "justice," these people say; there is just the use of different, self-serving claims about justice in a battle for power.

In this essay, I'll explain some of the basic ideas that we need to get straight in order to have clear and meaningful conversations about justice. I'll start by identifying a basic way of thinking about what justice is in human relationships; it is what people deserve. I'll then ask some deeper questions about how we work out our mental pictures of how human relationships should be and who deserves what. Finally, I'll look at some common errors that people make when trying to sort out questions of justice. With all these ideas in mind, the reader will be ready to analyze more closely the questions of this book on a particular sort of justice, called restorative justice.

Justice: What We Deserve

I mentioned before that some people think the whole idea of justice is an illusion. People will say, "It's just a dog-eat-dog world" or "It's survival of the fittest." Usually what they mean is that people don't treat others the right way, so you just have to take whatever you can get. These ideas are reflected in a famous argument in the writings of the ancient philosopher

Plato. The idea of justice is mocked by a thought experiment: What if you had a "ring of invisibility" and could get away with doing all sorts of things you'd otherwise consider unjust? Would you steal if you knew you couldn't get caught? Would you cheat on your partner if no one could see it? According to this thought experiment, everyone *would* take advantage of that invisibility, and simply throw their ideas of justice out the window. This shows that justice is just something we make up. We use the idea of justice to get people to behave correctly, even if no one is looking. But in reality, without fear of punishment, people don't really believe it.

Or do they? Let's consider this position—call it "justice-skepticism." Would you steal if you could get away with it? Most people often face opportunities to appropriate property without paying, but they don't do it. And I think this is because we recognize something about theft that is wrong—unjust. Yet I often ask my students if they illegally download music online. Some say they do, but others do not. Some downloaders indicate that this is not "really stealing" because no one gets hurt and because there is essentially no scarcity of downloads. But of course, this answer suggests they *do* have standards for justice, and we are really arguing about what justice is, in terms of property. That is, they have defined justice in terms of not harming others—if you can take property but not harm others, then it is not stealing.

Or take another example: Would you cheat on your partner? A lot of my students wouldn't, *even if* no one ever found out. Indeed, they are disgusted by the idea! And I typically needle them in response that no one is "hurt" physically by a little cheating, if no one ever finds out. Students push back, insisting that "the relationship" is hurt, regardless. But here again, they are relying on some standard for justice. The point is, it is very hard to sustain a complete skepticism about justice. Our behavior when faced with these rules suggest we may have different ideas about what justice requires, but all sides are working with *some* idea of justice.

Even in more everyday matters, our behavior suggests the skeptical position is wrong. There are many experiments suggesting that people usually do the right thing, even if they could get away with not doing the right thing. For example, experiments have shown that people leave the same tip, regardless of whether they are at a restaurant they go to frequently or they are in a distant city to which they won't return.[3] No punishment will happen, no future consequences will befall them, and yet they still leave

---

[3] David Johnston, *A Brief History of Justice* (West Sussex, UK: Blackwell, 2011), 10.

the same tip. If we are not to assume that these people are all just foolish suckers, then we should recognize that there does seem to be something to this idea of justice.

Of course, many people *don't* leave the same tip, if their service is bad. This observation can help us to see what is going on when determining a tip—what I called above the "standards for justice"—when people are making judgments about what another person *deserves*. This is a very traditional definition of what justice is at the most basic level. Justice is giving to each what is due, what is deserved. Saint Thomas Aquinas writes, "Justice is a habit whereby a man renders to each one his due by a constant and perpetual will."[4] What it means to do justice is to choose consistently to give others what they deserve. If the service is great, they deserve a better tip; if it's bad, they deserve less.

This sense of standards about deserving seems to be very deep within us. When children cry out, "It's not fair," what they mean is, "I'm not getting what I deserve." (They may be wrong, but they are appealing to the idea of deserving something.) The word "deserve" suggests a certain picture of what right relationship looks like. Even children have some sense of what a balanced, reciprocal relationship is supposed to look like, and they are convinced it has been violated. As we grow up, often our sense of justice matures, so that we become upset not only when we ourselves don't get what we deserve but also when we see others not getting what they deserve. Maybe we only do this for friends and family, or maybe we do it for strangers, too. But our sense of injury from people not getting what they deserve seems to extend beyond the self.

To say that people "deserve" something—or, as we sometimes put it, that they have "a right" to it—requires that we have a prior sense of what the appropriate, balanced, reciprocal relationship is among human beings. That picture, of how relationships are supposed to be, is the backdrop against which we make judgments about justice. In order to receive what is deserved, someone has to give what is deserved—even if the "giving" is just a matter of leaving someone else alone, letting them do what they have a right to do.

To this point, things are pretty simple. Two ideas are key: When we talk about justice, we are talking about people deserving something, and in order to talk about "deserving," we need to have a picture of what the right relationship is. Put this way, we can see that this justice thing is operating

---

[4] *Summa Theologica*, trans. Fathers of English Dominican Province (New York: Benziger Brothers, 1947), II–II, q. 58, a. 2.

all the time. Hopefully, we live in places where most of the time, everyone is in fact getting more or less what they deserve from others, but that's not happening automatically. It's really going on in our own behavior and the behavior of others. People are doing their jobs and getting paid, parents and children are getting along, friends are keeping their word to each other, buyers and sellers are engaging in roughly equal exchanges of goods and money. And we notice *injustice* because it is a break in that pattern: someone is acting to interrupt these ordinary relationships. For example, when we call something a "rip-off," we are saying that someone has just charged us more than we really think something is worth.

Justice: Rules of Roles and Relationships

However, let's make this a little more challenging by thinking about two problems that complicate the simple "deserve or not" picture. First, let's return to our tipping example. A tip is also called a "gratuity"—which means it is a kind of gift, something we are not required by law to pay. (Laws are ordinarily the tools we use to name more clearly what justice requires in different relationships.) Since we don't *have to* leave a tip, why do we do it? And why do we give a gratuity only sometimes, for some services and not others? There are clearly rules about who gets tips and who doesn't, but these aren't enforced by any laws. (Should super-friendly checkout clerks be outraged that there's no tip line on your credit card receipt at the local superstore? Justice in tipping seems rather mysterious. Yet it's still operating.)

And here's a second problem: Let's say we have these ordinary relationships going on, people doing their jobs, parents and children getting along, slaves obeying their masters . . . Wait a minute. That suddenly seems wrong to us, but to many people in many human societies, slaves working for masters didn't seem any stranger than a lot of other relationships. This is what masters deserved from their slaves. The same might have been true for women obeying their husbands. In those societies, "justice" would have meant women and slaves doing what they were supposed to do, just as workers ordinarily obey their bosses. And "injustice" would have been the opposite. Yet of course, we now think that in those cases (such as slavery) it was the ordinary, acceptable, taken-for-granted relationship that was actually the *unjust* one.

These examples (of formerly "just" but clearly unjust practices) make things more complicated, allowing us to dig deeper into how we form our judgments about who deserves what. How should we name this complication? These two examples are very different, yet each one makes the same point: Our sense of what people deserve has to do with *who they are*—that is, what role we see them in, in relation to others. The relationship of diner/server differs from the relationship of customer/cashier (as everyone seems to know). The relationship of master/slave we now reject entirely, because we have rejected the very category "slave." Differently, the relationship of husband/wife has been refined, so that the expectations of what is deserved are still there but have changed, and the relationship of boss/worker may still be one of obedience within legal limits. Students are still supposed to listen to their teachers and children to their parents, yet our framework for seeing these relationships has changed, too, and they also differ (though not completely) from one another.

Thus, we should draw an important conclusion: What we think people deserve backs up into who we think people are. Our sense of justice is based on the idea that people are not only "generic persons," but are specific people in specific roles. Plato, the ancient Greek philosopher, is well known for developing an order of justice in his work *The Republic*. His classic definition of justice imagined a balanced relationship among the three parts of a human soul, and then applied this balanced relationship to the three classes of people in a society: workers, warriors, and leaders. Each has a specific role, and "justice" describes the relationships where each is doing for the other and for the society as a whole what they are supposed to do. In more traditional societies, this complex set of roles and relationships was seen as much more fixed and overriding. For example, think of societies with kings and lords and other noble classes by birth. What they "deserved" was completely defined by who they were, and who other people were in relation to their fixed social rank. And "injustice" named actions that disrupted this stable order.[5] In these cases, retribution was a key part of justice, because it was seen as fixing the order. In our society, we still have hierarchies; yet, on the whole, we tend to see them as less fixed, as more a matter of what rank or position might be earned or chosen, and as less attached to the person in a fixed and total way. But even if our picture has become more fluid, notice that the examples of servers and slaves (or teachers, spouses, friends) still show how our sense of what is deserved in a given relationship is based on the *identities* of those in relationship. So while we might contest the contents of Plato's picture, we

---

[5] Johnston, *A Brief History of Justice*, 20–35.

nevertheless continue to understand just relationships in terms of people with a particular identity in relation to others with an identity. When we go on in this book to speak about "restorative justice," we mean to talk primarily about the particular identities of offender and victim, and thus how we determine what is deserved by each in their relationship.

Where Does Our Sense of Justice Come From?

So, when we ask how to determine what people deserve, we are looking for a correct, accurate set of identities. Who exactly are the people in this particular relationship, and how should such people give what is due to the other? These judgments about justice are among the most complex yet most essential things we do as a society. In our own day, it is helpful to sort such judgments into three categories, each of which assumes that we can no longer appeal to a claim such as "I am a lord"—to fixed status—in order to understand justice. Rather, in each case, there is a *kind of* equality we are trying to work out; there is something that is deserved by every person. Aristotle saw all claims of justice, whatever the particular relationship, in terms of some kind of equality, and what needed to be determined was what counted as equal in that particular relationship. Thus, he talks about an "equality of ratios" or a proper "proportionality."[6] If two people are paid by the hour, "equal pay" would mean not that each got the same thing, but that each got the proportion of pay that was equal to the hours they worked. Similarly, we tend to think it is fair for a more experienced or skilled worker to receive greater pay for the same number of hours worked; here, the "equal pay" is pay that is proportional not only to hours worked, but to skill and experience.

Here we meet another wrinkle: *exact* equality often isn't what justice means. I know for myself, growing up with one sister, very close in age, we were always very vigilant, crying out "it's not fair" if we perceived any difference at all in what was coming from our parents. As we matured, of course, we recognized that carefully making sure our parents gave us the same amount of Christmas presents was not a very good sense of equality! Instead the equality entailed that our parents would give each child what he or she truly needed; thus, more need might require being given more

---

[6] *Nicomachean Ethics*, ed. Lesley Brown, trans. David Ross (Oxford: Oxford University Press, 2009), 1131a10–1131b24. Aquinas follows this approach: *Summa Theologica* II–II, q. 57, a. 1.

attention. In a similar way, I am being fair and just to my students if I treat them all exactly equally in regard to some things, in terms of availability for office hours, the same level of difficulty of assignments, and basic personal respect. However, when I am grading their work, what counts as "fair" changes: it would not be fair to assign the same grade. The way I treat students equally in this way is to judge *their work*, rather than assign a grade based on other factors. But "equal" in this case doesn't mean they all get the same thing.

In these examples, we can see that there are different ways to understand what it means to treat people fairly or justly in the sense of equally. Thus, the first type of judgment about equality is like my process of being fair in grading. It is a judgment that people deserve whatever they can get—so long as everyone follows a fair *process*. It's the process that should be fair for everyone, but as long as the rules are fair (and enforced), what we deserve is based on what we do. Most commonly, we apply this to economic exchange. What is a fair price for an item at a garage sale or a fair wage? The answer may be, whatever a person can get the other person to pay, but without deception (which we usually call "fraud" in the economic sphere). People deserve what they achieve. In these types of scenarios, concerns about fairness typically center on whether the *procedures* followed to strike the bargain were fair—that is, one may claim that a wage or price is unfair if parties did not follow a common process to determine it, instead relying on force or fraud.

While this sort of judgment about what is deserved is quite common, the further concern about a "fair process" seems to rely on some other judgment about why anyone might "deserve" a fair process. For example, it is commonly believed that persons who commit crimes may be deprived of certain things that others ordinarily deserve—for example, the right to vote. But we also believe that offenders still deserve certain things, regardless of their alleged crimes—for example, a right to due process and a right to be punished in a way that is not "cruel and unusual." Hence, this sort of judgment about "deserve" as what you can earn or get almost never stands by itself.

Thus, a second type of judgment is that people deserve certain things *apart from* and *beyond* what they are able to get from others, or what their actions earn them. That's really why, whether I'm grading or leading class discussion, even poorly performing students still "deserve" something from me. Commonly, we apply this when we talk about ideas like civil rights or universal rights. But what is the basis for the idea that everyone deserves anything? It is often justified by reference to the philosopher Immanuel

Kant, or other thinkers who refined his argument. Kant suggested that persons treat themselves as ends in themselves, not just a means to some further end. What does that mean? This means that humans have an absolute value, not just a value relative to something they can do. Let's think about this: What worth does a pen have when it runs out of ink? It has no worth, because the pen is a writing instrument. Kant said that human beings have value not just because they are useful for some further end. It's clear that people treat themselves as if they are not just useful to get other things, but have some value beyond that. And if that is true of how I think of myself, it is correspondingly true of how others think of themselves. And it is unreasonable and inconsistent to believe this to be true about some people and not others. We might have worth as a means to some end, but we also have inherent value; we deserve something just because we are persons. For Kant, the most important value that humans have is best named as freedom, and so he concludes, "The universal law of justice is: act externally in such a way that the free use of your will is compatible with the freedom of everyone."[7] This constitutes a kind of limit on simply getting whatever you can, since there is a need to respect others' seeking of their own ends. If you want others to respect your human freedom, Kant basically says, then act so as to respect their freedom, too.

A third is a judgment that people deserve certain things because they are given as a gift by God, and so no human power can be justified in denying them or taking them away. The American Declaration of Independence suggests that people "are endowed with certain inalienable rights by their Creator," and this is used as a justification to reject certain aspects of the unjust rule of the British monarch. This third idea is particularly important within the Catholic tradition. The *Catechism* explains, "*Human life is sacred* because from its beginning it involves the creative action of God and it remains for ever in a special relationship with the Creator, who is its sole end."[8] Saint John Paul II in *Evangelium Vitae* states, "God proclaims that he is absolute Lord of the life of man, who is formed in his image and likeness (cf. Gen 1:26-28). Human life is thus given a sacred and inviolable character, which reflects the inviolability of the Creator himself."[9]

---

[7] "The Metaphysical Elements of Justice," in Jonathan Westphal, ed., *Justice* (Indianapolis: Hackett, 1996), 149–56, here 151.

[8] CDF, instruction, *Donum vitae*, intro. 5; quoted in *Catechism of the Catholic Church*, 2nd ed. (United States Catholic Conference—Libreria Editrice Vaticana, 1997), 2258.

[9] *Evangelium Vitae* (Vatican City: Libreria Editrice Vaticana, 1995) 53.

The idea that people deserve things simply because they are created and loved by God as children doesn't preempt the first two ideas, but it does fill in some notorious "gaps" in their conception of what any person deserves. For example, those who appeal to Kant's reasoning can suggest that those without the capacity of freedom, and especially free reasoning, perhaps do not deserve to live. And those who simply appeal to fair process sometimes think that those who "lose" in the process or break the rules can then be denied basic rights. By appealing to a source of deserving beyond anyone's characteristics or behavior protects even the weakest and the worst: they are still human, still in relation to God, and so still deserve to be treated with the dignity accorded all human beings.

What Mistakes Do We Typically Make about Justice?

Carefully reflecting on the foundations of justice can be challenging. Even if we adopt the view of the church that all humans deserve something because they are children of God, it does not then resolve the questions of what exactly each human being deserves. We still have to work through questions of tipping and child-rearing and responding to crime. Still, reflection on the deeper foundations of our sense of justice is important especially because we are apt to make certain errors in judging what is deserved, and careful reflection on a deeper sense of what people deserve can check these errors. Three temptations are particularly common:

Error #1: To go with our feelings. This is probably the most important error to watch out for. In our society today, we are bombarded by images and stories, and these images and stories often are shown in order to get us to feel something—in order to manipulate our feelings. And how we feel does have something to do with seeking justice. In the Disney movie *Inside Out*, the emotion of anger is depicted essentially as a reaction to unfairness, and feeling this kind of "righteous anger" when we see injustice or experience it is a mark of our humanity. For some thinkers, the experience of sympathy at another's joy or suffering—putting yourself in the other person's shoes and feeling what he or she is feeling—is a key motivator to action.

However, like all feelings, anger and sympathy are easily manipulated and can deceive us about what the right course of action is. In *Inside Out*, the main character, Riley, has understandable feelings of anger at her parents for a poorly planned and disruptive move to San Francisco that lead her to believe she should abandon her parents and go back home to Minnesota. What we feel may be very shortsighted, or based simply on our own prejudices, or on the predetermined conclusions about what is justly imposed by the person serving up the image. It may especially be affected by our individual experiences, however unrepresentative, and our immediate surroundings. We may not see the big picture. Take the issue of immigration: Both sides of this fierce and brutal debate claim they are on the side of justice, and both use stories and images to steer our emotions, to generate sympathy for their side and anger toward the other side. Who is right? Here we must seek the guidance of clearer practical judgments, judgments based on reason, and not simply on the strength of feeling.

Error #2: To rest with consequences. When we seek reasons to adjudicate conflicts over justice, we often see that people are quick to pull out "the data." We are a results-oriented society, and we want to know what will happen if we choose to do X or to do Y. Like experiencing feelings, thinking about various results isn't a bad idea. In fact, it's good. For example, many people are moved to act fairly by someone saying, "Well, what if everybody did that?" What if everybody littered or cheated on their taxes or tried to cut in line? We have an idea that it would be bad, and so we clean up, pay our fair share, wait our turn. The philosophy called utilitarianism is essentially this idea transformed into a general rule: do whatever brings about the greatest good for the greatest number.

However, there are two weighty reasons why consequences aren't enough in making a judgment about what people deserve. The first is this: The future is inherently uncertain, and we really can't grasp what will happen as a result of our individual actions. In fact, many people will point out that my cutting in line doesn't actually cause other people to do it—maybe some, but not others, and for other people, seeing someone cut in line may actually increase their willingness not to do the action. If this uncertainty about actual consequences is true for smaller actions, it is especially true for larger, society-wide questions. A lot of questions about economics in a society are difficult to work out because there are millions of interconnected choices that make up the economy—and it is not easy to understand how changing one thing will affect other things, especially in the longer run. This uncertainty is a challenging part of the issue of restorative justice, too. We can try to plan and have foresight, but we can't ultimately know how things will turn out.

But even more serious than the uncertainty problem is another problem of relying solely on consequences to determine the greatest good for the greatest number: We may have to do some horrible things in order to achieve the supposed consequences we want. The greatest good for the greatest number may be brought about by doing things to a smaller number of people that they don't deserve. Philosophers call these "lifeboat dilemmas" or "runaway trolley problems"—in which we are faced with a choice where we must kill one or two people to save five or six. Let's put it this way: If what is deserved is simply what produced the best overall consequences, then it is reasonable that a smaller number of people may be harmed to help a larger number. But does this sound just?

Well, it depends. What does "harm" mean? Here again, we cannot escape using reason, not simply in terms of what will happen—instrumental reason—but in terms of what should and should not happen: a sense of inherent dignity or natural rights. A politician who imposes a higher tax on wealthy people in order to build roads or parks or libraries for everyone is in a sense "harming" the wealthy. And people will argue whether it is fair to impose such a tax. But everyone will recognize that progressive taxation differs morally from dilemmas where we have to kill someone to benefit others. And that difference means we must be looking at something other than good consequences in order to determine what is just.

Error #3: To prefer "our people." A final temptation is to prefer our own tribe, and this one is very tricky—and to some extent stems from the first two errors. Emotional manipulations and calculations of what costs are worth paying to achieve certain benefits are often aimed at getting us to feel solidarity with those who are being harmed. If we feel like "our people" are getting hurt, we're more likely to rise up and call it an injustice.

However, we're also likely to be like a child who mistakenly cries out "it's not fair" when, in fact, it is fair, and we are just paying too much attention to our own concerns and not enough to others. It is a great moral achievement of our society that we are conditioned to think that everyone is equal and no one should get preferential treatment. No one should prefer "their own people." We relish the common interpretation of the Good Samaritan, the parable through which Jesus tells people to help their suffering neighbors across ethnic dividing lines.

As we saw above, Christians in particular have strong reasons to be wary of "preferring our own people." But here's where the tricky part comes in. What we mean in "not preferring our own" is clearly more complicated than it might at first appear. We do think our children deserve more *from us* than others do; we do devote more time and energy to our friends; we spend more time helping out in our own local community. In all these ways, we "prefer" some people to others. Thomas Aquinas calls this "the order of love," and he sees it as necessary for human life together.

What we need to do here—and again, we'll use our reason to do this—is identify the distinctions between where such preferences seem justified (and even necessary) and when they cross the line into being unfair. Take the question of a friend or family member being hired for a job. Should you "prefer" him or her? I don't think that's an easy question. My guess is you would seek to make further distinctions. If your friend was simply not qualified to do the job, and you hired her anyway, that might seem bad; on the other hand, if she is a strong, qualified candidate, it might seem unfair to not hire your friend—cold and heartless! Doing nice things for people you run across in your neighborhood—we call them "favors"— seems like a very good thing. But should you do this little extra only for some neighbors? for all? I live on a small, tight-knit city block of row houses with a Facebook group, where people routinely request favors of neighbors. What is a reasonable, fair request? What's too much to ask? What's taking advantage?

So, since I now seem to be saying it's quite right and good to show preferences, why do I label this a temptation? The complexity of the "hiring the friend" example helps start us thinking about where the limits are here. But there are a couple more important problems. First, historically, groups have identified "our people" in frankly unfair ways—most obviously to us in the United States, based on a person's skin color or gender. This kind of exclusion is usually what we mean by "discrimination," when we mean to call it unfair. It's not just that we discriminate in preferring some people to others, but we prefer *for bad reasons*. What reasons? Much of the debate about justice issues lies right here.

A second problem—which kind of encompasses the first—is that it's clear that not everyone is equal in terms of being a part of some group in the first place. For example, some people are born with better connections; some people develop better friendships. Perhaps most importantly, we are all part of a family, and people start out radically unequal due to family circumstances. For some part of human history, societies often were structured based on the view that your family was your destiny. There is a reason why visions of perfect societies, like Plato's *Republic*, think a truly just society must abolish the family and raise children in standardized environments! No doubt one of the powerful contributions of Christianity (as it combined with the philosophy of Stoicism) is the development of a different idea, that all humans are part of a single family, the idea of "the unity of the human race." And no doubt one of the most powerful founding ideas of America was a complete rejection of *inherited* titles and social hierarchies based on family origins. At least in theory, family lineage was not supposed to matter. As Robert Putnam explains it, Americans may be accepting of unequal outcomes (not everyone can win the race), but they really dislike unequal opportunity.[10] And in a world where "preferring" family, friends, and neighbors is an inevitable part of the life, we have developed the idea that it is only fair to watch out for those who are deprived of these connections—the "widows and orphans" of the Bible. In today's society, those we should attend to might be persons who are socially awkward, struggle with disabilities, or are simply strangers in a new place. We believe we should attend to those who may be vulnerable, marginalized, or neglected.

Conclusion: Toward Restorative Justice

This last idea—helping the vulnerable, marginalized, or neglected—forms an important bridge to the question of restorative justice, since among these are those in our society who have been imprisoned. In a sense our thoroughly and narrowly punitive approach to punishment leads to the extreme marginalization of persons in prison and after imprisonment. Prison intentionally cuts off prisoners from relations—with family, friends, and neighbors in one's community. Prisoners' criminal records follow them for the rest of their lives, defining them as outcasts in terms of their employment possibilities and voting rights. The permanent stigma of "convicted felon" defines prisoners for the rest of their lives. Is such marginalization fair?

The distinctive problem of restorative justice is what to do in response to an injustice that has occurred. Our first instinct is probably to fix it, to "make it right." But we should notice two problems that often get in the way. One, the injustice fundamentally affects relationships *between people* (even when it is just about things—like theft), and "fixing" these relationships involves more than just simple exchanges. Two, often (arguably, always) there isn't really the possibility of simply "restoring" the situation to its prior state—something has happened, time has passed, fractures and losses cannot be undone. In other words, one problem is that we can become narrowly focused on simple exchanges—*settling a score* between offender and victim—and lose the awareness that wrongdoing affects relationships *among people* on multiple levels in wide-ranging ways. The second problem is that we can become preoccupied solely with *an isolated act of wrong* that was done in the past. The wrongdoer has done an unjust

---

[10] *Our Kids: The American Dream in Crisis* (New York: Simon and Schuster, 2015).

act that can never be undone, and so our attention focuses narrowly on retaliating against the offender to right the wrong.

Restorative justice does not focus on exchanges that even scores and ways of paying back offenders. It does focus, primarily, on restoring the victim to wholeness and community. When possible, it focuses on ways that an offender can take responsibility to restore those he or she has harmed. Restorative justice broadly and deeply considers the issues raised in this chapter—how we should treat persons justly in ways that they deserve and how we should respond justly when someone has done something unjust. It also considers the linkage between these two issues and calls us to be attentive to both our responsibilities in treating persons justly and responding justly when persons fail to treat others justly. This book will draw you into a consideration of how restorative justice approaches these issues. Hopefully the considerations of this first chapter on justice have provided a general guide that will keep that consideration careful and thoughtful.

Review and Looking Forward

Editors

Justice is the virtue through which we sustain complex sets of relationship. Justice is giving others what they deserve, and judgments about what we owe to others and what is deserved depend upon our understanding of a person's place, standing, role, and relationships. As David Cloutier has explained, an individual "human being" is a place and standing in relationship to humanity, to creation, and to God (as God's image and likeness). Parent, child, neighbor, friend, boss, employee, legislator, citizen, and alien are all roles and relationships that also form the groundwork for the determination of what we and others need and deserve. In the Catholic tradition, this general definition includes sets of social relations.[11] Distributive justice is how those responsible for the whole (leaders and caretakers) allocate goods, services, and "what is deserved" to individual citizens, and social justice is how individuals contribute to the good of the whole. Commutative justice is how individuals relate to each other through contracts, commerce, and various sorts of interpersonal exchange. These three sets of relations are not easily disentangled, especially in a

---

[11] This account of justice is based on a classic in Catholic intellectual tradition, Josef Pieper, *The Four Cardinal Virtues* (New York: Pantheon Books, 1954), 43–113.

democratic republic like the United States. And this interweaving is a good thing; our acts of justice are deeply interconnected, as we are human beings, living in relation to others, God, and creation.

Restorative justice draws on this interconnectedness. (As you will see in chapters 5 and 6, it is the biblical model of justice.) Criminal justice, in its standard framework, is the preview of government; it is the manner by which fault, correction, and penalties are distributed—meted out—to citizens. Through retributive justice, the government takes revenge out of the hands of individuals. Indeed, retributive justice is not vengeance at all; in an impersonal fashion, a representative authority imposes a punishment—a measure of suffering—that is proportionate to the crime. Sometimes there is an attempt to combine retributive punishment with a reform and education of the offender; that is, there is an attempt at the rehabilitation of the criminal. Often, there is an attempt to shape retribution so that it is also a deterrent to would-be criminals. In comparison to restorative justice, an interesting thing about these forms of criminal justice is that they are interactions between an impersonal authority and an offender. The victims and their restoration are not in the picture at all.

Restorative justice begins with a focus on the ones who are harmed—first the particular victims, then the community, and finally offenders (who certainly harm themselves by harming others). While retributive justice is an exchange between a criminal and government (on behalf of a victim), restorative justice draws on the whole web of social relations. In addition to the concerns of governments, communities attend to the needs of victims and the fractures that crimes against individuals have created in the community itself. Restorative justice seeks the reform of criminals through their active and voluntary acceptance of responsibility for the injuries that they have caused. In other words, restorative justice includes both person-to-person exchange (commutative justice) and a call to the offender to contribute to the good of society as a whole (social justice). Because it is set deeply within a web of social relationships, restorative justice—you will discover throughout this book—is experienced as uplifting and healing for victims and communities, and it has great success in restoring offenders to community and setting them on a good path.

Questions for Discussion

1. A classic account of the social and individual responsibilities of justice are outlined in Pope John XXIII's encyclical *Pacem in Terris* (1963). The first section of the document (nos. 8–45) is titled

"The Order between Men." The section is not lengthy, and it is worth a look on the Vatican website.[12] The section begins with this proposition:

> [E]ach individual man is truly a person. His is a nature, that is, endowed with intelligence and free will. As such he has rights and duties, which together flow as a direct consequence from his nature. These rights and duties are universal and inviolable, and therefore altogether inalienable. (9)

From this principle, St. John XXIII outlines basic rights from "the means necessary for the proper development of life" (e.g., food, clothing, shelter) through the right of conscience and religious liberty to the "right to take an active part in public life, and to make his own contribution to the common welfare" (11, 26). These rights are accompanied by corresponding duties. "For example, the right to live involves the duty to preserve one's life; the right to a decent standard of living, the duty to live in a becoming fashion; the right to be free to seek out the truth, the duty to devote oneself to an ever deeper and wider search for it" (29).

Take a look at this first section of *Pacem in Terris* and consider the roles and relationships that set the context for justice and judgment about what we owe to one another.

2. Start with the point that sets of roles and relationships guide us in determinations of justice. From this point, consider various relationships at home, in town, and at work. How do these relationships and roles help us to determine what a person deserves from us? Consider our own children, neighborhood children, kids we coach; consider a boss or employee, priest or minister, mayor or citizen. What are the responsibilities of each of these individuals, given their role and place? Given who we are (our role and place), what do we owe to them? What do we owe to someone new in town—a stranger (a person we only know as "human being")? After you have gone through this exercise, imagine that each person has committed a crime. What do you want for each of them? What does each deserve?

---

[12] *Pacem in Terris* (Vatican City: Libreria Editrice Vaticana, 1963), http://w2.vatican .va/content/john-xxiii/en/encyclicals/documents/hf_j-xxiii_enc_11041963_pacem.html.

Chapter 2

Restorative Justice

Editors

Pope Francis understands the power of actions and gestures. He chose to end his September 2015 visit to the United States by visiting one hundred eighteen- to twenty-one-year-old inmates and their families in a gymnasium of the Curran-Fromhold Correctional Facility in Philadelphia. His words and gestures during the visit modeled a Christlike response to persons whose actions have harmed victims and their communities. They also embodied the Catholic understanding of restorative justice, which is the focus of this book. Such witness brought many Americans to reflect on our criminal justice system.

Always attentive to those who are marginalized or abandoned in society, Pope Francis began his visit by simply expressing his gratitude for the opportunity to be with the inmates and their families. He spoke as a pastor, explaining that he wished to share their situation and "make it my own," and cautioning that "any society, any family, which cannot share or take seriously the pain of its children, and views that pain as something normal or to be expected, is a society 'condemned' to remain a hostage to itself, prey to the very things which cause that pain."[1] Francis brought to these prisoners a message of hope—hope for redemption and

---

[1] Connie Awrey, "Pope Francis' Speech to Prisoners at the Curran-Fromhold Correctional Facility" (September 27, 2015), National Federation of Priests' Councils, http://nfpc.org/uncategorized/pope-francis-speech-to-prisoners-at-the-curran-fromhold-correctional-facility-philadelphia/.

restoration. He told the prisoners that as he came to them, so too Christ comes to meet all of us who suffer in order to restore our human dignity and help us "to set out again, to resume our journey, to recover our hope, to restore our faith and trust." By going to speak with these imprisoned offenders, Francis sought to clearly show that "confinement isn't the same thing as exclusion."

This book entails philosophical, theological, sociological, and public policy analysis. The hard work of such analysis is required for us to think critically about our criminal justice system. But Pope Francis made manifest the central point of the Catholic approach to criminal justice: that in the end it focuses on encountering and responding to the needs of persons—all persons—who suffer the impact of crime. In his words at the prison, Francis described how "it is painful when we see prison systems which are not concerned to care for wounds, to soothe pain, to offer new possibilities. It is painful when we see people who think that only others need to be cleansed, purified, and do not recognize that their weariness, pain and wounds are also the weariness, pain and wounds of society. The Lord tells us this clearly with a sign. He washes our feet so that we come back to the table. The table from which he wishes no one to be excluded, the table which is spread for all and to which all of us are invited."

Pope Francis's words address the much-needed reorienting of justice, which is the focus of this chapter. According to Catholic social teaching, the purpose of punishment must never be solely retributive. And it must never be a retaliative returning of harm with harm. Francis clarified to the Philadelphia prisoners, "This time in your life can only have one purpose. To give you a hand to getting back on the right road, to give you a hand to help you re-join society, all of us are a part of that effort. All of us are invited to encourage, help and enable your rehabilitation. A rehabilitation which everyone seeks and desires: inmates and their families, correctional authorities, social and educational programs, a rehabilitation which benefits the morale of the entire community and society."

Shaking hands with each of the inmates and conversing with many, Francis thanked them for the beautiful carved chair they had made for him. Fortunately this prison offers vocational workshops plus GED and remedial programs that begin to address the basic educational needs of 60 percent of the inmates who are barely literate, only reading at a third- or fourth-grade level. Pope Francis ended his comments by encouraging the inmates to foster a supportive attitude toward each other and all persons within the prison, to "make possible new opportunities . . . [and to resist] the lie that says no one can change." Rather than viewing these men as persons to be condemned and forgotten, he emphasized, "All of us have something that we need to be cleansed of or purified from. All of us. May the knowledge of that fact inspire us to live in solidarity, to support one another and seek the best for others." The pope's gesture in meeting with and personally greeting each of the inmates deeply affected many of them. But as he emphasized in *Evangelii Gaudium*, the Gospel is about living the kingdom of God rather than "small personal gestures to individuals in need." And, "To the extent that [God] reigns within us, the life of society will be a setting for universal fraternity, justice, peace and dignity."[2] Francis's words in this Philadelphia prison clarified that redemption and restoration in response to wrongdoing are the heart of the Gospel message. Hopefully the witnessing of the Gospel by Pope Francis can orient us as we begin to reflect on our criminal justice system in chapters 2 through 4.

Reorienting Justice

Trudy D. Conway

Many of us rarely think about crime and punishment. We care about justice and want to believe that our system of criminal justice is a just one, deserving of this name. Questions raised behind the secured doors of courtrooms and prisons likely don't preoccupy many of us. But members of our own community and seemingly distant communities have to grapple with questions shaped by these institutions on a daily basis. Local families in my own rural community, deeply troubled by a recent crime covered in the regional press, faced a range of particular questions: How are interactions with the prosecution team affecting victims? Does the judge and the offender understand the depth of suffering of the victims? Can a long prison term address the wrongs done to victims' families? What effect will imprisonment in a different state have on the young children of the offender? Does the offender understand the impact of this crime on our entire community? How can we prevent others from becoming victims of such a crime?

At bottom, these questions raised in our community point to a range of fundamental—but more abstract—questions explored in the previous chapter. What is justice? How is justice practiced? Are our criminal justice institutions focused on retributive justice (the assigning of what is justly due to violators of the law), restorative justice (the healing of persons

<hr/>

[2] *Evangelii Gaudium* 180, http://www.vatican.va/evangelii-gaudium/en/; and as cited by Margaret R. Pfeil, "A Theological Understanding of Restorative Justice," *Journal of Moral Theology* 5, no. 2 (June 2016): 162–63.

damaged by the wrongdoing of offenders), or the avoidance of injustice (the deterring of crimes)? Are our courts and prisons vehicles for manifesting state power, for promoting human well-being and the common good, or for maintaining entrenched social structures? Victims, offenders, and their loved ones and neighbors are thrust into thinking about and living such issues that rarely touch the daily concerns of so many persons.

Most of us rarely consider, let alone rigorously question, the rationale, reach, and extensive repercussions of the criminal justice system. The media's sensationalizing of crime is what grabs our attention—but only momentarily. And yet at times unexpected words and actions pull us into reflection. Our entire nation was riveted by what happened at a bond hearing in a Charleston, South Carolina, courtroom on June 19, 2015, two days after the brutal killing of nine members of the Mother Emanuel AME Church by a twenty-one-year-old driven by racist preoccupations. Families of the victims sat facing the video image of Dylann Roof projected from a nearby holding cell. At the invitation of Judge Gosnell, Nadine Collier rose to address the image of the young man who had murdered her mother, Ethel. She felt deep searing anger because "her mother had more living to do" and she knew the wide wreckage of human destruction caused by this young man's actions. And yet facing his image, she kept thinking that "he's a young man, he's never going to experience college, be a husband, be a daddy. You have ruined your life." To the shock of all who were riveted, she sobbingly said, "I forgive you. You took something very precious away from me. I will never get to talk to her ever again—but I forgive you, and have mercy on your soul."[3] The quality of mercy in response to these horrendous murders was not expected in that court that day. Neither was the call by many of the murder victim family members to take the death penalty sentence off the table.

Scarlett Wilson, the prosecutor, argued that "justice from our state calls for the ultimate punishment."[4] But to the surprise of many of us, a different sense of justice brought some members of the Emanuel AME community to be concerned about Dylann's confessing and turning inward to take inventory of his attitudes, actions, and life, especially what brought him to sit with his victims in a Bible study of the parable of the Sower (Mark 4:1-20) as he coldheartedly waited to draw his gun. They believed in the possibility of his coming to comprehend his evil actions that so damaged

---

[3] As quoted in D. Von Drehle, J. Newton-Small, and M. Rhodan, "Murder, race and mercy, stories from Charleston," *Time* (November 23, 2015): 43–68.

[4] As quoted in J. Newton-Small, "Why the Emanuel gunman may not get the death penalty," *Time* (November 23, 2015): 47.

their loved ones and beloved community and changing his life into one of meaning and value. Rose Simmons, the daughter of slain Reverend Daniel Simmons, spoke of her family's hope that Dylann's life in prison might sow the spiritual seed of a penitent transformation. These responses cannot be easily shaken off. Having recently endured the anguish of an extended sentencing hearing resulting from a crime committed against her father, the Emanuel community pushed her to examine the fluctuations of her personal responses and those of American society in response to crime. What is justice and how should it be practiced?

Just Retribution

Prosecutor Wilson's demand for just retribution for Dylann Roof's crimes did not shock or surprise anyone. Just retribution means giving the punishment that is due to violators of the law. As emphasized in the previous chapter, justice, in all its varied forms, concerns giving each person what is deserved. Just retribution is just one aspect of criminal justice, but in our society, it has come to represent the whole, for punishment has become the proxy for justice. There is agreement within relationships, families, communities, and civil societies that harmful wrongdoing should evoke response. Failure to respond manifests a callous disregard of persons who are, could have been, and may still be the targets of such action.

The demand for just retribution appears traceable to our elemental and visceral anger in response to harmful wrongdoing. In raising our children, failures to care about and respond to such wrongdoing, be it by children or caretakers, justifiably elicit concern. Aristotle describes anger as a response to perceived injustice, slight, or injury, while recognizing the great challenge of responding with righteous anger to the right person, at the right time, to the right extent, for the right duration, in the right manner, and for the right reason. Such virtuous expression of anger requires the exercising of practical wisdom—seasoned insightful deliberation about how to respond to the anger-evoking offender. Anger comes easily; righteous anger requires much of us. Without legal structure, anger quickly risks becoming retaliatory vengeance.

In order to limit the risk of vengeance, citizens came to hold states responsible for responding to harmful wrongdoing. This development took the responding to wrongdoing from victims and their communities and institutionalized it in a legal system that emphasized a retaliatory principle, requiring that the state mete out suffering to wrongdoers for their actions.

In so doing, the legal system asserted the power of the state against law-violating offenders, allowing victims and affiliated persons to play a role solely as witnesses in procedures focused on due process and the rights of offenders in determining guilt and meting out sentences for violations of the law. Such a *state vs. offender* approach, conducted through the adversarial roles of prosecutors and defense attorneys presenting argument and evidence, resulted in a legal system focused on payback for wrongdoing.

The present-day result is a legal system that often sidelines the needs and concerns of victims and other persons affected by crime. Justice herein requires the state to address the breaking of the law through a legal system directed to meting out just retribution through retaliatory suffering. Offenders must get what they deserve from the state, their punishment being seen as assurance that justice has been done. Personal and communal response has been replaced by a complex jurisprudence system directed by the state through a legal conduit of arrests, trials, and punishments governed by procedural rules. States have the responsibility to respond to wrongdoing codified as illegal and deserving of state-inflicted punishment. And states have the power and resources to ensure this is done.

Breaking the law angers citizens who refuse to commit such offenses. Acting as free-riders, offenders are seen as benefiting from, while violating, the rule of law enabling civic life. The desire for just retribution stems from the expectation that such persons be held accountable for such violations. Punishment exacted through a criminal justice system is thus seen as a matter of just retribution or deserved "payback" for offenders' crimes. Through just retribution society rights wrongs, measure for measure, by making the convicted offender suffer as the victim suffered. Punishment must entail the infliction of some kind of pain, harm, deprivation, or something normally considered undesirable and unpleasant. It must be administered by some legal authority according to reasonable standards and procedures to a person judged guilty of an offense that breaks the law. Retributive punishment thus has a retrospective focus—a condemning and righting of past wrongs by giving offenders what they justly deserve. Violations of society's law rationally *demand* just retribution, and such retaliatory response must be commensurate with the wrong done to be just. Not surprisingly, guilty verdicts and severe punishments often evoke spontaneous cheers in courtrooms, especially by victim family members.

The history of types of retributive punishment reveal evolving standards of decency. Today we look with horror on past punishments such as torturous stretching on the rack, public stockades, chain gang labor, stoning, disemboweling, quartering, gassing, and electrocuting. Over time our ways of administering punishment have shifted from corporeal forms of punishing to forms restricting the exercising of rights and range of freedom through imprisonment. Retributive justice is seen as demanding proportionate punishment that admits of a range. A punishment *beyond* what is deserved would be unjust to the convicted offender; a degree of punishment *below* what is deserved would be unjust to the victim. Such reasoning, drawing a limit to punishment, is seen in the constitutional review of punishment in light of the Eighth and Fourteenth Amendments of the Constitution, which state that "excessive bail shall not be required, nor excessive fines, nor cruel and unusual punishment inflicted," and no state shall "deprive any person of life, liberty or property, without due process of the law; nor deny to any person within its jurisdiction the equal protection of the laws."[5] Through such a court-administered system of retribution, we affirm the rule of law and the power of the state in upholding and enforcing it. Reading the words of our Constitution that established the groundwork for this system evokes admiration, but a study of our current-day criminal justice system reveals something is deeply amiss as far as our practice of justice.

From Retribution to Restoration

The reasoning of retributive justice is the default way of reasoning about crime and punishment in our society today. Because of this, any variant approach jars and confuses us. Not surprisingly, the Emanuel AME church members grabbed our attention. How can these members ask for anything but retribution for the wrongs done by Dylann Roof? And yet, at other times in our societal history our concerns differed, revealing other ways of responding to wrongdoing. Our seemingly antiquated terms "penitentiary" and "correctional facility" evoke different understandings of punishment. Some persons and communities have argued that the response to crime must be *more* than an exercise in retributive justice, and retribution itself must be transformed from merely retaliative matching of "like for like" to bringing offenders to recognize the harm they have done and the debt they owe to the harmed victim and community, and also bringing the community to examine the factors contributing to the crime. Here, the

---

[5] See http://www.archives.gov/exhibits/charters/bill_of_rights_transcript.html.http://www.archives.gov/exhibits/charters/constitution_amendments_11-27.html.

emphasis shifts from what the state *does to* offenders to what offenders and the community *owe* to those suffering harm caused by and tied to crime. What is done to offenders is transformed into what offenders must sacrifice and do and how the community must respond. Retribution is transformed into reparation and restoration.

Herein the focus subtly shifts from doing retaliatory harm *to* offenders to offenders suffering loss, pain, or sacrifice *for* harms done to others. To be so transformed, punishment must engage offenders as moral beings. And such a moral approach is premised on respect for persons as responsible agents capable of self-examination and reflection, as shown by the original purposes of a "penitentiary" and "correctional" institution. A purely retributive approach stresses legal obligations, prohibitions, and sanctions of violators who act outside the law. In our current system, the emphasis is not on offenders as persons capable of understanding the shared communal values, convictions, and responsibilities their actions have violated. The wrongdoer's recognition of wrongdoing does not come into play; the state charges, prosecutes, and sentences the criminal violator. The capacity of the offender for moral reflection, transformation, and reconciliation in the context of a community remains sidelined. Legal preoccupations with evidence, argument, and due process trump moral reflection and communication.

However, from our extreme preoccupation with retribution, the need for restoration emerges. Ironically, a purely retributive approach intends to limit retaliation and vengeance, but it risks only masking retaliatory vengeance enacted by the state. Long ago, the ancient philosopher Plato illuminated the contrast between retribution and restoration. His dialogue titled *Protagoras* presented Socrates's discussion of virtue. When the topic of punishment was raised, Socrates explained,

> In punishing the wrongdoers, no one concentrates on the fact that a man has done wrong in the past, or punishes him on that account, unless taking blind vengeance like a beast. No, punishment is not inflicted by a rational man for the sake of the crime that was committed—after all one cannot undo what is past—but for the sake of the future. . . . Whoever stays outside the lines [of the law], it punishes, and the name given to this punishment both among yourselves and in many places is correction, intimating that the penalty corrects or guides."[6]

---

[6] See Plato's dialogue *Protagoras*, segments 324b and 326e, in *The Collected Dialogues of Plato*, ed. E. Hamilton and H. Cairns (Princeton, NJ: Princeton University Press, 1963), in which he discusses the response of anger to wrongdoing.

Based on such reasoning, punishment itself becomes more a matter of restorative justice than the mere exercise of just retribution. Socrates, as presented in Plato's dialogue, offers us real insight in this passage. Today, some individuals, grappling with crimes that deeply harmed loved ones, struggle with our purely retributive approach and begin a journey of envisioning a potentially transformative, future-oriented set of restorative ideas and practices.

Restorative Justice Journeys

The members of the Pelke family were relieved that the judge "had the guts" to give Paula Cooper *exactly* what she deserved for the petty robbery and brutal murder of Ruth Pelke, the seventy-eight-year-old family matriarch and Bible teacher in Indiana. Initially, Bill Pelke felt justice had been served when Paula, a fifteen-year-old offender, was sentenced to death by electrocution in 1986 for his grandmother's murder.[7] Bill was passionately supportive of Paula's death sentence, but over time he became an equally passionate advocate of national and international efforts to overturn Paula's death sentence. Bill's journey was triggered by the haunting realization that his initial response violated all the Christian values his grandmother taught in her Bible studies. Bill was also haunted by questions about who Paula was and how she could commit a heinous murder. He sought out members of the Cooper family to understand Paula and then learned of her troubled childhood of abuse and neglect. He began to consider the possibility of her transformation. His subsequent correspondence with and visiting of Paula in prison played a role in encouraging that possibility. As his understanding of an alternative vision of justice deepened, he worked to create Journey of Hope . . . From Violence to Healing and other organizations focused on what he came to understand to be "restorative justice."

In 1989 the Indiana Supreme Court commuted Paula's sentence to sixty years, a sentence further reduced due to her good behavior and engagement in educational and service initiatives. During her imprisonment, Paula worked to transform her life, completing high school and college degree correspondence programs in addition to serving as a trainer of companion

---

[7] In 1986 Indiana law allowed defendants as young as ten years to be tried as adults and face a death sentence. In 2005 the Supreme Court banned the execution of juveniles in *Roper v. Simmons*.

dogs for disabled persons and a respected inmate counselor. She took advantage of such programs, which have become increasingly uncommon in prisons today. Based on her behavior, she received permission to participate in a work release program, enabling her to donate her earnings to victim-support programs. In June 2013, Paula, who was a sixteen-year-old sentenced to death by electrocution for murder, was released from an Indiana prison at the age of forty-three. Meeting her as she exited the prison, Bill reiterated his hopes for her beginning her life anew following twenty-eight years of imprisonment. In a 2004 *Indianapolis Star* interview, Paula stated, "Everybody has a responsibility to do right . . . , and if you do wrong, you should be punished. . . . Rehabilitation comes from you. If you're not ready to be rehabilitated, you won't be."[8]

Having served her punishment and made good of it, Paula sought to be reconciled with society. To everyone's surprise, Paula was instructed not to have contact with Bill Pelke, despite the fact that his support had played such a role in her transformation and release. Reentering society at midlife after decades in prison proved very challenging for Paula, as she struggled to deal with her childhood, the terror of her adolescent death sentence, three years of solitary confinement and prison sexual abuse, her continuing moral guilt for the harm she had caused as a teenager, and her being permanently labeled a convicted felon offender. Yet she managed to persevere in struggling to shape a good life, eventually becoming employed and mentoring persons who had served their felony sentences. Friends, including Bill, were devastated to learn that Paula, eventually defeated and depleted by her desire to be defined as more than the worst action of her life, took her own life two years after her release. Now, with even deeper resolve, Bill continues to seek out offenders and murder victim family members and to reorient our criminal justice system from retribution to restoration, banishment to reconciliation, violence to healing. Through his work on restorative justice, Bill encountered persons like Azim Khamisa who, on their own, had already shaped a similar understanding of justice and a way of living this understanding. Bill and Azim shared the same journey of being thrown into reflections on justice by personal tragedy.

On January 21, 1995, a nineteen-year-old California university student named Tariq Khamisa began the final run of his pizza delivery shift. As he began knocking on apartment doors, he realized he had been set up

---

[8] Tim Evans, "Former Death Row teen Paula Cooper—who is she now?," *Indy Star* (June 13, 2014), http://www.indystar.com/story/news/crime/2015/05/27/indiana-death-row-teen-paula-cooper/10420879/.

for a pizza hijacking. On the street in response to a teenager's demand for the pizzas, he threw them in his car and began to drive away. A single bullet shattered his car window, ending his life. Angered by Tariq's refusal to hand over the pizzas and egged on to hold a handgun and shoot, Tony Hicks fired that fatal shot. Police quickly searched for Tony since he had already been identified for stealing a shotgun from Ples Felix, his grandfather who had raised him. Tony had decided to sell the shotgun to support his running away from his strict grandfather. One last night of partying with friends would be his neighborhood farewell. Unknown to Tony, California recently had passed a severe "tough on crime" bill. Rather than being processed through a juvenile system with a maximum sentence of youth detention until the age of twenty-five, now adolescents under the age of sixteen could be tried as adults. This law dramatically changed the rest of Tony's life.

Tariq's father, Azim, could not comprehend how three fourteen-year-olds and an eighteen-year-old could be involved in his son's murder. The loud chorus of voices crying out for just retribution began to trouble Azim, a devout Sufi Muslim. From the paralysis of his sorrow came his inspiration. Rather than focusing on Tariq's killer as the target of his anger, he would commit to focusing on the forces that contributed to this senseless act of juvenile violence. Rather than being preoccupied with retaliatory justice, he threw himself into building a foundation committed to lessening youth violence. With the support of Tony's grandfather, Ples, and eventually Tony himself, the Tariq Khamisa Foundation began to take shape. Their shared foundation work transformed all their lives, helping them to heal and Tony to accept full responsibility for his actions. Pleading guilty to first-degree murder and expressing deep regret for his senseless act of violence, Tony hoped for Azim's forgiveness over time, which in turn gave Azim hope for this young man's moral transformation. After hearing Tony's sentence of twenty-five years to life, Azim recognized his efforts were rightly focused on restorative justice rather than retributive justice. He sought to relieve his anger by working to heal and restore all persons affected by Tariq's murder and to address conditions contributing to youth violence and prison recidivism. He sought an alternative way of responding to crime that encouraged responsibility, lessened offending, and promoted a broader quality of life in local communities.

Over time Azim and Ples shaped a school-based program, teaching that violence is a tragic choice causing deep suffering to a wide range of persons—victims, families of offenders and victims, and members of the community. Tony participated through letters, explaining his regrettable choices and their repercussions. Their programming led to national recognition and funding. Even more valued by Azim, the programming led to Tony's deepening commitment to living a good life of meaning and worth and repairing the harm caused by his action. Azim encouraged Tony to participate in every opportunity for educational programming and good behavior, leading to the possibility that he could work at the foundation if his transformation and commitment led to his parole after twenty-five years.

Azim gained great strength and motivation by coming to know other murder-victim family members. He joined Murder Victims' Families for Reconciliation, an organization that Bill Pelke helped shape to reorient our criminal justice system toward restorative justice. Over time these family members came to comprehend the conditions contributing to crime and the gravely unequal functioning of our criminal justice system as tied to interconnected hierarchies of class and race, which will be explored in the next two chapters. The narrow demands of retributive justice began to ring hollow the more they learned of the power of the state in selectively and inequitably prosecuting criminal behavior. They came to see that our current criminal justice processes were in many instances too rigid and often ineffective, if not destructive. They faced the fundamental question of whether our system truly furthered justice, broadly understood.

The journeys of both Bill Pelke and Azim Khamisa led them to sources within their Christian and Muslim traditions that shape a more restorative understanding of justice. Their deepened reflection on the meaning of their holy Scriptures, triggered by personal tragedy, brought them to live their religiously rooted commitment to restorative justice. Their personal journeys brought them to insights that have been lived in communities within our American tradition. Through their own experiences, they came to an understanding of restorative principles and practices that had begun to gain attention in the late 1970s and largely under the influence of religious communities. During that period, a range of writers and criminal justice practitioners began to articulate a quite different approach to crime and punishment—an approach that had deep roots in varying religious traditions, indigenous cultures, and localized communities. These voices grew in strength over the next three decades and gradually shaped a contrasting understanding of what justice is and how it should be practiced. This alternative understanding, focused on restorative justice, was seen as offering us rich resources as we begin to grapple with the very serious challenges posed by our current criminal justice system. It became clear that our criminal justice system needs to be fundamentally reoriented toward restorative justice. Only with such reorientation can we begin to address the depth of problems within our system.

Reorienting Our Criminal Justice System

Rather than narrowly focusing on retributive responses by the state to legal violations, restorative justice principles and practices focus on addressing human harms and needs—the needs of crime victims, local communities, and offenders. These principles and practices face the complexity and range of these harms and needs. They respond to

- the desire of crime victims and their loved ones to understand the truth about the wrongs done by offenders—what was done and for what reasons;

- the victims' and their loved ones' desire for acknowledgment of the harm done by offenders and the need for them to rectify the wrongs in some way;

- the community's need for recognition of the fact that crime violates shared values and damages all members, rendering them more vulnerable and less secure and trusting;

- the offenders' need to recognize and be held accountable for the harms they chose to do to persons and to provide restitution or reparation, even if only partial and symbolic due to penal restrictions on their actions; and

- the community's recognition of contributing factors of crime, even the extent to which harms done to offenders may have contributed to their choices.

And in affirming the need for these responses, supporters of restorative justice recognize that our current, adversarial judicial system often works against addressing such multiple needs. Judicial cases focus on the defense and prosecution teams winning court cases rather than disclosing the fullness of truth about crimes. Often even when sentenced, offenders are not encouraged to take responsibility for their actions, face the harms their actions produced, or envision ways to rectify their offenses. Moral and financial reparations for wrongs and harms go unattended. Offenders, defined by others solely in terms of their criminal offenses, often resist self-examination and transformation as they focus narrowly on winning appeals. And this is not surprising since our adversarial system focuses on winning or losing trials, negotiating retributive sentences, and winning or losing appeals. In such a context defined by wins and losses, multiple human harms and needs go unaddressed.

While the American criminal justice system remains focused on an adversarial approach strongly oriented toward retributive justice, restorative justice entails a paradigm or "lens" shift from purely punitive to reparative responses to harm done by persons to persons.[9] Such harms include physical and psychological damage to victims and their loved ones, the erosion of social trust and security, and damage done by offenders to themselves and their loved ones. A restorative justice approach fosters members of society addressing ways of preventing crime and rehabilitating persons who commit crimes, holding them responsible but also capable of transformation and social reintegration. Refusing to reduce offenders to their worst acts, such an approach opposes punitive measures that give up on offenders, defining them reductively and permanently as criminals and marginalizing them from society. It also focuses on harms that may have been done to offenders that played a role in their path toward wrongdoing, economic inequalities that influence crime, and the pervasive injustices of the system that result in disparate and wrongful convictions, which are explored in the next chapter. In shifting the lens through which we view crime and criminal justice, human harms and needs in all their complexity and range come into focus.

With such a shift, punishment serves multiple interwoven ends—(1) protection of the common good of persons in society, (2) restoration of public peace and order, (3) restitution for wrongs done to persons, and (4) rehabilitation of offenders. The fundamental orientation becomes future-focused on reparation and restoration rather than past-focused on payback for wrongs done through punitive retribution. As John Braithwaite emphasizes,

> Restorative justice involves a shift toward an active conception of responsibility, while still finding a more limited place for passive responsibility than is standard in criminal jurisprudence. While

---

[9] Howard Zehr, a leading writer on restorative justice, uses this image of "lens" in his *Changing Lenses: A New Focus for Crime and Justice*, 3rd ed. (Scottdale, PA: Herald Press, 2005). As a photographer, he recognizes that the lens one sees through shapes what is in the picture and the photographic outcome. So too viewing crime and justice through retributive or restorative lenses affects the elements and relationships at play and the outcomes (178).

passive responsibility means an offender being responsible for a wrong he has committed in the past, active responsibility is a virtue, the virtue of taking responsibility for repairing the harm that has been done, the relationships that have been damaged. Restorative justice is about creating spaces where not only offenders, but other concerned citizens as well, will find it safe to take active responsibility for righting the wrong done.[10]

Restorative justice is thus future-oriented toward responsibility, reparation, and restoration in response to actions that caused harm to persons— victims, offenders, loved ones, and community members. Such a shift in response to crime and criminal justice leads to shaping practices that bring persons and society to actively and responsibly work to right the wrongs done to persons by crime. It also leads to recognizing the role of community in actively responding to crime. As Howard Zehr stresses about those who have victimized or been victimized by crime, persons need social support characterized by both dignity and triumph that renews rather than humiliation and shame that defeats.[11]

In a fundamental sense, restorative justice is a perspective on how to form people and communities. Restorative justice is embedded in broad concerns for promoting justice in all its forms within communities. For this reason, it is not surprising that the two considered cases of Bill Pelke and Azim Khamisa focus on crimes by juveniles, even when tried as adults. Many practices of restorative justice center on crimes by juveniles, minor crimes by adults, and serious crimes by adults with significant mitigating factors. In many cases, restorative approaches complement or supplement the criminal justice proceedings. Current discussion of our criminal justice system across a wide political spectrum and by members of our society impacted by this system in very different ways is now beginning to raise the deeper question of whether our criminal justice approach should be subjected to a rigorous reconsideration of the most fundamental questions: What is justice, how is justice best served, and should our criminal justice system be focused on retributive justice exclusively or reoriented more toward restorative justice? A reorientation toward restorative justice in response to major adult offenses would entail a foundational shift

---

[10] "In Search of Restorative Jurisprudence," in *Why Punish? How Much?*, ed. M. Tonry, 342 (New York: Oxford University Press, 2011).

[11] John Braithwaite references these points made by Howard Zehr in a 2002 conference presentation titled "Journeying to Belonging" ("In Search of Restorative Jurisprudence," 343).

in our criminal justice system. And such a restorative approach may be unworkable in some cases, given recalcitrant offenders not open to self-examination, offenders with severe mental problems, and excessively vindictive victims. While recognizing this, the wide range of innovative restorative practices developed in specific countries (such as Canada and New Zealand), local communities, and particular corrections facilities provides an illuminating counterpoint to our settled, purely retributive approach to criminal violations. An exploration of them pushes us to critically examine what we are up to in our current practice of criminal justice.

Considerations of these practices also help us envision a more restorative approach that would modify, supplement, or provide alternatives to our state-pitted-against-the-offender adversarial model. In other societies such a restorative model has long been the norm, as exemplified in Afghani *jirga* practices, Navajo peacemaking courts, Maori conferencing practices, and aboriginal sentencing circles in native Canadian communities. In recent years international attention has been directed to noteworthy models of restorative justice, such as South Africa's Truth and Reconciliation Commission and indigenous practices fostering reconciliation following grave violence, such as the *Fambul Tok* practice following the Sierra Leone internecine war and the reconciliation practices following the Rwandan massacres. Numerous communities and local courts in the United States, many of which are featured in this book, have begun to institutionalize incrementally such restorative practices. Awareness of this alternative approach has very gradually increased in the United States, but for the most part American citizens continue to conceive criminal justice solely in terms of the retributive model.

This stark contrast raises another set of questions. Is it the case that more restorative models tend to be embedded in communities holding a far more communitarian conception of persons in contrast to conceptions emphasizing autonomous selves and procedural justice focused on protecting individuals' rights? The indigenous restorative practices emphasized in response to grievous harms found in the societies of South Africa, Rwanda, and Sierra Leone appear to be deeply rooted in the conception of *Ubuntu*, which conceives persons as inextricably embedded in an interconnected network of interpersonal relations. Emphases on restoration, reconciliation, rehabilitation, reintegration, and reparation stem from this fundamental core conception. Is it the case that a more atomistic conception of persons pulls in one direction and a more communitarian conception in another, lending toward more retributive or restorative approaches?

While we have seen increased awareness of the theory and practice of restorative justice in the United States, significant changes in the American criminal justice system work dramatically against moving this system in a restorative direction. As explored in the next chapter, mass incarcerations due to three-strike and rigid mandatory minimum sentencing practices have resulted in prisons being transformed into massive human warehouses of convicted felons. Escalating prison populations, massive overcrowding, and stretched fiscal resources work against restorative approaches. And in recent times the outsourcing of prisons to for-profit corporations that seek to minimize costs and maximize profits decreases the availability of counseling, spiritual ministry, and rehabilitative, educational, vocational, and reentry programming that contribute to the personal transformation seen in Paula Cooper and Tony Hicks. Such for-profit prisons risk reducing offender responsibility, transformation, and reintegration in communities. A profit-making business model, an overcrowded penal environment, and increasing budgetary pressures work against the orientation restorative justice encourages. In addition, relocating prisons from local communities to remoter rural settings diminishes the possibility of familial and communal relations that so often play a significant role in personal transformation and reintegration. The constellation of such factors greatly increases the likelihood of prisons being transformed into debilitating and crime-ridden holding cells for recidivist offenders. And yet awareness of these developments is what has prompted reflections on restorative justice today.

Failure to reorient the criminal justice system in a restorative direction will likely result in pushing this system toward the other end of the spectrum—toward a more punitive system that increasingly warehouses an endlessly increasing supply of offenders whose actions once evoked justifiable anger, who have been removed from local communities and are seen now as best forgotten, so long as they get what they deserve. Such an approach fosters recidivism and indifference to the plight of both victims and offenders, and manifests a glaring failure to address the complexity of the sources, realities, and consequences of crime that harms persons. Such a system tragically ends up only remotely connected with the noble concern of justice. Since justice is administered in our name and through our tax dollars, we are called to examine our criminal justice system and to transform it for the good of all.

We rightly take pride in being part of a society committed to justice. To be committed to justice calls us to devote ourselves to examining our conceptions and practices of justice—in our families, work environments, communities, and society. Responding to this call helps us to live more justly with one another. To fail to examine our current criminal justice system means we risk not knowing whether it truly promotes or undermines justice. To respond to the call to examine our conceptions and practices not only enhances our practicing of justice but in the end our capacity for even thinking about justice. As Plato rightly recognized in response to Socrates's conviction and punishment, our humanity is in peril if we fail to attend closely to justice. As persons who live with others in community, we are all served by our being attentive and responsive to calls to reflect on our assumptions about justice as practiced in our society.

The responses of the Mother Emanuel AME community members alerted us to this call as we listened to the news that one early summer day. So too Pope Francis's actions and words in Philadelphia gripped our nation for a week in 2015. His powerful gesture of visiting prisoners and their families on the forgotten fringes of that city inspired us to reflect on the justice that shapes our criminal justice system—and not only for a day, a week, or an entire Jubilee Year of Mercy, but in ongoing reflection tied to our personal, familial, communal lives. For it may be the case that our lives are filled with grace and hope through our commitment to understanding justice and living more justly in relation to each other.

Review and Looking Forward

Editors

If we conceive of justice on a spectrum with retributive justice at one end and restorative justice at the other, chapter 2 calls us to work to push our criminal justice system more toward restorative justice. Trudy Conway offers reasons for doing this; the subsequent two chapters will add sociological and economic data to strengthen this case. As our society begins to grapple with the needed repair of our criminal justice system, such arguments and data will be debated. Meanwhile practitioners of restorative justice will continue their daily work in local communities because they have seen the positive effects of restorative justice in addressing the fundamental needs of offenders, victims, and their communities. Repeatedly, practitioners tell us that restorative justice is all about relationships, an understanding that resonates with Pope Francis's frequent comments that the Gospel message centers on encounters among persons. Father David Kelly, who participates in a restorative justice ministry on the south side of Chicago, knows this all too well. Viewing crime as not primarily a violation of a criminal code, but rather a violation of relationships, he is convinced that we, as members of a church, a society, and a local community, must strive to repair the harm done to relationships by crime. For him, restoration is ultimately a work of God, and we must be workers within that field of God's work.

Often it is personal encounters that open people to the possibilities that arise through restorative justice. Father Kelly tells the story of his being invited to participate in one kind of restorative justice victim-offender circle, which will be discussed in later chapters.[12] This was a sentencing circle arranged in coordination with the court system. Participants in the circle included the young offender and his mother and the father of the family whose home the young offender had robbed. The father happened to be a police officer. He agreed to participate since he wanted the young offender to know what he had done to his family and to hear the strong words he had for him. During the dialogue, the police officer learned about the young man—how he never had a father growing up, the challenges he faced living on the south side of Chicago, and how he had gotten himself expelled from school. His mother spoke of her deep love of her son, her embarrassment over his crime, and the deep fears she had for him as he faced the violence in their community. The police officer described how he grew up in very similar circumstances without a father. All participants could observe the gradual changes in the officer's demeanor as he began to engage the young man. He explained that the harm done to his family had little to do with the stolen computer and damaged door. The harm was tied to the pain he experienced in regard to his five-year-old son. Since he had not had his father's protection as a child, he wanted always to be there for his son. He vowed to keep his son safe and was crushed when after the robbery, his son no longer wanted to live in their home and had to be sent to his grandmother's house. The young man had stolen the sense of safety and comfort that had defined his home. On hearing this, the young man apologized profusely; it was obvious that they had come to see each other very differently. Father Kelly asked the father how the harm that had been done could be repaired. The

---

[12] Fr. David A. Kelly, CPPS, recounted this story in his keynote address at the 2014 "Restore Justice! Encounter and Mercy" conference on restorative justice sponsored by the Catholic Mobilizing Network (CMN), held at Catholic University, Washington, DC, on November 21, 2014. Fr. Kelly is a Catholic priest of the Missionaries of the Precious Blood. He has worked for Kolbe House, a parish-based jail ministry of the Archdiocese of Chicago, since 1985. For more than thirty years he has worked as a chaplain in Cook County Jail and Cook County Juvenile Temporary Detention Center. In 2002 Fr. Kelly, along with other members of his religious congregation, began the Precious Blood Ministry of Reconciliation (PBMR) to reach out to and support those who have been impacted by violence and conflict.

officer said he had everything he needed. But then seeing his own young self in this youth, he explained that he wanted to do something. It was important to him that this boy go back to his school, a school that refused his return. A retired school principal in the circle explained that she could do something to make this happen. As the officer left the circle, he turned to the young man and handed him his card. Everyone present saw the irony and humor of the gesture since the boy clearly knew the location of the home he had burglarized. He also invited the young man to shoot hoops at the gym where he coached, having heard the boy describe his love of basketball. The officer went on to become his mentor, staying faithful to the relationship that began in that circle. It is hard to conceive such an encounter happening in a courtroom. Restorative justice cannot be reduced to a repeatable formula or to the application of a method or strategy. Rather it is a dialogical process that orients participants away from doing harm and toward restorative healing. And it is the absence of such restorative healing that too often characterizes our current criminal justice system.

Questions for Discussion

1. Retributive justice focuses on righting past wrongs by inflicting punishment on offenders. Justice requires that such wrongs be righted. Discuss whether restorative justice abandons this requirement or reconceives what is entailed in "righting wrongs."

2. Discuss the ways our criminal justice system often sidelines the needs and concerns of victims of crime.

3. Public defenders who serve the poor have to grapple with a criminal justice system in which persons of wealth fare far better than persons who are poor. Discuss the ways in which a criminal justice system narrowly focused on retribution fails to attend to the disparities concerning wealth that plague our society.

4. In what way does our criminal justice system (trials, sentences, appeals) not encourage offenders, who have committed the crimes for which they have been sentenced, to come to grips with their offenses and the harm they caused individuals and communities? Discuss in what ways restorative justice is different.

Chapter 3

Criminal Justice

Editors

Timothy Wolfe begins this chapter with a clear statement of what our current criminal justice needs. He presents a troubling overview of the interrelated and reinforcing problems that undermine social justice and human dignity in our current system. He is not alone in thinking that we can no longer avoid addressing these needs and problems. But he is also hopeful because he witnesses growing awareness of what concerns him and shared determination to work on improving this system. He is convinced that such improvement requires that we reorient our criminal justice system in the direction of restorative justice.

A 2016 PBS *NewsHour* broadcast considered jurisdictions across the country that are turning to restorative justice to address criminal cases.[1] Many of these jurisdictions began by applying restorative justice approaches to juvenile cases and, then, based on their positive outcomes (especially in regard to recidivism rates), subsequently applied them to adult cases. The program highlighted the case of two teenagers who attempted to steal a $600 power saw in a Boulder, Colorado, hardware store. Both were charged with theft, but their parents responded in dramatically different ways. One of the teen's parents took the route of fighting the

---

[1] This introduction draws a segment of the two-part PBS *NewsHour* series on restorative justice. Rebecca Beitsch, "States consider restorative justice as alternative to mass incarceration" (July 20, 2016), http://www.pbs.org/newshour/rundown/states -consider-restorative-justice-alternative-mass-incarceration/.

charge in court by hiring an expensive private defense attorney. This family was drawn into a lengthy legal battle as the attorney filed motions, looking for ways of getting the case thrown out. Rather than focusing on why their son engaged in stealing property, they focused on legal challenges, such as whether the security guard's searching of the boy's backpack was an illegal violation of his rights. The parents of the other teen sought to address their son's crime through a restorative justice process. They and their son participated in a restorative justice conference that included someone from the hardware store and a restorative justice facilitator. The dialogue focused on what the teen had done, why he did it, and how he could take responsibility for his action and repair the harm he caused. The conference produced an agreed-upon plan that enabled him to address his responsibilities in righting the wrong he had committed. The experience was very positive for everyone involved, and the young man avoided the collateral consequences of spending time in prison. The broadcast reviewed how thirty-five states have passed legislation encouraging the use of restorative justice for teens and adults both before and after they served time in prison. States are facing the massive costs and range of problems generated by mass incarceration—issues explored in this and the subsequent chapter. Recognizing the value of restorative justice programming, states are welcoming the assistance of local nonprofit organizations in developing and facilitating these programs. Some states, such as Vermont and Colorado, have passed legislation enabling the development of agencies to oversee and support restorative programming.

States have developed various ways of introducing restorative justice approaches within their judicial systems. Some states give judges the authority to direct adults, who have been sentenced to probation rather than prison, for assessments regarding participation in restorative justice programming. The broadcast offered viewers a glimpse into how restorative justice programming can work in addressing crime. It also showed how restorative justice can play a formative role in bringing offenders to understand what is reprehensible about their actions. Greg Brown, Boulder's chief probation officer, stresses the importance of such self-examination. He cites a case in which a man wearing a yarmulke was assaulted by two other men in a bar. The men resented being charged with a hate crime. In the context of a restorative justice conference, a bias specialist explained to the offenders the reasons why they were so charged. They finally understood what they had done only when the victim asked one of the offenders whether he would have assaulted him if he had not been wearing a yarmulke. This encounter led to a transformative dialogue about the impact of hate crimes. Prior to the presentencing conference, the victim sought to have the offenders serve the maximum permissible sentence. Following the dialogue, he no longer sought the maximum and supported the judge's decision to let the main attacker serve his sentence in separate segments so that he could keep his job. The dialogue also brought the bar owner to examine why he had allowed his bar to become a rough place in which such offensive behavior occurred. The other attacker helped him explore ways to transform the bar's reputation, even designing for him a bar mural promoting diversity and inclusion. The positive effects of such a restorative justice approach were evident to all the participants.

Attitudes are definitely affected by engagement in restorative justice programming. State Representative Pete Lee of Colorado is a lawyer who helped create Colorado's restorative justice pilot program for juveniles. He credits such programming with transforming the attitude of persons who go through such programming in contrast with regular court proceedings. He emphasizes, "The rest of the justice system doesn't work like that [as far as bringing persons to accept responsibility for their actions]. Lawyers are telling their clients not to talk to the victim or admit guilt. It's all denial, denial, denial until the plea agreement."[2] Restorative justice gives offenders the opportunity to examine and accept responsibility for their actions, work collaboratively to repair the harm they have done to victims and their community, and shape a future not defined by their worst actions.

The broadcast also raised concerns about attitudes regarding racial minorities and the poor that permeate our criminal justice system being carried over into restorative justice programming. Persons who organize and facilitate restorative justice programs must be vigilant in ensuring such biases do not influence assessments of persons as good candidates for such programming. The following two chapters bring us to recognize how attentive we must be regarding the role economic class and race play in all aspects of our justice system.

Restoring Our Justice System

Timothy W. Wolfe

We desperately need a better approach to dealing with crime, victimization, and rehabilitation. It is clear that what we are currently doing in the United States, what we have been doing for the past several decades, is not working. There has been wide questioning of whether our current system

---

[2] As quoted in Beitsch, "States consider restorative justice."

furthers the ends of justice, broadly and deeply understood, as discussed in chapter 1. Dissatisfaction with the status quo has never been higher. Conservatives, moderates, and liberals seem to be in agreement that our criminal justice system is broken. In a rare show of political unity, elected officials from both sides of the aisle are working together to address at least some aspects of our broken criminal justice system:

> Last year, Sens. Cory Booker, D-N.J., and Rand Paul, R-Ky., together wrote legislation aimed at helping nonviolent offenders seal their records. In February, Sen. John Cornyn of Texas, the No. 2 Republican in the Senate, and Sen. Sheldon Whitehouse, D-R.I., introduced legislation aimed at cutting prison populations by allowing eligible prisoners to reduce their time.[3]

These are relatively rare acts of political cooperation in hyperpartisan Washington. Clearly something is capturing the attention of policy makers of all political stripes, and the American public appears to be in agreement with them. Attitudes toward offenders are changing, as evidenced by growing support for eliminating mandatory minimum sentences, as well as allowing some offenders to regain their right to vote. As recently reported,

> The alliance of liberals and conservatives seeking reform of our criminal justice system seems to have public opinion on its side. A recent Reason-Rupe poll found that 77 percent of Americans now favor eliminating mandatory minimum sentencing, while 73 percent support allowing nonviolent drug offenders who have served their sentences to vote.[4]

So, what exactly is wrong with our criminal justice system? What about it is broken, in need of reform (or, perhaps more accurately, transformation)? These are the kinds of questions to which my initial response is, "There are so many problems that it is hard to know where to begin." The criminal justice system is vast and complex. Its major components include law enforcement, the court system, and corrections. And there is not one criminal justice system. All fifty states and the District of Columbia, plus the federal government and the US military, have their own laws and systems. And "system" suggests a level of orderliness and efficiency that

---

[3] Allan C. Brownfeld, "Bi-Partisan Agreement: The Criminal Justice System is Broken," *Communities Digital News* (May 12, 2015), http://www.commdiginews.com/featured/bi-partisan-agreement-the-criminal-justice-system-is-broken-41336/.

[4] Ibid.

is hardly the actual case in many jurisdictions across the nation. Still, I will use the term "criminal justice system" as it is typically used to refer to the broad patterns of policing, convicting, sentencing, and punishing offenders that are well known and of great concern to many observers.

Identifying the Problems

So while it is hard to know where to begin, we have to begin somewhere, of course. The purpose of this chapter is to provide an overview of some of the most broken aspects of our criminal justice system. I will show that the most significant problems in our criminal justice system include, but are certainly not limited to, (1) persistent and pernicious racial and class bias, (2) a so-called war on drugs and resultant mass incarceration that has been devastating to communities and corrupting of our police, (3) insufficient commitment to rehabilitation and reentry programs, the result of which is high rates of reoffending, and (4) insufficient attending to the needs of victims of crime (broadly defined to include the direct victims of crime, the families of victims and offenders, and the local community, all of whom suffer the impact of crime).

Taken together, the first three interrelated and reinforcing problems undermine social justice and human dignity, and they allow corruption to flourish. Most importantly, the third problem is tied to the fact that our criminal justice system has created (by design or by accident) a large and growing group of offenders, ex-offenders, their families, and neighbors who get pushed further and further to the margins of society, cast aside and seemingly forgotten, unable to effectively cope in a changing, competitive economy. In a similar way our system often marginalizes and even abandons victims of crime in communities due to the fact that funds directed to punishing vast numbers of offenders cannot be used to meet the needs of crime victims, such as victim support programming and preventive and rehabilitative measures that lessen the ongoing threat of crime in local communities. Too often such persons are left to cope on their own with the repercussions of crime in their lives and communities.

The effects of involvement with the criminal justice system can be devastating and long-lasting, persisting over generations, and they can even drag down entire neighborhoods. Every dollar spent on the war on drugs and the attendant aggressive policing, harsh sentences, and reliance on incarceration is a dollar that cannot be spent on victim support, crime prevention, housing, education, health care, job training, and infrastructure needs. "Million-dollar blocks"[5] refer to census units where the cost of incarceration for residents of that block exceeds a million dollars. Mapping software allows researchers to match inmates with their home addresses to show how much money we spend in a wasteful cycle of arrests, convictions, stints of incarceration, release, rearrests again and again for technical, nonviolent offenders in our poorest communities. As a result of this powerful visualization tool, policy makers and others have begun to think differently about how finite resources are used. For example, researchers with the New York-based Justice Mapping Center reported,

> One of the things we noticed right away when legislators and others started to see this, is they talked about this issue differently. Instead of getting stuck in the "being soft, get tough [on crime]" paradox, they started to talk about neighborhoods. . . . For example, in Connecticut, legislators started to talk there about the Hill neighborhood [in New Haven] . . . and why were we spending $6 million a year to remove and return a whole range of people for technical violations, when we could be investing some of those dollars in the social and economic well-being of those places?[6]

While there is growing awareness of the economic waste and human suffering that result from our ill-conceived war on drugs, the problems in our criminal justice system are still massive; the prison-industrial complex built over decades is still largely intact; and the need to dismantle and replace it is staring us in the face. There are signs of movement in the right direction, but we are only at the beginning of a social movement that will take time to transform our broken criminal justice system.

Related problems—from erroneous convictions and clear racial disparities in the application of the death penalty, to plea bargaining that has gone awry, inadequate funding of public defense, and the privatization and commercialization of prisons—persist and need to be addressed as well. Because all of these problems are interrelated and symptomatic of larger underlying problems, simply addressing one or even a few aspects of our broken criminal justice system will not be sufficient. We need change that is broad and deep. In order to properly change practices and policies, we need to change hearts and minds.

---

[5]As reported on Cities Project: NPR's Series on Urban Life in the 21st Century, Diane Orson, " 'Million-Dollar Blocks' Map Incarceration's Costs" (October 2, 2012), http://www.npr.org/2012/10/02/162149431/million-dollar-blocks-map-incarcerations-costs.
  [6] Ibid.

Rethinking Criminal Justice

All of the major components of our criminal justice system—cops, courts, and corrections—contribute to these problems. Why? The short answer is because we, the public, have accepted, even sometimes supported enthusiastically, this wrongheaded approach to crime and justice. This approach can be described as "retributive" as you may recall from reading the previous chapter. Therefore, to successfully change the system, we must address all components. We need a truly *systemic* or system-wide approach, a transformation if you will. We need a better way to think about crime and justice. We need to face the fact that our reliance on a heavily retributive philosophy has gotten us into this situation. Restorative justice principles and practices offer the best way forward.

One of the most thoughtful, provocative, and insightful analyses of our criminal justice system has been conducted by Michelle Alexander in her important and widely read book, *The New Jim Crow*.[7] Alexander lays out the historical and racial context that helps makes sense of our criminal justice policies over the past four decades. She shows in compelling fashion how one form of social control and marginalization has been replaced by a new one. Her view, shared by many who observe and study our criminal justice system, can be hard to accept at first. But after looking carefully at the evidence and the strength of her argument, it becomes easier to see how our supposedly color-blind justice system, in fact, perpetuates racial discrimination. In effect, our entire criminal justice system—from the enforcement of laws on the streets to prosecution and sentencing in our criminal courts to the warehousing of inmates in our prisons—serves to maintain a racial and class hierarchy.

I want to drive home a key point before getting into the next part of this chapter: There is a window of opportunity to make bold changes to our criminal justice system. It is crucial that reform-minded policy makers, activists, and citizens move quickly and effectively, before our collective attention is diverted to other issues. *Now* is the time to change our way of thinking about crime and justice, to discard those principles and practices that undermine genuine justice and instead embrace principles and practices that truly promote community safety, victim rights, rehabilitation of offenders, and real social justice. I hope that you will sense and embrace this urgency and do all that you can to push for reforms. David

---

[7] *The New Jim Crow: Mass Incarceration in the Age of Colorblindness*, rev. ed. (New York: New Press, 2012).

Cloutier brought us to understand justice in all of its interrelated aspects. In a similar way we need to think about the challenges we face in all the interrelated aspects of our criminal justice system. We have tried so-called get tough policies for decades. Enough of get tough, let's start to get smart.

Law Enforcement: What's Wrong with Policing in America?

Michael Brown. Eric Garner. John Crawford. Ezell Ford. Rumain Brisbon. Jerame Reid. Phillip White. Eric Harris. Walter Scott. Freddie Gray. Tamir Rice. Sandra Bland. Laquan McDonald. Philando Castile. It would be easy (too easy, sadly) to add more names to this list, but I think the point has been made: some of these have become household names, as Americans have learned over the past couple of years that policing in America is broken. The lack of trust and respect for police in many communities is profound. Too often police engage in misconduct that can be deadly and that deepens the community's mistrust of police in particular and the broader criminal justice system more generally. If you support the Black Lives Matter movement, or if you are suspicious of this movement and, instead, place yourself in the camp of those Americans who are "pro-police," you will still most likely agree that police-community relations are strained (to say the least). How strained?

There are several ways to answer this question. For one, protests—often peaceful, sometimes violent—in cities and towns across America that we have all witnessed on the screens of our televisions and electronic devices make clear just how strained police-community relations are. Chants of "No justice, No peace, No racist police" capture the sentiments of many of our citizens, particularly our fellow Americans of color. People take to the streets when they are fed up, when they sense that something needs to be done now. Those who are content do not march in demonstrations.

The discontent expressed by protesters and demonstrators is also revealed in polling data. For example, a scientific poll conducted by CNN/ ORC in February 2015 asked, "In general, do you think that the country's criminal justice system treats whites and blacks equally, or does it favor whites over blacks?" Only about half (49 percent) of white respondents answered that the criminal justice system treats whites and blacks equally, while about a fifth (19 percent) of black respondents answered that treatment of the races was equal.[8] In a different poll that asked, "How confident

---

[8] CNN/ORC Poll (February 12–15, 2015), as reported by PollingReport.com, http:// www.pollingreport.com/race.htm.

are you that the police in this country treat whites and blacks equally: very confident, somewhat confident, not so confident, or not confident at all?" the results once again show a clear racial and ethnic divide: 17 percent of whites responded that they were "not confident at all" that police treat the races equally compared to 57 percent of blacks and 29 percent of Hispanics.

When this same scientific poll asked the question, "Do you think the recent killings of unarmed African American men by police in Ferguson, Missouri, and New York City are isolated incidents, or a sign of broader problems in treatment of African Americans by police?" a similar pattern emerged. That is, 60 percent of whites responded that these incidents were isolated, while 35 percent of whites said these cases were indicative of broader problems. For black respondents, 18 percent reported that these were isolated events, while 74 percent indicated that these cases were signs of broader problems in the treatment of blacks by police. For Hispanics, 45 percent reported these were isolated events and 51 percent thought these incidents were signs of a broader problem.[9] When we look at the criminal justice system in America, what we see depends on who we are and what our experiences have been. For many white Americans, the system seems fair, unbiased. For many black and brown Americans, the system (particularly law enforcement) seems unjust.

While protests and polling data, it can be argued, are really measures of perception that may not accurately reflect what actually occurs, we know that police do, indeed, treat people differently, depending on the race and social class of the people they encounter. Research has shown us, for example, that police are more likely to stop minority motorists than white motorists.[10] In one study of more than 250,000 traffic stops over thirteen years in Durham, North Carolina, researchers found the following:

> Our review of racial differences in traffic stops in Durham reveals some very troubling patterns and trends. Consistently, no matter whether we look at univariate correlations or conduct a more sophisticated multivariate regression analysis using every available control, Blacks are subject to much greater odds of search and therefore arrest. This is particularly true among men, and

---

[9]ABC News/Washington Post Poll (December 11–14, 2014), as reported by Polling Report.com, http://www.pollingreport.com/race.htm.

[10] Frank R. Baumgartner, Derek A. Epp, and Bayard Love, "Police Searches of Black and White Motorists," UNC-Chapel Hill (August 5, 2014), https://www.unc.edu/~fbaum/TrafficStops/DrivingWhileBlack-BaumgartnerLoveEpp-August2014.pdf.

especially so among younger men. Further, the trends are growing, not disappearing, over time.[11]

Other carefully conducted social scientific research studies find this same pattern: police are more likely to stop minority motorists. We also know that police in large cities (e.g., NYC) and smaller towns (e.g., Ferguson, MO) across the country are more likely to stop and frisk young minority males than any other demographic group. It is this persistent problem and the related killings of minorities at the hands of police that has given rise to the Black Lives Matter social movement and the "Hands up, don't shoot" expressions many of us have heard and observed (and, perhaps, said ourselves).

In addition to surveys and rigorous scientific studies that examine large samples, control for relevant variables beyond race and gender, and use the latest and most sophisticated statistical techniques, we also know from insider accounts that some police departments have a culture that encourages brutality, especially toward minorities and the poor. Michael A. Wood Jr., a white, war-tested US Marine and former Baltimore police officer, recently exposed the Baltimore Police Department's racist attitudes and conduct via a series of tweets, interviews with the media, and blog posts on his website (michaelawoodjr.net). He has made painfully clear how he and his Baltimore PD colleagues targeted minorities in order to "make their numbers" or meet expectations of their supervisors. If any reader is skeptical that police officers intentionally target and brutalize minorities, all you have to do is listen to Wood's interviews and read his tweets and blog posts. In plain and compelling fashion, Wood explains how he and his colleagues would never think about arresting white people in wealthy neighborhoods for drugs and other related offenses. Instead, they would go into "the hood" to make those arrests. Further, Wood makes the crucial point that the problems he observed and sometimes took part in are not adequately explained by "a few bad apples" as is often invoked to explain away police misconduct. Instead, he rightly points out that these problems are deeper, they are systemic, and they have their roots in our war on drugs.

All of these sources of data—polls, sophisticated quantitative studies, and insider accounts—confirm what many of us have known for a long time: police brutality, especially toward poor minorities, is real, hardly a fabrication of the media or of the citizens and activists who reside in low-income neighborhoods. Think back to the list of names at the beginning

---

[11] Ibid., 28–29.

of this section and all of the media attention those police killings generated. How many middle-class and unarmed whites died at the hands of police? How often do white people in the suburbs complain about police brutality? The answers are obvious.

Having identified the problem of police brutality, we are still left with the question of what drives this. Why do some police engage in brutality, especially toward our younger black and brown citizens? Part of the answer is to be found in our war on drugs, militarization of law enforcement, and deep commitment to a retributive approach to crime and justice that emphasizes punishment, that promotes a "lock 'em up" mentality. Waging war quite naturally leads to an "us against them" way of thinking and acting. In war, there are allies and there are enemies, our side and their side. It is hard to imagine police taking seriously the call to "serve and protect" when their supervisors are pressuring them to "make numbers," to "increase arrests," to "win the war on drugs." We need to change how we think about crime. We need to reform policing so that rapport and trust can be established between officers and the communities they serve. Reorienting our system from retributive justice toward restorative justice, as discussed in the last chapter, will go a long way in helping us make such changes.

Courts: What's Wrong with Our Criminal Courts in America?

Other aspects of our criminal justice system are likewise broken. Two specific areas are addressed in this section: sentencing disparities, whereby minorities are disproportionately charged and convicted of crimes relative to their white counterparts, and overly harsh sentences that can permanently stigmatize and cripple offenders such that they have a very difficult time reentering society with bright prospects. We will look at each in turn.

Sentencing disparities have been the topic of social scientific research for many decades, while sentencing reform has become a topic of conversation among policy makers only in recent years. Similar to the patterns and trends mentioned above in a previous section, research studies reveal that one's race and social class, independent of other key factors such as strength of evidence and severity of crime, are key predictors of how one will be treated by the courts. One of the most respected and influential groups to examine these issues is The Sentencing Project. Having been established in 1986, The Sentencing Project "works for a fair and effective U.S. criminal justice system by promoting reforms in sentencing policy, addressing unjust racial disparities and practices, and advocating for alternatives to incarceration."[12] In their thirty years of conducting high-quality scientific studies, they have provided some of the most widely cited research findings and policy analysis. What they have consistently found is a serious problem with racial disparities. Summarizing what they have found over the years, they report the following:

> More than 60% of the people in prison are now racial and ethnic minorities. For Black males in their thirties, 1 in every 10 is in prison or jail on any given day. These trends have been intensified by the disproportionate impact of the "war on drugs," in which two-thirds of all persons in prison for drug offenses are people of color.[13]

The war on drugs, in general, and sentencing policies, like mandatory minimum sentences and three strikes, account for the vast increase in our jail and prison populations and the accompanying overrepresentation of racial and ethnic minorities (who are often poor). Beginning in the 1970s and picking up momentum in the 1980s and '90s, drug laws became increasingly punitive. Discretion in sentencing offenders was largely taken away from judges, replaced with some of the harshest sentences we have witnessed in recent times. Examples of this include not only so-called three strikes and mandatory minimum sentences, but also "truth in sentencing" policies that increased the average length of time served in prisons. Politicians competed with one another to demonstrate that they were tougher on crime than their opponents. The equivalent of an arms race in criminal justice policy, especially sentencing, led to what we now call mass incarceration.

The effects of this "arms race" and resultant mass incarceration hit minority and low-income communities particularly hard. While research consistently reveals that drug use is fairly evenly distributed across racial and ethnic groups,[14] the criminal justice system treats minorities much more harshly for drug offenses. No serious observer of our criminal courts disputes this. It is widely recognized now that the war on drugs and its draconian sentences have devastated individuals, families, and communities. As a recent report put it,

> the criminal justice system evolved into a highly punitive system designed to distance people from society. It neglects the strengths

---

[12] The Sentencing Project, "About Us," http://www.sentencingproject.org/about-us/.

[13] Ibid., http://www.sentencingproject.org/issues/racial-disparity/.

[14] A number of sources, such as "Monitoring the Future" surveys of youth, find that whites and minorities have similar rates of drug use.

of individuals and communities and generally leaves individuals worse off than before they entered the system. The consequences of this era are staggering: the United States is the world leader in incarceration with 2.3 million adults in jail or prison on any given day and an incarceration rate of more than 100,000 citizens. . . . Mass incarceration disproportionately affects vulnerable segments of the country's population. People of color, those in poverty, and those with behavioral health disorders are grossly overrepresented in U.S. jails and prisons.[15]

So, we know that our criminal courts, much like the police in many communities, treat people differently. This is a clear example of how our criminal justice system is broken. A related and very serious problem with our criminal courts is the severity of sentences imposed, particularly for nonviolent crimes. Racial disparities in sentencing have shaped who is held in our prisons, while the comparatively harsh length of sentences for a variety of offenses ensures they will be there for a long time.

Compared with other wealthy, developed democratic nations around the world, we in the United States have particularly harsh and lengthy criminal sentences. As reported in a *New York Times* article,

> The United States has less than 5 percent of the world's population. But it has almost a quarter of the world's prisoners. Indeed, the United States leads the world in producing prisoners, a reflection of a relatively recent and now entirely distinctive American approach to crime and punishment. Americans are locked up for crimes—from writing bad checks to using drugs—that would rarely produce prison sentences in other countries. And in particular they are kept incarcerated far longer than prisoners in other nations. Criminologists and legal scholars in other industrialized nations say they are mystified and appalled by the number and length of American prison sentences.[16]

Close study of our current criminal sentencing systems reveals an extreme focus on retributive justice, applied in sentences that undermine rather than promote justice.

---

[15] Matthew W. Epperson and Carrie Pettus-Davis, "Smart Decarceration: Guiding Concepts for an Era of Criminal Justice Transformation," Center for Social Development at Washington University in St. Louis (2015), 2.

[16] Adam Liptak, "Inmate Count in U.S. Dwarfs Other Nations," *The New York Times* (April 23, 2008).

Corrections: What's Wrong with Our Correctional System in America?

Similar to the problems with police and the court system, our correctional institutions are broken. For one, many are overcrowded because we incarcerate more people in the United States, both as a raw number and as a rate, than any other country for whom we have reliable data. This is not an area in which the US should want to be number 1. As mentioned above, we have more than 2.3 million adults locked up in our jails and prisons. About half of all of these inmates are there for low-level drug offenses. Our correctional institutions are filled, largely, by brown and black males who are typically poor and poorly educated. Many have drug and other behavioral health problems.

Additionally, there is too little "correction" or successful rehabilitation in our jails and prisons. Instead, they have become human warehouses. Inmates' problems—like addiction, mental health issues, and lack of skills and education—go largely unaddressed. In many respects, we effectively give up on some offenders. Treatment for mental and behavioral health disorders are severely lacking. Educational and job training programs are relatively few and far between. As a result, when inmates are released they have the same problems coming out of the institution they had going into it. Actually, they may return to their communities in even worse shape, as a criminal conviction stigmatizes them and makes it extremely hard to find employment and become reintegrated into their local communities. The message seems clear: once a felon, always a felon. Howard Zehr, a prominent writer on restorative justice, emphasizes the difference between indelible stigmas that debilitate and reintegrating shame that enables offenders to accept responsibility for their past choices and begin shaping a different future through better choices.

The case of Paula Cooper discussed in the last chapter gives us a sense of the immense challenges faced by persons at the end of prison sentences. Due to exceptional support systems in prison, Paula underwent positive personal transformation, was able to prepare well for reentry into society, was employed by Five Guys (a company committed to employing former offenders) upon release, and eventually became an admired legal assistant in a public defenders office. But no matter what she did, she felt she was permanently defined as a felon. It is no wonder, then, that many released prisoners, lacking such supportive networks in and outside prison, quickly experience despair as they try to navigate reentry and reintegration into their communities. Far too many end up returning to the streets and the problems that put them in prison. Rates of recidivism or reoffending are particularly high, with two-thirds of those released from our "correctional" institutions returning in a short period of time.

Given the dearth of treatment, education, job training, and reentry programs, plus the permanent stigma of "ex-con," it is no wonder that rates of reoffending are high. Underlying risk factors and deficits are not routinely and effectively addressed. What is more, some inmates are kept in solitary confinement, cut off from regular human interaction. As a result, their mental health deteriorates, their prospects for returning successfully to their communities decline, and their lives are made increasingly difficult. As former Democrat Senator Jim Webb from Virginia wrote,

> Our overcrowded, ill-managed prison systems are places of violence, physical abuse, and hate, making them breeding grounds that perpetuate and magnify the same types of behavior we purport to fear. Post-incarceration reentry programs are haphazard or, in some places, nonexistent, making it more difficult for former offenders who wish to overcome the stigma of having done prison time and become full, contributing members of society.[17]

Rather than addressing our criminal justice problems, too often our correctional systems are part of the problem.

Victims: What's Wrong with Our Response to Victims in America?

Our get-tough-on-crime approach that resulted in our country's mass incarceration situation reveals a criminal justice system focused on meting out punishment to those charged with violating laws. Here, justice risks being reduced to retributive justice, as pursued by cops, courts, and corrections in our criminal justice system. Such preoccupation with getting and punishing lawbreakers often risks marginalizing and neglecting persons victimized by crime.

The experience of being victimized by crime, whether it be a minor or major offense, can be traumatizing and can produce long-term effects ranging from fear, immobilizing anxiety, anger, and financial losses to a sense of loss of control, withdrawal, and alienation. With attention focused on pursuing, prosecuting, and punishing the criminal, victims can feel forgotten and marginalized. Victims often say they want the offender to admit responsibility for the wrongs done to them, some reparation (real

---

[17] "What's Wrong With Our Prisons?" *Parade Magazine* (March 29, 2009).

or symbolic) for the harms suffered, and better understanding of why the crime was committed against them. Victims also emphasize their need to recover a sense of respect and agency, which the criminal act violated. These responses are tied up with their need for justice to be done—that their situation as victims of crime is being acknowledged, responded to, and addressed. But far too often, the victims of crime and their loved ones are called to play a part in the criminal justice system only in their capacity as witnesses for the state. At times when they do not support the goals of prosecutors, as in the case of family members of murder victims who oppose the seeking of a death sentence, they can feel silenced and discounted.

With the historical rise of our professionalized criminal justice system at the beginning of the twentieth century, interrelated bureaucratic agencies functioned to control and respond to crime.[18] Police tracked down offenders, prosecutors oversaw court proceedings, and corrections officials controlled the sentencing process. Crime victims and the community played a minimal role in such a system. The current criminal justice system far too often fails to address, even ignores, the needs of persons affected by crime, be they narrowly defined as the needs of victims, their family members, and the larger community victimized by crime. The exorbitant costs of our system leave little funding for victim support services and community programming to address the devastating effects of crime.

As we saw in the last chapter, in contrast to this retributive approach, restorative justice views crime fundamentally as a violation of persons and relationships. What, then, matters is the righting of the wrongs that entails offenders understanding and taking responsibility for the harms they caused, the community understanding what factors contributed to the crime and how to address the needs of persons affected by crime, and effective ways for diminishing crime and its devastating effects. As Howard Zehr explains,

> Restorative justice is an approach that involves, to the extent possible, those who have a stake in a specific offense and to collectively identify and address harms, needs and obligations, in order to heal and put things as right as possible.[19]

A more restorative approach will push our criminal justice system to expand our reflections on justice beyond the narrow confines of a purely retributive approach.

---

[18] Daniel W. Van Ness and Karen Heetderks Strong, *Restoring Justice: An Introduction to Restorative Justice*, 5th ed. (Waltham, MA: Anderson, 2015).

[19] *The Little Book of Restorative Justice* (Intercourse, PA: Good Books, 2002).

Summary and Conclusions

We desperately need to address the problems in our criminal justice system from broken trust between police and the people they are sworn to serve and protect to the mass incarceration of millions of Americans predicated on a war on drugs that has been devastating. There is rare agreement among elected officials across the political spectrum that we must fix this broken system. The public agrees. Now is the time to make the changes we need so badly.

Restorative justice, I believe, represents our best hope of addressing and reducing many of the problems we now face. As presented and argued in other chapters in this book, restorative justice principles and practices will help us improve the lives of crime victims, community members, and offenders. After reading this book, I think you will realize that we *must* reorient our understanding and practicing of justice. Our experiment in waging war against our own people has been a dismal failure. We stand at a moment in time when we can transform the system, making it more humane and more effective at truly protecting us from violence, assisting crime victims in meaningful ways, and offering offenders real opportunities to change their lives for the better. What is stopping us? What is stopping you from getting involved in this important work in some way?

Review and Looking Forward

Editors

Some cities and counties recognize the importance of improving the current state of law enforcement, the courts, and corrections. Given the tensions and confrontations that recently have surfaced across the country, thinking about how local communities view the police is a good starting point. One New Jersey county is engaged in such thinking. Camden county police chief Scott Thomson recognizes the importance of having his police officers out in the community, interacting with people as they go about their daily lives.[20] He prefers to have his police force viewed as a version of the Peace Corps rather than a military force. Problems arise

---

[20] This account draws on National Public Radio coverage of developments in Camden, New Jersey, in an *All Things Considered* segment by Jeff Brady. For the complete story, see http://www.npr.org/2015/05/22/408824877/obama-camden-n-j-police-a-model-for-improving-community-relations.

when police officers are seen as storming into the community only in response to incidents of violence.

One of Thomson's goals is to figure out ways to promote mutual understanding between officers and local residents. A major initiative is to promote daily encounters between local residents and police officers. This requires that officers get out of their patrol cars and start walking on the streets of Camden, interacting with the people they serve. President Obama cited Camden as a "symbol of promise" for the whole country. Camden county police officers line up daily for morning roll call at an office located in a trailer. Thomson says, in addition to the downtown central headquarters, he wanted to extend the department out into the community, with two offices located closer to where people live. Officer Virginia Matias already can see the positive effects of such an initiative. Walking in an area that once was busy with drug dealing, she now sees people coming and going, while doing their shopping in local stores. She chats with the local shop owners in Spanish, pleased to hear that they are no longer facing drug traffic problems. The act of daily walking helps build community interactions and relationships. Louis Tuthill, a professor of criminology at Rutgers University, knows the impact of such daily encounters. He describes what his research shows: "What I found was that for all crimes, generally, the foot patrols decreased crime between about 10 percent and 19 percent, depending on the quarter. . . . Robberies with a firearm had a decrease of 51 percent." Camden's murder rate has been cut in half. While there are still numerous problems that need to be addressed, the local community appreciates that there are some signs of progress.

Many of the issues raised in this chapter are overlooked in policy discussions of our criminal justice system. Timothy Wolfe walks us through many aspects of our criminal justice system that are in dire need of reform. But consistent with other chapters in this book, his final message is one of hopeful resilience. He is convinced that we can marshal the stamina and determination needed to address these problems. And he is convinced that restorative justice offers a path to improving the lives of crime victims, community members, and offenders. This book references numerous programs that begin to address these problems.

Restorative justice practitioners are also hopeful for a different reason. In his book *Changing Lenses*, Howard Zehr argues that a restorative paradigm of justice preexisted our current retributive paradigm.[21] We have

---

[21] *Changing Lenses: A New Focus for Crime and Justice* (Scottdale, PA: Herald Press, 1990), 97–125.

not always handled crime the way we do today. The narrowly retributive approach, which developed during the Enlightenment period, views crime as an offense against the state that must be rectified by the state through retributive punishment. Offenders are judged as guilty by the state and punished by the state. Responsible restitution, reparation, and restoration are no longer of central concern; neither are the healing of persons and repairing of relationships. Howard Zehr is convinced such a system generates endless problems that require continuous reforms. Timothy Wolfe and Alejandro Cañadas, the author of the next chapter, identify and analyze our current problems. Most importantly, they remain hopeful about our capacity to reorient our understanding and practicing of justice. The practicing of restorative justice, referenced in so many concrete instances in this book, enable them to sustain their hope in the possibility of the reforms they envision and work to promote.

Questions for Discussion

1. For many people, exposure to the criminal justice system is through films and television shows that focus on crime. Timothy Wolfe's chapter may disclose to readers aspects of our criminal justice of which they were not previously aware. Discuss which aspects of our justice system were disclosed to you for the first time through the chapter. Why might many Americans not be aware of what occurs in our criminal justice system?

2. In Hebrews 13:1-3 we are called to "Let mutual love continue. . . . Be mindful of prisoners as if sharing their imprisonment, and of the ill-treated as of yourselves." In Matthew 25:31-46, we encounter Jesus explaining to his followers the criteria by which he will judge them. Consistent with the statement in Genesis 1:26-27, that every human being bears the "image and likeness of God," Jesus reminds his followers, then and now, that it is his face they see when he states, "For I was . . . in prison and you visited me" (Matt 25:35-36). When we visit prisoners, we learn about what is happening in our prisons and criminal justice system. Discuss whether you think all citizens, especially those who are Christians, have a responsibility to learn about mass incarceration in our society and its effects on individuals, families, and communities. Discuss your reasons for thinking as you do.

3. This chapter speaks of the gulf that exists in some locales between the police and members of the community. This "us against them" gulf has been captured in billboards proclaiming "Blue Lives Matter" in contrast to signs and chants announcing "Black Lives Matter." Pope Francis repeatedly calls us to promote encounters between persons. Discuss how honest dialogue and personal encounter can help begin to build trust and rapport within our communities.

4. Fiscal budgets have moral dimensions in that they express our values and priorities. Discuss what might be morally problematic and shortsighted about our spending exorbitant funds on mass incarceration while inadequately meeting the needs of persons dealing with mental or drug problems, facing crime victim trauma, and facing reentry challenges after serving prison sentences.

Chapter 4

The Criminal Justice Economy

Editors

Chapters 3 and 4 bring into clear focus a criminal justice system in dire need of extensive reform. Rarely do we hear urgent calls for such systemic reform from the highest ranking members of our judiciary. But such a call was voiced by Supreme Court Justice Anthony Kennedy in his testimony on March 23, 2015, before a House appropriations subcommittee on the 2016 federal judiciary system and Supreme Court budget. Justice Kennedy could not have been more direct in his assessment of our criminal justice system when he stated, "In many respects, I think it's broken."[1] In agreement with Kennedy, Republican Representative Steve Womack of Arkansas described the corrections system as "one of the most overlooked, misunderstood institutions we have in our entire government," adding that it focuses solely on issues of guilt and innocence rather than "corrections" that should follow. Kennedy concluded, "This idea of total incarceration just isn't working and it's not humane." In reporting on the hearing, *The New York Times* editorial board supported Justice Kennedy's conclusions, raising an issue central to this chapter. Their editorial argued that "all too often decisions about sentencing and corrections are made without meaningful consideration of their long-term costs and benefits, or of

---

[1] "Supreme Court Fiscal Year 2016 Budget," C-Span (March 23, 2015), www.c-span.org/video/?324970-1/supreme-court-budget-fiscal-year-2016.

their effect on the millions of people who spend decades behind bars."[2] Despite repeated attempts to introduce bipartisan sentencing reform bills, Congress continues to face the challenge of passing needed reforms. Yet despite such legislative inaction, on a daily basis individuals working in our criminal justice system and restorative justice programs advocate for and try to do all they can to further such reform within their local communities and courtrooms. And they often do so with great success, helping us to envision what is possible. One such case is the story of Justice Cathy Serrette and Chris Wilson, who model well the method of "seeing, judging, and acting" featured by Alejandro Cañadas. A video made during the 2016 presidential campaign captures well their inspirational story.[3]

Chris Wilson faced what is a far too common life of extreme poverty and neglect in our poorest urban communities. Born and raised in Washington, DC, Chris faced a life surrounded by violent crime and drug addiction. At a young age he was subjected to a kidnapping at gunpoint and saw his mother raped and beaten by a police officer she had been dating; years later his father would be murdered. As a teenager, Chris was caught up in a world characterized by turmoil and illegal activities, which brought him to the day that shaped the rest of his life. Surrounded daily by violent interactions, he fired lethal shots in response to a threatening interaction with heavily armed teens. That choice led to his being convicted of murder, following his having been charged as an adult.

Facing a life sentence at the age of seventeen, Chris began a process of self-examination triggered by a promise to his dying grandfather that he would turn his life around. His participation in victim-impact conferences finally brought him to face what he had done and to contact the family of the young man he had killed. His reflections eventually produced his "positive delusion" that his future could improve by committing himself to bettering, in some way, the lives of individuals in poverty-stricken communities he knew so well. Hope in this possibility drove all his subsequent choices. Fortunately because of his age, he was serving his sentence in a Maryland prison that offered educational and rehabilitative programming. Vowing to take advantage of every opportunity to develop his skills, strengthen his positive attitude, and further his education, he eventually produced what he called his ten-year "master plan" for shap-

---

[2] See "Justice Kennedy's Plea to Congress," *The New York Times* (April 4, 2015), www.nytimes.com/2015/04/05/opinion/sunday/justice-kennedys-plea-to-congress .html?emc=eta1.

[3] "Be Bold, Change the System" (June 2, 2016), www.youtube.com/watch?v=UUVmeg V69og.

ing his future. His belief in the possibility of his being given a redemptive second chance to live a productive life of service sustained him. He threw himself passionately into daily efforts to fulfill his outrageously optimistic, overly ambitious plan, which impressed all who knew him in prison. And then he began to check off the goals listed on his plan. While imprisoned, Chris successfully completed high school equivalency and vocational shop programs, learned Spanish, and went on to earn an associate degree in sociology through a local community college program. Amazed by his success, prison officials allowed him to function as a mentor to other inmates, run a book club, and develop a career center directed toward reentry of inmates into local communities. He managed to acquire subscriptions to *Fortune*, *Forbes*, and *The Wall Street Journal*, which helped him to further refine his plans for the future. Reading an article on digital cameras in *Popular Science* gave him his initial idea for a business serving others. Confident of his emerging entrepreneurial talent, he and another inmate got permission to develop a photography business selling photos of prisoners and their visiting loved ones. To the amazement of prison officials, the business raised $40,000 in three years, funds Chris hoped would be used to refurbish the prisoners' gym.

Fortunately, Judge Cathy Serrette, the judge conducting his ten-year sentencing review, was able to "see, judge, and act" regarding Chris's impressive transformation. Seeing his accomplishments and judging the remaining goals of his plan to be truly amazing, she commuted his sentence to twenty-five years and agreed to release Chris if he showed continuing progress in completing his detailed master plan. Her belief in him deepened his resolve and dedication. Judge Serrette upheld her promise, freeing Chris after he had served sixteen years of his sentence.

Living in a halfway house and working at Strong City Baltimore, Chris still faced obstacles challenging his resolve. His caseworker discouragingly told him he should abandon his plan and be satisfied with a job pumping gas. But Chris kept to his plan of shaping a productive life of service that would help lift others in Baltimore City from the cycle of poverty and crime he knew all too well. And then he encountered other individuals also willing to give him another chance. When Chris walked into the administrative offices at the University of Baltimore and explained that his master plan included obtaining a business degree from this university, the dean was receptive. He set the conditions for his admission and offered financial support if Chris met them and was academically successful. Knowing the stigma associated with imprisonment, Chris asked that his past not be disclosed to members of the community. He wanted a fresh start before letting classmates know his story. After finishing his degree and beginning a number of service-related ventures, he eventually fulfilled his dream of creating a business that linked local small-size entrepreneurs and ex-offenders facing the challenge of finding work.

He is currently the founder and director of Barclay Investment Corporation, a contracting company that connects unemployed Baltimore residents with contracting clients who need their services. His corporation meets the needs of two sectors of the local community—community members facing steep challenges of finding employment and local maintenance, cleaning, and renovation businesses needing dedicated workers. Chris's own ethic is mirrored in the corporation's statement of what it does:

> We deliver work on schedule, and in the process we provide a sorely needed social function. The success of Barclay as a mission-oriented business hinges on deep, lasting relationships with our clients and our community.
>
> The Barclay team has decades of experience in the construction trades and cleaning industry, and they are motivated. Our people come from disadvantaged communities where sustained employment is tough to find. Often, their personal backgrounds present further challenges in seeking work. We can help them because we've been where they are now.[4]

Chris has been sought out by Johns Hopkins and Harvard universities for their MBA programs. But his enduring commitment to Baltimore City pulls him to continue and expand his successful service to the community.

Chris often explains in interviews that all he is accomplishing would not be possible if he had not been given a second chance. His satisfaction comes from being able to give back by helping others get that same chance. Given the staggering rates of vacant properties and unemployment in Baltimore City, he knows there will be a continuing need for his future-oriented plan that "bridge[s] the growing economic disparity between the lower and middle class population" of his city.[5] In addition to these economic initiatives, he actively supports sentencing reform, especially regarding juveniles, and a major shifting of our economic priorities. Redirecting public spending from mass incarceration to poverty and employment initiatives has the power to transform impoverished communities and lessen the devastating economic and human impact of mass incarceration. His story is an inspirational one of how both officers

---

[4] "What We Do," Barclay, http://www.barclayinvestmentcorporation.com/services -c21w2.

[5] "The Need," Barclay, http://www.barclayinvestmentcorporation.com/the-need.

of the courts and offenders can work effectively to transform individual lives and communities.

Economic Concerns and Our System of Criminal Justice

Alejandro Cañadas

One of the most damaging problems affecting our criminal justice system is its massive economic and social costs, which, relative to its benefits, signal an inefficient allocation of scarce resources and a source of many injustices produced by the high level of inequality in the system. There is a very strong correlation between inequality in income and social and human inequality, which produce social injustices at various levels in society. Knowing about important economic problems in our justice system is essential for two main reasons: first, it will help us better understand the reality of this system, and second, it will motivate us to find real and feasible ways to change and improve our criminal justice system. In this chapter I want to implement a three-step methodology for analyzing the main economic concerns about the criminal justice system in the United States. These steps are "seeing => judging => acting."[6]

The rest of the chapter is organized in this way: First, I start with the first step of *seeing*, where I describe some known facts about inequality and its effects in the criminal justice system in the US. Second, I use the step of *judging* to explain why inequality is a multidimensional economic problem that we have to address in order to improve our criminal justice system. Third, I use the step of *acting* in order to propose a useful framework of analysis to reduce inequality and the excessive costs of the criminal justice system in the US.

Step 1: Seeing *the Reality of our Justice System*

The American Civil Liberties Union (ACLU) estimates that the US, with only 5 percent of the world's population, has more than 20 percent of the

---

[6] Pope John XXIII describes the "seeing, judging, and acting" method in *Mater et Magistra*: "First, one reviews the concrete situation; secondly, one forms a judgment on it in the light of these same principles; thirdly, one decides what in the circumstances can and should be done to implement these principles. These are the three stages that are usually expressed in the three terms: look, judge, act" ([Vatican City: Libreria Editrice Vaticana, 1961] 236).

world's prison population, which makes the US the world's largest jailer. From 1978 to 2014, the US prison population has risen 408 percent, which means that 1 in 110 adults is incarcerated in a prison or local jail in the US, the highest rate of imprisonment in American history. It also means that 1 in 35 adults is under some form of correctional control, counting prison, jail, parole, and probation populations.[7] This situation did not develop by chance; we could say that the US has created a large-scale social experiment with enormous and very costly consequences. We have increased the per capita rate of imprisonment sixfold. After nearly fifty years of stability, the rate increased dramatically since the early 1970s, climbing from 110 per 100,000 in 1973, increasing to 470 per 100,000 in 2001, and reaching 612 per 100,000 in 2014. In 2001, America held in prison 1.3 million people and that number went up to more than 1.5 million[8] by the end of 2014.[9]

The number of prisoners held in state and federal correctional institutions by the end of 2014 was 1,561,500 individuals. "On December 31, 2014, state and federal correctional authorities held 1,508,600 individuals sentenced to more than 1 year in prison."[10] When we look at the capacity of prison facilities we discover this:

> Eighteen states and the [federal Bureau of Prisons] were operating at more than 100 percent of their maximum prison facility capacity at year end 2014, and seven states housed at least 20 percent of their prison population in privately operated facilities (New Mexico, Montana, Oklahoma, Hawaii, Mississippi, Vermont and North Dakota). Since [the Bureau of Justice Statistics] began tracking the number of prisoners in private prisons on an annual basis, the size of this population has grown 90 percent—from 69,000 prisoners in 1999 to 131,300 in 2014. . . . An estimated 516,900 black males were in state or federal prison on December 31, 2014, on sentences of more than one year, which was 37 percent of the sentenced male prison population. White males made up an

---

[7] See "The Prison Crisis," ACLU, https://www.aclu.org/prison-crisis.

[8] Some statistics show that the number of people in prisons in the US is closer to 2.2 million, including individuals in federal and state prisons as well as local jails. See, for example, Bureau of Justice Statistics, "Prisoners under state and federal jurisdiction, 1980–2015," https://www.bjs.gov/index.cfm?ty=kfdetail&iid=488.

[9] This information has been collected by the Bureau of Justice Statistics, "U.S. Prison Population Declined by One Percent in 2014" (September 17, 2015), https://www.bjs .gov/content/pub/press/p14pr.cfm.

[10] E. Ann Carson, "Prisoners in 2014," Bureau of Justice Statistics (September 17, 2015), https://www.bjs.gov/index.cfm?ty=pbdetail&iid=5387.

additional 32 percent of the male population (453,500 prison inmates), followed by Hispanic males (308,700 inmates or 22 percent). White females in state or federal prison at year end 2014 (53,100 prisoners) outnumbered black (22,600) and Hispanic females (17,800) combined.[11]

In 2012, real total government spending on the criminal justice system totaled "over $274 billion, or $870 per capita, a 74 percent increase relative to spending in 1993. In 2013, 11 states spent more on corrections than on higher education."[12] The rise in incarceration increases the economic burden on our society, resulting in the fact that "direct expenditures on the criminal justice system have increased substantially. Similarly, in 2012, real per capita criminal justice spending was $872 per year, up 43 percent over the same time period. Real expenditures on corrections were $83 billion, representing over a quarter of total criminal justice spending in 2012."[13] Research on the cost of the justice system in the US shows that criminal justice is the second fastest-growing category of state budgets, behind only Medicaid, and 90 percent of that spending goes to prisons. We are wasting trillions of dollars on an ineffective and unjust criminal justice system. According to a White House study,

> In addition to its direct costs, the criminal justice system also imposes substantial collateral consequences on individuals with criminal records, their families, and their communities. Having a criminal record makes it more difficult to find employment and depresses earnings. Criminal sanctions can also have negative consequences for individuals' health, debt, transportation, housing, and food security. These consequences can add up to large and lasting negative impacts for incarcerated individuals' families and communities. The probability that a family is living in poverty increases by nearly 40 percent while a father is in prison, and children with incarcerated parents face an increased risk of

[11] Bureau of Justice Statistics, "U.S. Prison Population Declined."

[12] Executive Office of the President of the United States, "Economic Perspectives on Incarceration and the Criminal Justice System" (2016), 7; https://obamawhitehouse.archives.gov/sites/default/files/page/files/20160423_cea_incarceration_criminal_justice.pdf. See also Bureau of Justice Statistics, "Employment and Expenditure," https://www.bjs.gov/index.cfm?ty=tp&tid=5; and Michael Mitchell and Michael Leachman, "Changing Priorities: State Criminal Justice Reforms and Investments in Education," Center on Budget and Policy Priorities (October 28, 2014), www.cbpp.org/research/changing-priorities-state-criminal-justice-reforms-and-investments-in-education.

[13] Executive Office of the President, "Economic Perspectives on Incarceration," 10.

a variety of adverse outcomes, including antisocial and violent behavior and lower educational attainment. . . .

These costs fall most heavily on Black and Hispanic men, poor individuals, and individuals with high rates of mental illness and substance abuse. Although Black and Hispanic Americans account for only 30 percent of the population, they comprise over 50 percent of the incarcerated population. . . . One-third of the prison population has received public assistance, and one in ten incarcerated Americans were homeless in the year before entering prison. . . . Criminal justice sanctions can compound existing disadvantages for these populations, reinforcing patterns of intergenerational poverty.[14]

What is noteworthy is that the incarcerated population has grown dramatically in the last thirty-five years, despite declining crime rates. Research shows that "adjusting for population, the incarceration rate grew by more than 220 percent between 1980 and 2014. The U.S. incarceration rate is higher" than the similar rate in any of the thirty-five countries in the Organisation for Economic Co-operation and Development, and "is more than four times the world average." However, "at the same time, crime rates have fallen sharply; between 1980 and 2014 violent crime rates fell by 39 percent" since 1980, and "property crime rates fell by 52 percent" from their peak in 1991.[15]

What is especially noteworthy is that research has found that incarceration growth is not the "cause of the drop in crime. Instead, the decrease in crime may be [associated with] a number of other factors, including demographic changes, changes in policing tactics, and improving economic conditions" (e.g., falling unemployment). Further research also solves this puzzle, showing that growth in US incarceration has been driven by criminal justice policies. On the one hand, "changes in the severity of sentencing and enforcement—longer sentences and higher conviction rates for nearly all offenses—have been the primary drivers of the incarceration

[14] Ibid., 8. Also see Rucker C. Johnson, "Ever-Increasing Levels of Parental Incarceration and the Consequences for Children," in *Do Prisons Make Us Safer? The Benefits and Costs of the Prison Boom,* ed. Steven Raphael and Michael A. Stoll, 177–206 (New York: Russell Sage Foundation, 2009); Doris J. James and Lauren E. Glaze, "Mental Health Problems of Prison and Jail Inmates," Bureau of Justice Statistics (December 14, 2006), https://www.bjs.gov/content/pub/pdf/mhppji.pdf ; and E. Ann Carson, "Prisoners in 2014."

[15] Executive Office of the President, "Economic Perspectives on Incarceration," 3.

boom."[16] On the other hand, "changes in arrest patterns have also likely contributed to incarceration growth. As crime rates have fallen, arrests have also declined but at a slower pace, resulting in increases in arrests per crime, for both violent and property crimes."[17]

High incarceration rates for nonviolent crime are a problem. A recent report from the ACLU shows that there are at least 3,278 people serving sentences of life without parole for nonviolent crimes. Around 79 percent of them were convicted of drug crimes. ("Drug arrest rates grew by over 90 percent between 1980 and 2014."[18]) Long sentences have been imposed for having a "small amount of cocaine in a pocket, selling $10-worth of crack to a police informant and mailing small amounts of LSD [to a friend]. Property crimes that earned offenders a permanent home in prison include shoplifting three belts, breaking into an empty liquor store and possessing stolen wrenches."[19] One of the problems of our criminal justice system is that by law, judges are bound by sentencing requirements even when they appear to be extreme and unjust. Along with the injustice of it, constantly imprisoning people who commit petty crimes is expensive. The ACLU estimates that life-without-parole sentences for nonviolent offenders add $1.8 billion to the cost of incarcerating those to whom they apply. "In the past 20 years, it has quadrupled, even as violent crime has declined."[20] Taxpayers spend almost $70 billion a year on corrections and incarceration.

The fact that "interactions with the criminal justice system are disproportionately concentrated among Blacks and Hispanics, poor individuals, and individuals with high rates of mental illness and substance abuse" reveals inefficiencies, ineffectiveness, and injustice in the system. For instance, even though "Blacks and Hispanics represent approximately 30 percent of the population, they comprise over 50 percent of the incarcerated population." What is more, "a large body of research finds that, for

---

[16] Executive Office of the President, "Economic Perspectives on Incarceration," 8. In particular, the increase in convictions likely reflects the "get tough on crime" movement in the 1980s and 1990s that caused cultural changes in the criminal justice system. The "war on drugs" expanded resources for fighting drug crime and placed an emphasis on incarcerating individuals arrested for drug crimes.

[17] Ibid., 3–4.

[18] Ibid., 4.

[19] "Throwing away the key: A shocking number of non-violent Americans will die in prison," *The Economist* (November 16, 2013), www.economist.com/news/united -states/21589868-shocking-number-non-violent-americans-will-die-prison-throwing -away-key.

[20] "Throwing away the key," *The Economist*.

similar offenses, Blacks and Hispanics are more likely than Whites to be stopped and searched, arrested, convicted, and sentenced to harsher penalties." If we consider the level of education of prisoners, "approximately 65 percent of prisoners have not completed high school and 14 percent have less than an 8th grade education." Research shows that people with mental health problems and the poorest are more likely to be imprisoned. "Over a third of the prison population has received public assistance at some point in their lives, 13 percent grew up in foster care, and over 10 percent experienced homelessness in the year prior to entering prison. Over 50 percent of the incarcerated have mental health problems, while approximately 70 percent were regular drug users and 65 percent regularly used alcohol prior to being incarcerated."[21] The inefficiencies and injustices of our criminal justice system also impose an economic burden on taxpayers and society in general.

Step 2: Judging *the Reality of Inequality as an Economic Problem*

To get an estimate of the costs of the US criminal justice system including its local, state, and federal government levels is challenging, especially given its "complex and interconnected structure." Based on the 2016 report on economic perspectives on incarceration and the criminal justice system, the estimate of "real total criminal justice spending increased by 74 percent, from $158 billion to $274 billion," between 1993 and 2012. "Approximately 50 percent of this spending is attributable to local governments, 30 percent is spent by States and 20 percent is spent by the Federal Government. Police are the largest outlay with real spending of $130 billion in 2012, followed by $83 billion in corrections spending and approximately $60 billion in judicial and legal government spending."[22]

When we consider the statement that the real total government spending on the criminal justice system totaled over $274 billion in 2012, we have an estimation of the minimum cost of the total (real) cost of the criminal justice system. In other words, this $274 billion does not include the social costs imposed on the whole society beyond the price paid by various levels of government. If we analyze the spillover cost of incarceration, research shows real cost estimates should include the multiple burdens imposed by

[21] Executive Office of the President, "Economic Perspectives on Incarceration," 4.
[22] Ibid., 43.

sending a person to jail, such as those imposed upon his or her children, spouse, family, and community in general. For instance, research shows that incarceration inflicts psychological and emotional costs. Prisons are very difficult places to endure. Adaptation brings psychological costs, and these psychological costs and pains can serve to impede post-prison adjustment.[23] In practice, incarceration separates individuals from their families and relationships. Research has shown that the psychological impact of imprisonment affects the relationships between the parent and children, the development of children as they cope with the loss of a parent, and the relationships between the parent and children after prison. Incarceration has a very negative impact on family relationships, and this negative impact also affects the local community.

Prison-related social problems include "problems with separation, caretaking, schooling, antisocial behavior during childhood, educational failure, precocious sexuality, premature departures from home, early childbearing and marriage, and idleness and joblessness during adolescence and early adulthood. . . . The withdrawal or loss of a parent can result in the loss not only of economic capital, but also of social capital involving relationships among family members and the organization of family life toward the maintenance and improvement of life chances of children."[24] Because "the majority of prison inmates come from and return to disadvantaged, minority communities, . . . high rates of incarceration might weaken already fragile inner-city neighborhoods. At low levels, the experience of incarceration [is] largely an individual and family matter. However, at high levels of incarceration, communities must support increasing numbers of economically and socially impaired men, women, and children. That burden may exacerbate existing strains within the community, such as unemployment and crime."[25]

In sum, the reality is that mass incarceration has had clearly negative social impacts. Research has found "various ways in which prison may have inadvertently affected crime rates. . . . Social factors known to contribute

[23] See, for example, R. Robin Miller, "Various Implications of the 'Race to Incarcerate' on Incarcerated African American Men and Their Families," in *Impacts of Incarceration on the African American Family*, ed. Othello Harris and R. Robin Miller (New Brunswick, NJ: Transaction Publishers, 2006).

[24] John Hagan, "The Next Generation: Children of Prisoners," *Journal of the Oklahoma Criminal Justice Research Consortium* 3 (August 1996): 19.

[25] Joan Moore, "Bearing the Burden: How Incarceration Weakens Inner-City Communities," *Journal of the Oklahoma Criminal Justice Research Consortium* 3 (August 1996): 43–54.

to criminality such as broken families, inequality, and social disorder increase with high rates of imprisonment, especially in certain communities." In addition, within organized crime the incarceration of gang members does not reduce crime but creates an incentive to start "an earlier and more sustained recruitment of young people into criminal careers." Further, "as more people acquire a grounded knowledge of prison life, the power of prison to deter crime through fear of the unknown is diminished. Extensive reality-based experience of prisons in certain communities exponentially increases the significance of this problem."[26]

If we focus on the microeconomic costs, research shows that earning "mobility depends on stable employment in career jobs [and] incarceration reduces ex-inmates' access to steady jobs" and reduces their wage growth. Using data from the National Longitudinal Survey of Youth and interviewing one-quarter of the black noncollege males in the survey between 1979 and 1998 while in prison or jail, the study showed that "the effect of imprisonment on individual wages also increases aggregate race and ethnic wage inequality."[27] Research focused during the prison boom (between the 1980s and 1990s, which coincided with growing polarization of the American labor market) showed that wage inequality increased during these decades, and wage declines were particularly large among men with little education, especially among black and Hispanic men.[28] Likewise, "declines in unemployment rates reduce crime levels, and crime is particularly sensitive to employment opportunities for low-skilled men. . . . Similarly, evidence suggests that recessions can lead to cyclical increases in crime."[29] All this data shows that the microeconomy is not isolated from the macroeconomy; incarceration affects an individual's opportunities (microeconomy effect on their individual household) and

[26] Todd R. Clear, "Backfire: When Incarceration Increases Crime," *Journal of the Oklahoma Criminal Justice Research Consortium* 3 (1996): 7–18.

[27] Bruce Western, "The Impact of Incarceration on Wage Mobility and Inequality," *American Sociological Review* 67, no. 4 (2002): 526–46.

[28] Annette Bernhardt and others, *Divergent Paths: Economic Mobility in the New American Labor Market* (New York: Russell Sage Foundation, 2001).

[29] Executive Office of the President, "Economic Perspectives on Incarceration," 41–42. Also see Shawn D. Bushway, Philip J. Cook, and Matthew Phillips, "The Net Effect of the Business Cycle on Crime and Violence," Duke Department of Economics Research Paper (2010), https://papers.ssrn.com/sol3/papers2.cfm?abstract_id=1655741; Keith R. Ihlanfeldt, "Neighborhood Drug Crime and Young Males' Job Accessibility," *The Review of Economics and Statistics* 89, no. 1 (2007): 151–64.

high numbers of individuals in prison will negatively affect the aggregate level of income in the whole community (macroeconomy).[30]

To summarize, there are four main mechanisms explaining why prison or jail time is linked to slow wage growth. First, incarceration is stigmatizing, and it erodes human and social capital. Employers are less likely to hire ex-offenders than comparable job applicants without criminal records. Second, the stigma of conviction is especially prohibitive of entry into high-status or career jobs. Men in trusted or high-income occupations before conviction experience especially large earnings losses after release from prison. The stigma of conviction thus reduces ex-convicts' access to jobs characterized by trust and continuity of employment. Third, time out of employment prevents the acquisition of skills gained through work experience. As a result, for some categories of federal prison inmates, earnings decrease as sentence length increases. Thus ex-offenders are relegated to spot markets with little prospect for earnings growth. Finally, the social contacts that provide information about job opportunities may be eroded by incarceration. Juvenile detention and juvenile crime itself weaken social connections that correlate to stable employment opportunities. "If prisons are criminogenic, adult incarceration may have a similar negative effect on job referral networks."[31]

The final step in the process of explaining the cost of current incarceration practices is the analysis of private prisons. Federal and state government has a long history of contracting specific services to private firms, including medical services, food preparation, vocational training, and inmate transportation. The 1980s, though, ushered in a new era of prison privatization.[32] "Private companies in the U.S. operate 264 correctional facilities, housing almost 99,000 adult offenders."[33] Proponents of privately run prisons contend that cost savings and efficiency of operation place private prisons at an advantage over public prisons and support the

---

[30] David Garland, *The Culture of Control: Crime and Social Order in Contemporary Society* (Chicago: University of Chicago Press, 2001).

[31] Shawn Bushway, Michael A. Stoll, and David F. Weiman, *Barriers to Reentry? The Labor Market for Released Prisoners in Post-Industrial America* (New York: Russell Sage Foundation, 2007), 341.

[32] With the increase of prison population resulting from the war on drugs and increased use of incarceration, prison overcrowding and rising costs became increasingly problematic for local, state, and federal governments.

[33] Adrian Smith, "Private vs. Public Facilities, Is it cost effective and safe?" *Corrections.com* (June 11, 2012), www.corrections.com/news/article/30903-private-vs-public -facilities-is-it-cost-effective-and-safe-.

argument for privatization. Recently, however, the Department of Justice ordered the Bureau of Prisons to stop using private prisons. Unjust and unfair treatment has been found to be more likely when profit is the goal of prison operations. In addition, the cost-savings justification of private prisons has been challenged:

> Evidence has shown that private prisons are neither demonstrably more cost-effective, nor more efficient than public prisons. An evaluation of 24 different studies on cost-effectiveness revealed that, at best, results of the question are inconclusive and, at worst, there is no difference in cost-effectiveness. . . . Evidence suggests that lower staff levels and training at private facilities may lead to increases in incidences of violence and escapes. A nationwide study found that assaults on guards by inmates were 49 percent more frequent in private prisons than in government-run prisons. The same study revealed that assaults on fellow inmates were 65 percent more frequent in private prison.[34]

Research leads to the conclusion that private-run facilities are "no more cost saving effective or safer than a state run facility."[35]

The failure of private prisons suggests that the economic markets will not solve social problems, particularly those produced by mass incarceration. Any serious endeavor to improve the whole justice system has to deal with the problem of inequality. So, it is imperative to take important economic concerns very seriously. Nobel Prize winner Joseph Stiglitz has written, "Of the 1 percent, by the 1 percent,"[36] which describes the enormous increase in inequality in the US and a political system that seemed to give disproportionate advantage to those at the top.[37] Stiglitz goes on to say,

---

[34] Ibid.

[35] Ibid. A study by the US Bureau of Justice Statistics found that the cost savings promised by private prisons "have simply not materialized." James Austin and Garry Coventry, *Emerging Issues of Privatized Prisons* (US Department of Justice Office of Justice Programs, 2001), 29. Also see Brendan Fisher, "Violence, Abuse, and Death at For-Profit Prisons: A GEO Group Rap Sheet," *PRWatch* (2013), www.prwatch.org/news/2013/09/12255/violence -abuse-and-death-profit-prisons-geo-group-rap-sheet.

[36] Joseph E. Stiglitz, "Of the 1%, By the 1%, For the 1%," *Vanity Fair* (May 2011), www.vanityfair.com/news/2011/05/top-one-percent-201105.

[37] See " 'Hell no! We won't go!' Bloomberg backs down over dawn 'eviction' of Wall Street camp after mob storms his restaurant," *DailyMail.com* (October 2011), www.dailymail .co.uk/news/article-2048754/Occupy-Wall-Street-Bloomberg-backs-dawn-eviction.html.

While there may be underlying economic forces at play, politics have shaped the market, and shaped it in ways that advantage the top at the expense of the rest. Any economic system has to have rules and regulations; it has to operate within a legal framework. There are many different such frameworks, and each one has consequences for distribution as well as growth, efficiency, and stability. The economic elite has pushed for a framework that benefits them at the expense of the rest, but it is an economic system that is neither efficient nor fair. . . . Our inequality gets reflected in every important decision that we make as a nation. . . . Given a political system that is so sensitive to moneyed interests, growing economic inequality can lead to a growing imbalance of political power, a vicious nexus between politics and economics. And the two together shape, and are shaped by, social forces—social mores and institutions—that help reinforce this growing inequality.[38]

After *seeing* the facts of incarceration in the US, one can conclude that the call to reform our criminal justice system must also involve a rethinking of our political and economic system—not in order to create a revolution, but to create an evolution that contributes to an economic opportunity for all. Such a point is articulated by Pope Francis in his encyclical *Laudato Sì*: "Since everything is closely interrelated, and today's problems call for a vision capable of taking into account every aspect of the global crisis, I suggest that we now consider some elements of an *integral ecology*, one which clearly respects its human and social dimensions."[39]

Step 3: Acting *with a More Effective Framework of Reality*

In our analysis we used the second step of *judging* to understand the problem of inequality, its complexity and its consequences, which sustains and perpetuates an unjust economic and political system that corrodes our justice system. Because inequality is a multidimensional problem that needs serious analysis and debate directed toward finding real, practical, and effective solutions, we need courage to act to bring about the needed

[38] Joseph E. Stiglitz, *The Price of Inequality: How Today's Divided Society Endangers Our Future* (New York: Norton, 2013), l–li.

[39] Francis, *Laudato Sì* (Vatican City: Libreria Editrice Vaticana, 2015) 137, http://w2.vatican .va/content/francesco/en/encyclicals/documents/papa-francesco_20150524_enciclica -laudato-si.html.

changes in our criminal justice system that will make it more efficient and just.

A courageous way to start to improve our justice system is to turn to restorative justice as a practical way of reducing the problem of inequality and its consequences and at the same time creating a more just and efficient system. Restorative justice is based on a more efficient framework for seeing reality. Today the justice system is commonly seen as entailing a primary and direct one-on-one relationship between a perpetrator and the victim, which can be captured in this image:

Here the number 1 means one individual who is affecting and also is affected (<=>) by another individual (another number 1). The effects between these two individuals can be positive or negative. For example, let us suppose these two individuals are neighbors who live beside each other in the same neighborhood. If one of them improves the landscape of his property, this action will improve the value of his property, and this in turn will have a positive effect on his neighbor's property. This would create an incentive for the second individual to also work on improving his own landscape as well, which will reinforce the positive effect on the increased value for both individuals. The second individual would also have an incentive to motivate the "good" behavior of his neighbor. This is called a positive externality in economics because there is a positive effect from individual one spilling over to individual two.

On the other hand, we can have an example of a negative effect between these two individuals such as if the first individual decides to sell illegal drugs at her home. This action will decrease the value of her property, and it also will have a negative effect on her neighbor's property. This would create an incentive for the second individual to try to stop his neighbor's actions by seeking help from the justice system. It is clear that if the second individual cannot change his neighbor's behavior, he also has an incentive to seek protection against the "bad" behavior of his neighbor. This is called a negative externality in economics because there is a negative effect from individual one spilling over to individual two, and the only way to solve this problem is by seeking protection from the justice system.

The current justice system spends countless resources trying to resolve claims between individuals regarding particular violations to the legal system. Once the justice system determines the facts and prosecutes the offender, it tries to find the right punishment for the offender, which should be proportional to the crime committed. So, now the individual number 1, who has committed a crime, is being punished for his crime by being put away in prison. This is represented by the line that crosses the 1. Such punishment is supposed to restore the well-being of the second individual (the victim of the crime).

$$\boxed{\; \cancel{1} <=> 1 \;}$$

Here, the main idea is that if the justice system works, we should have winners (society and the victim) and losers (criminals). This one-on-one relationship of the justice system might also acknowledge that there might be some unintended consequences to the communities and families that we have to tolerate for the system to function properly. Something like collateral damage is seen as inevitable. This idea is represented by the thick black border that defines the one-on-one relationship between the criminal and the innocent victim. This view of the justice system focuses mainly on retribution as a way to "pay back" harm done to the victim. Based on that unilateral cost the system believes that it does the best job in re-repaying the unilateral cost between a perpetrator and the victim.

In practice our judicial system takes a primarily retributive approach to crime. The power of the state is brought to bear on criminals convicted of violating its laws and thereby deserving of its punishment. The determinations of justice are made by professionals of the courts. The victims who suffered the crimes are not the main focus of this state-versus-the-criminal dynamic.

$$\boxed{\; \cancel{\text{Offender}} <=> \text{State Power} \;}$$

Consequently, while the victim is the person who suffers the harm, the relationship shifts its main focus to the power of the state in determining the punishment that rectifies the wrong done when the offender breaks the law. As a consequence the victim is not the main focus in the retributive justice system, and often the punishment has little to do with addressing the harm done, except in the punitive sense of payback. This process could become mechanistic, simplistic, and static (as is clearly shown in judges having to follow mandatory sentencing guidelines). Therefore, the shift to restorative justice as an alternative to retributive justice is in practice a major and fundamental change in the focus of the process, since it focuses directly on the harm that has been done to persons, most especially the victims of the crime.

Let me now present an alternative framework for restorative justice. In order to refocus the system back to the victim and emphasize the deep ripple effect of crime on many persons who are in networks of relationships with the victim, let us represent a person by a set of relationships with other people. As human beings we are not only individuals, but also relational beings open to transcendent fulfillment (social, moral, and spiritual). In order to add these ideas to my previous graph, the human person is now designated as "p," representing a person now seen as multi-relational—as an individual in relationships because he/she is a father, mother, son, daughter, friend, spouse, and a member of a family, community, and society. Such a conception of persons as relational is central to the restorative justice approach.

$$p <=> p$$

This is not a simplistic, static, and mechanistic relationship between two individuals but a more complex, dynamic, and transcendent relationship. With this dynamic set of relationships in view, the justice system has a more complex problem to solve. It is not a one-on-one relationship between a perpetrator and the victim, but many-to-many relationships. Here, we also have a criminal now represented by "p," describing many-to-many relationships of an individual who is affecting and is affected (<=>) by another "p" who is also a many-to-many relationships individual. Now both p(s) are not isolated from their many-to-many relationships because there is not a border separating them from the rest of their communities.

Now in a restorative system the job of the justice system is to focus on harms done to persons by crime and to seek to rectify the wrongs on a deeper level that takes place on the level of persons. While a retributive system focuses on finding the right punishment for the offender, the alternative restorative approach focuses on repairing the harm done to persons, especially the victims of the crime.

Now the punishment is not viewed only in terms of the costs to the individual but also in terms of the multiple costs to the many-to-many relationships. The criminal, now seen as an individual existing within many-to-many relationships (represented by "m"), is being punished for his crime by being put away in prison (as represented by being crossed out). Not only is this person impacted by incarceration, but all the persons with whom he or she has relationships are also impacted.

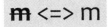

The characteristics of the retributive justice system have very important consequences for the economics of the whole system. Since it focuses narrowly on the punishment of offenders, its cost considerations center on the costs of the judicial processes leading to incarceration and incarceration itself. In contrast, since restorative justice focuses on addressing the harms caused by crime, its cost considerations center on addressing the causes of crime, the needs of victims, ways to rehabilitate offenders, and the long-term impact of incarceration on individuals and communities.

When the justice system wants to take into consideration the many-to-many relationship costs to reestablish justice (after a crime), restorative justice is an excellent alternative, for this new paradigm is based on an "ecological approach" that tries to capture the real complexity of human relationships in order to measure the real impact of new reforms, identifying their real benefits and real costs to the individual, the community, and the society.[40]

Conclusion

Fortunately, concern about these issues has been generated in our society. "The upsurge in incarceration, together with a growing recognition of the costs of current criminal justice policies, have led many policymakers, researchers, and advocates, across the political spectrum, to conclude that the criminal justice system needs to be comprehensively reformed" in a way that takes into consideration all its explicit and implicit costs along with its real benefits for the whole society, in the context of comprehensive sense of justice and fairness, in an ecological efficient allocation of resources.[41]

This requirement for urgent reform in our criminal justice system is necessary in order to reverse the negative vicious cycle of increasing inequality in our society, which has been eroding our fundamental concern for real justice and fairness in our criminal justice system, and which

---

[40] Joyce Arditti, Sara Smock, and Tiffaney Parkman, " 'It's Been Hard to Be a Father': A Qualitative Exploration of Incarcerated Fatherhood," *Fathering* 3, no. 3 (October 2005): 267–88.

[41] Executive Office of the President, "Economic Perspectives on Incarceration," 7.

in turn creates further instability in our political and economic system. Furthermore, serious reform of our criminal justice system is necessary from a pure economic point of view that focuses on improving our federal, state, and local allocation of resources in a time of budget constraints, low economic growth, and future growth in budget liabilities. "Within this context, economics can provide a valuable lens for evaluating the costs and benefits of [a] criminal justice" system and particular policies. Of course, the criminal justice system has a clear goal of "reducing crime and maintaining the safety of citizens." However, as our examination in the *see* and *judge* segments has shown, our criminal justice system has many efficiency problems, which increase its total social costs by "hundreds of billions of dollars each year."[42]

Using the *acting* analysis, our claim is that in order to create an efficient reform of our criminal justice system, it is necessary to implement a different paradigm of thinking. This new paradigm should be based on an "ecological approach" that tries to capture the real complexity of human relationships in order to measure the real impact of new reforms, identifying their real benefits and their real costs (explicit and implicit) to the individual, the community, and the society. Finally, we claim that a new paradigm of thinking for effective reform should reduce the level of inequality in the society in order to reduce its negative cycle of vicious effects. Reform of our criminal justice system requires that we address the economic and racial inequality that contributes to the occurrence of many crimes.

We believe that this reform can be realized in the US. Our criminal justice system should keep communities safe, reduce crime, and treat people fairly and justly, regardless of the color of their skin, the level of their education, and the size of their bank accounts. This reform of the criminal justice system must be cost-effective; it must be accomplished by using our taxpayer dollars and public resources wisely and effectively. It must further a context of decreasing inequality in the whole society, which in turn brings about greater political and economic stability. Recent racial tensions, which focused on relations between local communities and the police, have increased our understanding of these important issues. In order to evaluate policies through such an ecological approach, more interdisciplinary research is also "needed to understand how to best improve the effectiveness of the police and build constructive relationships

---

[42] Ibid., 7.

between communities and law enforcement." According to a study by the federal government,

> Model policing tactics are marked by trust, transparency, and collaborations between police and community stakeholders, but more work is needed to identify and replicate best practices. Calls from citizens, policy-makers, and advocates to address issues related to police use of force, protection of constitutional rights, and police militarization stress the need to invest in policing strategies that both build trust and keep communities safe. . . . To further these goals, investments in police hiring should be accompanied with support for community policing and an emphasis on identifying effective policing strategies through [ongoing] evaluation. . . . Economic models of criminal behavior underscore another way that public policy can reduce crime: through establishing viable and meaningful alternatives to criminal behavior.[43]

In this important area, interdisciplinary research combining economics with behavioral sciences and law enforcement is another example for promising partnership. "Crime and poverty are correlated, and criminal behavior is often motivated by a lack of economic opportunity. If legitimate employment opportunities with sufficient wages are available, then the necessity and relative attractiveness of criminal activity will decline."[44]

There is already available research that could be integrated to reform the criminal justice system in many areas. For instance, we know that investments in education can reduce crime by improving future labor market opportunities and by altering the propensity of children to engage in risky behaviors, even though they are not specifically designed to reduce crime:

> Investments in education can reduce crime by expanding employment opportunities, and thereby improving non-crime alternatives. . . . The research on education and crime has found broad and meaningful effects. . . . Improvements in school quality can also have large returns in reducing criminal activity through both improving labor market outcomes and altering student behavior. . . . Targeted education and jobs programs are also effective tools to prevent crime. By enhancing non-cognitive and behavioral skills and improving educational attainment, preschool education initiatives can have large crime-reducing effects.[45]

---

[43] Ibid., 41.
[44] Ibid.
[45] Ibid., 42.

Finally, we have seen that a narrowly retributive justice system has very important economic consequences. By focusing narrowly on the offender, the costs are heavily oriented toward the processes for the imposition of punishment and the incarceration of the offender. This distribution of costs limits the real benefits for society, for example, more people being incarcerated versus more victims' needs being addressed. On the other hand, by placing a great emphasis on addressing the needs of persons harmed by crime, the costs of restorative justice focus on programming that meets the needs of victims (through counseling and support services) and programming that rehabilitates offenders (many of whom were once victims of crime) and prepares them for reentry into society. Both kinds of programming benefit our communities. If we want to be smart in reducing the costs and improving the benefits of our justice system, we have to shift from being tough on crime to being smart on crime. We need to shift from an exclusive focus on retribution to a focus that includes restoration of persons impacted by crime. We need to shift to a restorative approach that is focused effectively on preventing and responding to crime that harms human persons, relationships, and communities.

Review and Looking Forward

Editors

Alejandro Cañadas has provided a very detailed overview of the economic and social consequences of mass incarceration for individuals, families, and communities. Included among these are victims and their families since this system funnels into prisons resources that otherwise could be used to support victims and prevent persons from becoming victims. His analysis challenges the shortsighted and deeply flawed assumption that our current incarceration system results in winners (society and victims) and losers (offenders). In their work *Invisible Punishment*, Meda Chesney-Lind and Marc Mauer capture succinctly the effects of such a policy:

> Imprisonment was once primarily a matter of concern for the individual prisoner, but the scale of incarceration today is such that its impact is far broader—first, on the growing number of families affected financially and emotionally by the imprisonment of a loved one; beyond that, by the way incarceration is now experienced by entire communities in the form of broad-scale economic hardships, increased risk of fatal disease, and marked economic and social risk for the most vulnerable children. And ultimately, a society in which mass imprisonment has become the norm is

one in which questions of justice, fairness, and access to resources are being altered in ways hitherto unknown.[46]

These realities and their consequences often remain hidden from many citizens, and yet they impact all our lives. The alarming financial cost of our criminal justice system finally has brought legislators to the point of concern. But Catholics' concern about these issues goes much deeper than fiscal preoccupations. Generating an ecological reform espoused by Pope Francis and supported by Alejandro Cañadas is the challenge our society now faces. Initial governmental steps toward such reform are beginning to be seen in the gradual closing of private, for-profit prisons.[47] But piecemeal, incremental steps cannot address the interrelated challenges we face. This chapter ends with a call to Catholics to become concerned about these realities, and then to become more informed about the ways in which Catholic social teaching addresses them. Once Catholics can see and make informed judgments about these realities, then they, individually and collectively, can pressure legislators to act on needed reforms rather than passively perpetuating a broken system that harms human persons and communities. Consistent with Catholic teaching, they also can demand that state and federal government officials put high on their agendas educational and employment initiatives that reduce the economic inequalities through which so much crime festers. As Alejandro notes, the method of "seeing, judging, and acting" can become a highly effective pastoral and communal tool linking faith and justice and leading to actions on the behalf of communities that truly promote justice.

Questions for Discussion

1. *Seeing.* In *The Name of God Is Mercy*, Pope Francis expresses his desire for the church to become a field hospital where as Catholics, we "go outside and look for people where they live, where they suffer, and where they hope."[48] In going forth, they can respond

---

[46] *Invisible Punishment: The Collateral Consequences of Mass Imprisonment* (New York: New Press, 2003), 1–2.

[47] Sally Yates, former deputy attorney general, explained that these prisons do not substantially reduce costs and offer fewer rehabilitation services (education and job training) that reduce recidivism and increase public safety: Charlie Savage, "U.S. to Phase Out Use of Private Prisons for Federal Inmates," *The New York Times* (August 18, 2016), https://www.nytimes.com/2016/08/19/us/us-to-phase-out-use-of-private-prisons-for-federal-inmates.html?_r=0.

[48] *The Name of God Is Mercy: A Conversation with Andrea Tornielli*, trans. Oonagh Stransky (New York: Random House, 2016).

compassionately to human suffering in all its forms. Pope Francis recognizes that compassion—the act of suffering with another—first requires that we see such suffering. Perhaps the greatest barrier to the cultivation of compassion is our not seeing the suffering of others in our society. In what specific ways has this chapter's discussion of the realities and consequences of mass incarceration brought you to see suffering that was previously unseen?

2. *Judging.* Judging is often not a taxing activity; we easily draw conclusions and move on in our thinking, be it in conversation, news viewing, or headline reading. The Buddhist monk Thich Nhat Hanh makes important points about our process of judging, which at times leads to the condemning of persons whom we know and do not know. He says that before condemning, we must judge; but before judging, we must understand; and when we understand, we often end up not condemning persons. How was this approach to judging reflected in the encounter of Judge Serrette and Chris Wilson? How might such an encounter play out between other judges and less amazing offenders? How might this narrative and the entire chapter influence your judging of persons within our criminal justice system?

3. *Acting.* In a homily for the Jubilee for Prisoners in St. Peter's Basilica, Pope Francis urged prisoners to maintain the gift of hope, "for hope is the *power to press on* towards the future and a changed life. It is the *incentive* to look to tomorrow."[49] He also spoke of the hypocrisy of those who view prisoners only as wrongdoers and disregard the possibility of rehabilitation. In chapter 6 Sr. Mary Kate Birge analyzes Luke 19:1-10, which focuses on Jesus' response to Zacchaeus, a person already despised in society for doing harm to other persons. Before reading her chapter, reflect on how Jesus' words and actions open for Zacchaeus the possibility of "a future of hope" (Jer 2:9-11). Consider how the Luke passage speaks to both the journey of Wilson and the lives of persons and communities caught up in the devastating effects of mass incarceration as analyzed by Cañadas.

---

[49] Ann Schneible, "Pope Francis to prisoners: Never lose hope in God's mercy," *Vatican Radio* (June 11, 2016), http://en.radiovaticana.va/news/2016/11/06/pope_francis_to_prisoners_never_lose_hope_in_god%E2%80%99s_mercy/1270460.

Part II

Responsibility, Restoration, and Reform

Chapter 5

Scripture—Old Testament

Editors

"In March, 1994, the members of Temple B'nai Jeshurun of Des Moines, Iowa awoke to find neo-Nazi graffiti and swastikas scrawled on their synagogue."[1] The vandals—a nineteen-year-old man and his seventeen-year-old girlfriend—were apprehended and charged for their felony hate crime. He was troubled, and she was tagging along. A few years before, he had run away from home and found a place among members of the Aryan nation. When he returned to Des Moines, he hoped "to become the leader of the disparate groups of neo-Nazis in the area. The desecration of the Temple was his first public 'action' against the enemy." She was under his tutelage. The people of Des Moines were outraged and called for retribution. With the prompting of Rabbi Steven Fink and the temple leadership, the congregation of Temple B'nai Jeshurun put the matter to debate. Some argued that the full weight of the criminal justice system should be set against the offenders. "Others argued that simply putting these individuals in jail would only create true hard-core neo-Nazis, or victims of another sort."[2]

The two accused pleaded guilty, but the sentencing hearing was postponed so that a prearranged meeting could be held with the defendants and the temple membership. During a four-hour "facilitated session,"

---

[1] David Lerman, "Restorative Justice and Jewish Law," *VOMA Quarterly* (Victim-Offender Mediation Association) 9, no. 1 (Winter 1998): 1.
[2] Ibid.

the community "explain[ed] to them the damage done by their act of hate-vandalism" and set about "to work out a sentence." After much discussion, the members of the synagogue came to a consensus, and the offenders accepted their solution:

> 100 hours of service to the synagogue under the supervision of the Temple's custodian, 100 hours of study of Judaism and Jewish history with the Rabbi, a referral to a hearing specialist for the young man [he had a hearing disability], a requirement that the young man remove the nazi tattoos on his arms, and attainment of employment skills and psychological assessment of both the offenders as well as fulfillment of requirements for a GED. After successful completion, the charges against them would be dismissed.

In the end, the two offenders did attain high school diplomas, were married, and started a family. In the process, they "learned about Jewish history and culture, including the Holocaust, had individual needs met, and took responsibility for their actions."[3]

In the chapter that follows, Richard Buck shows that the restorative justice solution developed by the congregation of Temple B'nai Jeshurun is fully in line with the Scriptures. He discusses biblical law within the context of Jewish life and the rabbinical traditions—from observance to the Sabbath to righting day-to-day wrongs within a community to dealing with great harms done to others. Purification, healing, and making whole again are fundamental goals—both for the offender and for those who have been violated or injured. Richard puts to rest the mistaken idea that the Old Testament imposes strict retributive punishments. He puts the oft-cited "eye for an eye" (Lev 24:20) in its proper religious and legal context. He indicates, through a careful study of texts, that restoration of the victim rather than retribution against the offender is the primary intention of Torah law. Not only that, but a corresponding end of the restoration of the victim—a goal of repairing harm—is that the offender is called back within the community.

Restorative Justice in the Hebrew Biblical Tradition

Richard Buck

At first glance, the concept of restorative justice may seem entirely foreign to the view of law and justice found in the Hebrew Bible. After all, the Hebrew Bible is well known for its harsh and apparently straightforward

[3] Ibid.

statements commanding strict punitive measures ("an eye for an eye") as well as capital punishment for various crimes, ranging from the desecration of the Sabbath to murder.[4] But what is often overlooked or ignored are the many passages in the Hebrew Bible and throughout the Talmud and the rabbinic commentaries that present a much different view about the aims and methods of punishment.[5] The aim of this chapter is to explore the Hebrew biblical tradition in order to learn what it tells us about both how those who commit sins or crimes against persons are to be punished and the general view of justice that underlies this approach to punishment. This investigation will show that although the Hebrew biblical tradition does require severe punishments (including death) for some crimes, the aim of such punishments is always restorative.

"Let Him Repent and He Shall Be Forgiven": Offenses Against G-d

The offenses discussed in the Hebrew Scriptures can be divided into offenses against another person (known as *bein adam l'chavero*) and those offenses committed against G-d[6] (known as *bein adam l'makom*). From the perspective of the modern state—what I will call the *criminal justice perspective*—these two kinds of offenses are clearly different. Indeed, one could argue that this distinction is one of the hallmarks of a modern society, since it would be an affront to basic freedom for the sinner to be compelled to make good to the state for his or her offense. In other words, from the criminal justice perspective, punishment is about retribution or *paying back* the offender for what he or she has done, and since sins are between the individual and G-d, it is up to G-d to pay back the sinner for his or her offense. To be sure, the Hebrew Scriptures require severe punishments—

---

[4] See, for example, Leviticus 20:1-5; 21:24; 27:29.

[5] For the purposes of this chapter the phrase "Hebrew biblical tradition" will be used to refer to the Tanakh (the Torah, book of Prophets, and the Writings—which includes Psalms, Proverbs, the book of Job, the Five Scrolls, and the books of Daniel, Ezra-Nehemiah, and Chronicles), the Talmud, as well as numerous commentaries on the Tanakh and Oral Law. For observant Jews, the Torah, Mishnah, and the Gemara are all part of the revelation at Sinai. Without these texts, the Torah would be difficult, if not impossible, to understand. Indeed, as we will see, it is lack of attention to the discussions of punishment in the Mishnah and Gemara that leads to serious misunderstandings of its justification and practice.

[6] Editors' note: The author's use of "G-d" here is consistent with the Jewish tradition of refraining from writing or speaking the name of the divine.

death, for example—for the most serious of offenses against G-d (for example, idol worship and public desecration of the Sabbath). Perhaps this is the reason that advocates for severe punishments for criminal offenses often use the Hebrew Scriptures as support for their view. But as it turns out, even the severe punishments required for offenses against G-d are not to be understood as a form of revenge or payback to the offender, but as part of a process of atonement for the offender.

Discussions of restorative justice usually focus on offenses committed against other persons. We will discuss how such offenses are treated in the Hebrew biblical tradition later in this chapter. We begin with a brief discussion of offenses against G-d because they provide a useful model for understanding the obligations of those who commit offenses against other persons. Offenses against G-d can be either intentional or unintentional. While both kinds of offenses require repentance, punishments for intentional sins are, for obvious reasons, much more severe. Perhaps the most common of the offenses committed against G-d are unintentional, for example, accidentally performing one of the forms of work prohibited on the Sabbath.[7] The book of Leviticus provides a detailed discussion of how one achieves atonement for such sins through bringing sacrificial service and repentance (see Lev 4:2-35). Leaving aside the intricacies of the laws of sacrifice (the type of animal that must be brought, the manner in which the animal is prepared for sacrifice, etc.), what we see from the discussion in Leviticus is that a person who unintentionally sins against G-d has indeed committed a wrong by not giving proper attention to his or her actions. The proper response by the offender is to seek a purification of his or her soul from the "stain" of such a sin, as opposed to undergoing a punishment that would, in some way, serve to pay back the sinner for what he or she has done. What G-d demands, then, is not restitution but a cleansing process, through which the sinner can come to understand how he or she can learn to become less careless about the actions he or she performs. When undertaken in the right state of mind, the sin-offering should result in an improvement to the offender's character.

Intentional sins against G-d are much more serious and cannot be rectified through sacrifices. Instead, the sinner receives a severe penalty, in some cases death and in others *kares* or "cutting off of the soul." The penalty of *kares* is sometimes described as excommunication, but this is misleading because excommunication as we understand it today is typically imposed on the person by a court or other religious authority. The

---

[7] Unintentional or inadvertent sins (*shogeig*) are to be distinguished from sins that were committed by accident. Sacrifices are only required for inadvertent sins.

commentaries to the Old Testament typically understand *kares* as either being cut off from life in the world to come or suffering an early death. And while this certainly looks like a severe punishment, it is important to note that *kares* is essentially self-imposed. For example, in Exodus 12:15, *kares* is imposed for (willingly) eating leavened food during the Passover holiday. One might ask why the penalty for eating a certain type of food should be so severe. The reason is clear: the Passover holiday is a *communal* celebration of G-d's freeing the nation of Israel from slavery in Egypt. By willingly violating the ritual commandments related to this celebration, the sinner is effectively saying, "I don't want to be part of this community." Thus, the sinner is willingly *separating him or herself from the community*. But repentance is still possible for such offenses by acknowledging the sin and changing the attitude that allowed the sinner to knowingly and willingly violate G-d's law. The Hebrew word for "repentance" is *teshuvah*, which literally means "return." Thus, in the context of intentional sins, the sinner must commit to a return to the community and, thereby, to G-d.

Offenses Against Others

From the modern perspective, what we have called offenses against G-d that do not result in any harm to another person are a private matter. But offenses that harm another person physically or financially are a public matter, regardless of whether the act in question violates a religious law. Such offenses harm both the person who is victimized as well as the society at large because such acts undermine the order and stability needed for the welfare of the society and its members. We will now consider what the Hebrew biblical tradition tells us about the response to such offenses. As we will see, the goal of punishing the offender in such cases is not to repay the offender for what has been done, but to *restore* the damage that has been done, both to the victim(s) and the larger community.

Despite the harsh punishments prescribed in the Hebrew Bible for serious offenses, it is interesting to note that one crucial instrument of modern criminal justice systems—the prison system—is not part of the biblical justice system. This is borne out by the fact that there are very few references to prisons in the Hebrew Bible: Joseph's imprisonment *by his Egyptian master*, after being falsely accused by his master's wife of attempted sexual assault[8]; the temporary incarceration of the man found gathering

---

[8] Genesis 39:20.

wood on the Sabbath;[9] and the imprisonment of the prophet Jeremiah (which was a violation of Jewish law).[10] The lack of punitive incarceration clearly shows that in the view of Jewish law, putting criminals in prison for long periods of time does not satisfy the demands of justice for either the offender or the victim.

So what, then, does Jewish law prescribe for those who commit offenses against other persons? We can begin to answer this question by taking a closer look at one of the most often quoted passages from the Old Testament, which we mentioned at the very beginning of this chapter:

> Whoever takes the life of any human being shall be put to death . . . Anyone who inflicts a permanent injury on his or her neighbor shall receive the same in return: fracture for fracture, eye for eye, tooth for tooth. The same injury that one gives another shall be inflicted in return. (Lev 24:17, 19-20)

This passage is often taken as proof that the Hebrew Bible requires retribution—paying back the offender for his or her crime by doing the very same thing to the offender. This view is contradicted by numerous passages in the Talmud that clearly show the text actually calls for monetary compensation of the victim.[11]

Other rabbinic sources add more detail to the responsibility of the offender. For example, the Medieval Jewish philosopher and sage Rabbi Moshe ben Maimon (Maimonides) cites Exodus 21:18-19 as evidence that the offender must make restitution to the victim:

> When men quarrel and one strikes the other with a stone or with his fist, not mortally, but enough to put him in bed, the one who struck the blow *shall be acquitted*, provided the other can get up and walk around with the help of his staff. Still, he must compensate him for his recovery time and make provision for his complete healing.

---

[9] Numbers 15:32-36. Gathering wood is one of the types of work prohibited on the Sabbath, and *public* desecration of the Sabbath is, according to the Hebrew Bible, a capital offense. The verse states that "they put him [the offender] in custody, for there was no clear decision as to what should be done with him."

[10] Jeremiah 37:15. The Babylonian Talmud, tractate *Sanhedrin* discusses the use of prisons as part of carrying out an execution, but not as method of punishment in itself. See 81b.

[11] See, for example, Rabbi Shimon Bar Yochai's argument in Tractate Bava Kama, 83b–84a.

This passage clearly shows that even in a case of assault, what is called for is not retribution, but that the offender makes the victim "whole" by compensating the victim for the time it takes to recover (and being unable to work during this time) and the costs incurred for treatment of the injury.[12] The Talmud further stipulates that the offender must also recompense the victim for pain and any humiliation caused by the injury.[13]

Although at first glance the Old Testament endorses a fairly strict view of justice according to which offenders receive harsh punishments, upon closer examination we see that this is not the case. Properly understood, the Old Testament view actually focuses more on what must be done to heal the victim—both physically and emotionally—than on what must be done to the offender.

The Cities of Refuge

The approach we have just discussed seems reasonable for offenses involving damage to property, emotional harm, and even physical harm. But what is required for more severe offenses, such as killing? For such offenses, the Old Testament requires the offender to flee to a city of refuge. These cities were set up so that a person who unintentionally killed another person could be protected from the vengeance of the deceased's family.[14] The killer was required to remain in the city of refuge until the death of the current High Priest, after which time the family of the deceased was no longer permitted to avenge the blood of their relative.

The discussion of the cities of refuge in the Talmud and various rabbinic commentaries shows that the purpose of these cities was not to punish through isolation, but rather to provide for the killer a safe and easily accessible place to reflect on what had been done and to embark on a process of *teshuva*, leading, ultimately, to atonement.[15] For example, the cities of refuge were located throughout Israel so that a killer who needed refuge

---

[12] See *Mishneh Torah, Hovel U'Mazik (Injuries and Damages)*, chap. 1.

[13] See, for example, Baba Kama, 85a.

[14] See Exodus 21:13; Numbers 35:11; and Deuteronomy 4:41 and 19:1. It is important to distinguish an unintentional killing—which is a result of lack of concern about one's actions—from an *accidental* killing, which is beyond the killer's control. Accidental killers did not need to flee to a city of refuge because the relatives of the deceased were not permitted to seek vengeance. It appears from the Talmud that negligent and intentional killers also fled to these cities. See Babylonian Talmud, tractate *Makkos*, 9b.

[15] See tractate *Makkos*, 2b.

could readily find a city regardless of where he or she lived. In addition, the roads leading to the cities had to be much wider than the standard road;[16] bridges had to be built to allow for travel to the cities over hills and through valleys. Specific road signs were erected and, in some cases, major roadwork was required in order to ensure that the cities were relatively easy to reach.[17] Compliance was ensured through mandatory yearly inspections set up by the *beis din* (Jewish court). The obligation of the *beis din* to ensure that all of the requirements of the cities of refuge were met was taken very seriously. Failure to meet this obligation was tantamount to shedding blood.[18]

It was no doubt traumatic for a person to move away from home and family and be confined to a strange city for an unspecified amount of time. But the requirements for the cities of refuge demonstrate clearly that their function was not punitive. Indeed, as indicated by Maimonides, the cities were to have all the characteristics of a normal city:

> They should be located solely in trading places, where water is found. If there is no water near them, water should be diverted toward them. They should be located solely in a populated area. If the surrounding populace is reduced, it should be increased. If the number of inhabitants of the city of refuge decrease, priests, Levites, and Israelites should be brought to live there. Snares may not be set in such a city, nor may rope traps be set there, so that the blood redeemer will not come there.[19]

Note that the population of these cities was not restricted to those who had to flee there, and that even *kohanim* (priests) and other members of the tribe of Levi (assistants to the priests) were required to live in these cities. Far from being banished to some remote location, those seeking refuge in one of these cities were to live among Jews who were appointed to perform religious rites in the holy temple in Jerusalem.[20] Beyond this,

---

[16] See tractate *Baba Basra*, 100b.

[17] For example, hills and valleys on the roads leading to these cities had to be removed. See Maimonides, *Mishneh Torah, Rotzeach uShmirat Nefesh* (*Laws of Murder and the Protection of the Soul*), 8:5-7.

[18] See tractate *Mo'ed Katan*, 5a.

[19] *Mo'ed Katan*, 8:8. Translation from Chabad.org, www.chabad.org/library/article _cdo/aid/1088924/jewish/Rotzeach-uShmirat-Nefesh-Chapter-Eight.htm.

[20] In addition, those seeking refuge in the city were not permitted to pay rent for their residence. See *Sefer HaChinuch* (*The Book of Education*), vol. 5, trans. Charles Wengrove (Jerusalem, Israel: Feldheim Press, 1984), 113. See also Babylonian Talmud, tractate *Makkos*, 13a.

efforts were made to ensure that these cities had a reasonable population so that the refuge-seekers would not live isolated lives.

The regulations governing the cities of refuge go beyond normative structural features and demonstrate that the aim of sending offenders to these cities is to encourage *teshuvah* and atonement. According to commentaries on the Torah and rabbinic authorities, this view of the cities of refuge can be gleaned from the end of Deuteronomy 4:42, which states that the killer should flee to the city of refuge *and live*. The phrase "and live" is taken to mean that the daily life of the offender is to resemble, as much as possible, the life he or she lived before fleeing to the city. Thus, if the offender was married and had children, they accompanied him to the city. If an offender had a teacher, he was to be sent to provide instruction and guidance through the duration of the offender's stay in the city, since without the teacher rehabilitation and *teshuvah* would be exceedingly difficult. Residents of these cities were not to treat refugees with disdain or ill will. Thus, if the residents of one of these cities wished to honor a killer who fled to a city, the killer can accept the honor so long as he or she publicly declares that he or she has killed and the residents still insist on granting the honor.[21]

It is also important to note that the law of the city of refuge also reflects a concern for the family members of the victim. According to the *Sefer HaChinuch*, the city of refuge provides healing for the entire community of the victim since "in this way he [the killer] will be rescued from the hand of the blood-avenger, that he should not kill him when there was no violence in his hands."[22] Further, requiring the killer to go into exile spares the family and friends of the victim the pain of seeing the killer and knowing that the killer remains in their midst.

Restoration and Reconciliation

And though I say to the wicked that they shall die, if they turn away from sin and do what is just and right—returning pledges, restoring stolen goods, walking by statutes that bring life, doing nothing wrong—they shall surely live; they shall not die. None of the sins they committed shall be remembered against them. If they do what is right and just, they shall surely live. (Ezek 33:14-16)

[21] Babylonian Talmud, tractate *Makkos*, 12b.
[22] *Sefer HaChinuch*, vol. 4, 225.

Two things should be clear from the discussion up to this point. First, offenses against G-d or other persons are serious matters; this is reflected in the harsh punishments described in the Hebrew Bible, Talmud, and rabbinic commentaries. Second, the practice of punishment in the Hebrew Bible is rooted in the view that human beings are capable of change and improvement, even those human beings who commit serious crimes. This idea is at the heart of the concept of *teshuvah* or return: human beings can repair the damage they have done and return to the proper way of life in communion with others. As we have seen to this point, offenders must go through a prescribed legal process in order for *teshuvah* to be possible. This process allows the offender to make restitution to the community that he or she has offended through the criminal act. But the process of *teshuvah* is not complete until the offender has made amends to the individual persons he or she has harmed.

If the offender wishes to completely atone for the harm done, he or she must first make an appeal to the victim for forgiveness. In what is today regarded as the authoritative text on the process *teshuvah*, Maimonides argues that even in the case of verbal offense, the offender must request forgiveness from the offended party in person: "If a person hurt someone's feelings by what he said, he must placate him and approach him again and again until he forgives him."[23] Maimonides makes clear that without the personal appeal to the offended or harmed party, *teshuvah* and, ultimately, atonement are impossible.

But *teshuvah* also requires the willing participation of the offended party, which includes (depending on the nature of the offense) the community as a whole. The victim must accept the sincere plea from the offender for forgiveness regardless of the severity of the offense:

> One should be easy to appease and hard to anger. When the person who wronged him asks for forgiveness, he should forgive him wholeheartedly and willingly. Even if he was grievously wronged, he should neither seek revenge nor bear a grudge against the offender.[24]

Forgiveness and reconciliation are fundamental Jewish moral commitments. Maimonides points out that refusal on the part of the victim to respond to a sincere appeal for forgiveness is a grave sin. Indeed, the one

---

[23] *The Laws of Repentance*, trans. Rabbi David Shure (New York: Institute of Research for Biblical Talmudic Law, 2004), 2:9.

[24] Ibid., 2:10.

who refuses to forgive has rejected a central obligation of Judaism and has embraced the moral corruption of those who reject monotheism and embrace idol worship.[25]

In fact, reconciliation and restitution, both between individuals and between individuals and the larger community, are so important that the victim is actually obligated to inform the offender of the harm that has occurred. This is done so the offender is given a real opportunity to acknowledge the wrong, seek forgiveness, and engage fully in *teshuvah*.[26] This process is known as *tokeach* or rebuke, and must be undertaken with the sole aim of encouraging the offender to engage in *teshuvah*. That there is an obligation to rebuke the offender shows that the rebuke aims not simply to provide a wronged individual relief by pushing the offender to apologize. Rather, the rebuke is seen as an obligation to the community, since a stable social order is impossible if offenders do not recognize their crimes and try to improve their character.

Conclusion

As we have seen throughout this discussion, the Hebrew biblical tradition endorses a restorative model of justice. Although the various texts of the tradition describe harsh penalties for severe offenses against G-d and other persons, when understood properly it is clear that punishment is only one aspect of a complex system of justice. Punishment in the Hebrew biblical tradition is not punitive or retributive; its aim is to bring relief and healing to all of those involved in and impacted by the criminal act. Put simply, the purpose of punishment is not to harm the offender, but rather to repair what has been broken and bring the offender back into the community.

Review and Looking Forward

Editors

When a Jewish cemetery was desecrated in Auckland, New Zealand, the response of the Jewish community was much like the reaction of the congregation of Temple B'nai Jeshurun in Des Moines, Iowa (described

---

[25] Ibid.
[26] See Leviticus 19:17.

at the beginning of the chapter). Several headstones were painted with swastikas and covered in profanities and anti-Semitic slogans. Some called for harsh punitive measures, while others argued for a more constructive solution. Like in Iowa, a restorative justice meeting was held after one of the perpetrators pleaded guilty. (Another defendant pleaded not guilty and did not enter into the restorative justice process.) After the meeting, Geoff Levy, chairperson of the Jewish Council of New Zealand, had to answer questions when word got out that someone at the meeting offered to pay tuition so that the offender could take engineering courses at Auckland University of Technology.[27]

Levy's explanation fits well with the discussion of Jewish approaches to harm and injury in Richard Buck's chapter. The community members took the defendant's acts of hatred and vandalism as inexcusable, but they still looked for ways to find restoration. Levy noted,

> I was very pleased with the way people around the table responded . . . and the way he [the offender] interacted with everybody, that was good. On the other hand, I still have some doubts. I feel pretty negative about the damage he did. He said he'd been drinking . . . he manifested all the attributes of a drunken lout.

Naida Glavish, a community leader who attended the meeting, added,

> Desecration of graves is a terrible thing. . . . [The Jewish representatives] were angry, but they expressed their anger very calmly, and at the end offered this young man an avenue to get to know them.

About the offender Glavish said,

> It was a very courageous thing to do. He admitted youth and stupidity. He was cross-examined by them. I thought he learned a very valuable lesson and received an opportunity as well at the end of it.

Levy continued,

> He's going to have to want to do something himself. If we can help him, we're happy to do that. But it's got to be consistent with realising the damage he's done, paying the price that society demands of him and making sure it will not happen again.
> Hopefully we can provide him with support, mentoring and assistance in getting an education, so that he will be able to make the best decisions next time when faced with a choice . . . to make

---

[27] Tony Wall, "Merciful Jews Forgive Nazi Grave Vandal," *Stuff* (January 20, 2013), www.stuff.co.nz/national/crime/8199918/Merciful-Jews-forgive-Nazi-grave-vandal.

sure he had every chance to reform himself. It doesn't derogate from the need for him to pay a penalty for what he has done, or the need to restore the cemetery or the anger and upset we feel as a community.

Levy echoes Richard Buck's conclusion about the goal of restoring the offender to community. The Hebrew Bible speaks "of the need to help all citizens of a city. . . . His parents split up at an early age, he then goes from pillar to post . . . he goes to different schools, he's shifted around, he has no stability, no base to call his own." In a sense, the Jewish community was willing to offer the defendant a refuge—as described by Richard—"a safe and easily accessible place to reflect on what had been done and to embark on a process of *teshuva*, leading, ultimately, to atonement." Richard notes that *teshuva*, or repentance, literally means "return."

In the next chapter, on restorative justice in the New Testament, Mary Kate Birge, SSJ, will discuss the return of Zacchaeus to the people of God (Luke 19:1-10). When Zacchaeus repents of his extortion and disregard for the poor, Jesus proclaims, "Today salvation has come to this house because this man too is a descendant of Abraham. For the Son of Man has come to seek and to save what was lost" (Luke 19:9-10). In her detailed analysis, she notes that Zacchaeus—through the hospitality of Jesus—turns his life around by committing himself to live in accord with Jewish law. Living by the law and his new life are one and the same. As you work through chapter 6 keep referring back to this chapter on Jewish law.

Questions for Discussion

1. In the chapter, Richard Buck corrects a common misunderstanding of biblical law. Too often, we think of the Torah law as exacting punishment so that a person or the people will have to pay through suffering for what they have done. The misconception is that God's justice is merely retributive. To set up a contrast and to correct this misconception, Mary Kate Birge, in the next chapter, will introduce the biblical concept of *shalom*. In chapter 6, Sr. Mary Kate explains, "This concept, *shalom*, reflects a vision of wholeness, unity, and integrity that God desires for all of creation." In terms of *shalom*, Jewish law and ritual observance have the purpose of turning the people toward God. Likewise, the wrath of God is brought forth through love; divine demands and commands have the purpose of renewal and restoration.

As an example of restorative justice in the Bible, consider the return of Jacob to Esau in Genesis 32–33. The two brothers were in competition from the start (from within the womb) and eventually Jacob swindles Esau, his older brother, out of his birthright and his father's blessing (Gen 25:19-34; Gen 27:1-45). Immediately, Jacob flees to another land. Years later, when he sets about to return to his homeland, it is clear that Esau—who is richer and more powerful than Jacob—intends to kill him. Jacob sends gift after gift of appeasement. Offering so many gifts that it seems he will have nothing in the end, Jacob eventually bows before Esau, who has a change of heart and welcomes Jacob back home. Because Esau is rich and has no need, he refuses to take his brother's gifts. But Jacob entreats him: "If you will do me the favor, accept this gift from me, since to see your face is for me like seeing the face of God—and you have received me so kindly" (Gen 33:10). When all is said and done, Jacob—for his own good—gives, appeases, and repents for his own good. Giving is a gift to him.

Consider Jacob's words to Esau in terms of Jacob's encounter with an angel the night before (Gen 32:23-33). What is the connection between Jacob's return to Esau and his rededication to God? What is the connection between Jacob's struggle with the angel and his desire for unity and peace with Esau?

2. There is an interesting interplay between anger and mercy in the story of Esau and Jacob, in the encounter between Temple B'nai Jeshurun and those who vandalized their synagogue, and the biblical framework of restorative justice presented in the chapter as a whole. Consider the pronouncements against Jerusalem and Judah in Isaiah 3:1-4:6. What is the reason for God's wrath? What is God's hope of the people of God and the goal of his judgment?

Chapter 6

Scripture—New Testament

Editors

"Tommy, an agitated 14-year-old high school student in Oakland, Calif., was in the hallway cursing out his teacher at the top of his lungs." Tommy's story is told by Fania Davis, who is the executive director of Restorative Justice for Oakland Youth (RJOY). Fania notes, after describing the incident instigated by Tommy, that "RJOY's 2007 middle school pilot eliminated violence and expulsions, while reducing school suspension rates by 87 percent."

> After two years of training and participation in RJ practices, whenever conflict arose, RJOY middle school students knew how to respond by coming to the RJ room to ask for a talking piece and space to facilitate a circle. Today, at one of the RJOY school sites, student suspensions decreased 74 percent after two years and referrals for violence fell 77 percent after one year. Racial disparity in discipline was eliminated. Graduation rates and test scores increased.[1]

With the help of the RJOY program at his school, Tommy—after his outburst—was able to find a constructive pathway. The evening before the incident he discovered that his mother's drug addiction had taken hold of her, that he was parenting his two younger siblings, and that he was

[1] Fania Davis, "Discipline With Dignity: Oakland Classrooms Try Healing Instead of Punishment," *Yes! Magazine* (March 7, 2014), www.truth-out.org/news/item/22315 -discipline-with-dignity-oakland-classrooms-try-healing-instead-of-punishment.

feeling exhausted, anxious, and alone. The RJOY facilitated a restorative justice circle with Tommy, his mother, his teachers, and the principal of the school. As a result, his mother reentered treatment for her addiction, his home gained stability, and he was able to focus on school. In chapter 12, more attention will be given to the restorative justice programs in Oakland schools. At this point, we turn to Fania Davis's struggles with justice and working for a better world.

Fania has her own story of restoration. She was a teenager in 1963 when two of her friends were murdered in the now infamous Ku Klux Klan bombing of a church in Birmingham, Alabama. In 1970, her sister was put on trial (later acquitted) for murder and conspiracy in the armed takeover of a California courtroom. Fania was sympathetic with the Black Panther movement, and after her sister's trial, she went to law school and became what she calls an "enraged" civil rights lawyer. Looking back, she notes, "I had too much fire and too much anger." In the mid-1990s, she realized that she needed a change, for her own "peace of mind." When she discovered and learned about the restorative justice movement, she experienced "a life-changing epiphany, one that 'integrated the warrior and the healer in me.' "[2] Inspired by the success of the Truth and Reconciliation Commission in South Africa, Fania set about to propose such methods and processes for dealing with racial injustice in the United States.

In 2005, Fania succeeded in establishing Restorative Justice for Oakland Youth:

> Punitive school discipline and juvenile justice policies activate tragic cycles of violence, incarceration, and wasted lives for youth of color. Founded in 2005, RJOY works to interrupt these cycles by promoting institutional shifts toward restorative approaches that actively engage families, communities, and systems to repair harm and prevent re-offending. RJOY focuses on reducing racial disparities and public costs associated with high rates of incarceration, suspension, and expulsion.[3]

Restorative justice practices have been embraced by Oakland schools (www.ousd.org/restorativejustice). The organization has had a profound effect on communities in metropolitan Oakland and, of course, on the young people who are able to grow and develop their gifts and talents.

---

[2] Micky Duxbury, "Circles of Change: Bringing a More Compassionate Justice System to Troubled Youth in Oakland," in *Restorative Justice Today: Practical Applications*, ed. Katherine S. van Wormer and Lorenn Walker, 109, 108 (Los Angeles: Sage Publications, 2013).

[3] "Mission," Restorative Justice for Oakland Youth, http://rjoyoakland.org/about/.

Fania—through her lifelong struggle with racism and its debilitating social effects—has found a way of restoration and the formation of life-giving community.

In the chapter that follows, Sr. Mary Kate Birge discusses Jesus' ministry, his announcement of the coming of the kingdom of God, his encounter with the oppressive tax collector Zacchaeus, and the succor he gives to an adulterer who was about to be stoned for her violation of God's law. We have told Fania's story as an apt image of God's way of restoration. We began her story with Tommy's outburst at school and end with the hope and positive change spurred by the RJOY. In the middle is Fania's own liberation. She finds what Sr. Mary Kate defines as *shalom*—wholeness, unity, peace, and justice. About her own turning point, Fania says, "I could no longer pursue a vision of social transformation that didn't include spiritual transformation."[4]

Jesus, the Kingdom of God, and Restorative Justice

Mary Katherine Birge, SSJ

The restorative justice that you have been reading about in this book, especially the previous chapter on the Hebrew Bible, and the justice that Jesus taught and practiced are one and the same. How is this restorative justice of Jesus different from the justice taught and practiced throughout the law schools and court systems of the United States? Jesus begins from the biblical vision of the kingdom of God, whereas our legal system begins from a stance that immediately seeks out whom to hold guilty for the crime.

In the United States we are most familiar with the kind of justice represented in film and television courtroom dramas such as *Law and Order* and its various manifestations throughout the last three decades (*SVU*, *CI*, *Trial by Jury*, and *LA*). This kind of justice, forensic justice or criminal justice, is "the procedure by which criminal conduct is investigated, evidence gathered, arrests made, charges brought, defenses raised, trials conducted, sentences rendered and punishment carried out."[5] At times, but more often than not, in the punishment phase (prison time for serious crimes) there is some kind of attempt at rehabilitation of the "criminal." In this

---

[4] Duxbury, "Circles of Change," 109.
[5] Gerald and Kathleen Hill, "Criminal Justice," *The People's Law Dictionary*, Law.com, http://dictionary.law.com/Default.aspx?selected=405#ixzz3yYP6avUQ.

system of justice the state becomes the injured party. The victim, while often acknowledged in the court proceedings by the prosecution, seldom participates in the process, unless he or she is called as a witness by the prosecution. Perhaps at the sentencing phase of the trial, the victim may even be invited to give a victim impact statement. Beyond these instances, the victim has no contact with the offender and does not participate in this "justice" process. In fact, the whole focus of the system remains steadily and unremittingly on the one accused of the crime. The victim of the crime remains isolated from the proceedings and uninformed about them. The state gives the victim no opportunity to move from victim to survivor of the crime, except, perhaps, for a chance to offer a victim impact statement at the sentencing phase of the trial.

The purpose of this process is to punish the perpetrator, to achieve a kind of retaliation against the one who committed the crime, to hurt back the one who hurt the order of the state (under whose umbrella the actual victim is subsumed). The state presumes that the perpetrator, after having been hurt himself in return, will never again resort to criminal action: "lesson learned." The essays in this book by my colleagues in sociology and criminal justice, and the statistical evidence they share, demonstrate clearly that this presumption is false.

The kingdom of God that Jesus taught, preached, and enacted during his ministry on earth begins at a point very different from where our nation's criminal justice does; it begins from a conviction that God's deepest hope for humanity—that we live with God and with one another in relationships that are just—is possible. We know what this vision looks like from the first two stories in Genesis about the first man and first woman. In Genesis 1, the man and the woman are created in the image and likeness of God (v. 27), from whom they receive their charge to be fruitful as God has been fruitful with creation (v. 28), in order to relate to all of creation as God has done. "Because they bear the image of their divine creator, who is the source and summit of all justice, when human beings act with justice they reveal both the justice of God and their own fidelity to living out of that image of God in them. When they fail to act with justice, that is, to mirror the likeness of God in their dealing with one another or with God, the rightness or trueness of their relationship both with God and other human beings is affected adversely."[6] When a person fails to meet

---

[6] Mary Katherine Birge, "Biblical Justice," in *The Heart of Catholic Social Teaching: Its Origins and Contemporary Significance*, ed. David Matzko McCarthy, 20 (Grand Rapids, MI: Brazos, 2009).

the demands of a particular relationship, either with God or with other people, justice fails, too. In Genesis 2:5-25, we encounter the other story of creation in which the man and the woman first live with one another and with God in right relationships that illustrate, as the story of Genesis 1:1–2:4 does, the very image of the word *shalom*, peace with the practice of justice (cf. Ps 85:10; Isa 32:17; Zech 8:16-19).

The idea of peace, which the word *shalom* translates, is not simply the absence of violence. Rather this concept, *shalom*, reflects a vision of wholeness, unity, and integrity that God desires for all of creation. When the man and the woman fail in their vertical relationship with God, they also fail in their horizontal relationship with one another, and shame, violence, deceit, mistrust, and suffering become the daily companions of creation (Gen 3:1-24). From there the Old Testament spends the rest of its pages recounting the story of God calling humanity back into right relationship, back to the practice of justice, through restoration and reparation of the relationships that humanity has broken, the methods for which my colleague, Richard Buck, explained in his essay. Gradually, over centuries, the concept of *shalom* as the hope that God has always desired for humanity becomes the basis for the symbol that we encounter so often in the New Testament, the kingdom of God. It is a time, a space, and an experience in which God's rule is experienced directly by all of God's creation. It is this time, space, and experience in which all that has become broken in creation shall be restored at last by God.[7]

In the New Testament Jesus lives, teaches, preaches, and demonstrates to all who are willing to listen to him this same kingdom of God, the image of *shalom*. He makes the kingdom of God present every time he performs a miracle of healing (e.g., Mark 1:29-31), drives out evil spirits from someone they possess (e.g., Matt 9:32-34), and brings back to this life a person who has died (cf. Mark 5:21-24, 35-43; Luke 7:11-17; John 11:1-44). Through his own hospitality and openness to the alien and the enemy (cf. Matt 5:43-48; Luke 6:27-36), to those who would put him to death (cf. Luke 22:49-51; 23:33), he makes it possible for others to join him in building the kingdom of God, building *shalom*, in the present age. Until Jesus' return to earth brings to completion the kingdom of God that began with his earthly life, this is the task of those who would follow Jesus: to live in just relationships with one another, to work at restoring

---

[7] "In the lifetime of those kings the God of heaven will set up a kingdom that shall never be destroyed or delivered up to another people; rather, it shall break in pieces all these kingdoms and put an end to them, and it shall stand forever" (Dan 2:44).

to wholeness those people and relationships that they and others have broken, and to repair as best they can what cannot be restored. This practice of restoring and repairing relationships between people and God and among people themselves is not unlike that in which the contemporary practice of restorative justice engages. Like Jesus' own work to establish the kingdom of God, to bring about the fullness of *shalom*, through the practice of right relationships and the healing of those people who are "broken," restorative justice focuses on the present and future needs of the victim, the perpetrator, and society in order to repair what has been broken or stolen from the victim, to bring the perpetrator to acceptance of responsibility, and to mend the threads that hold society together. This is one of those stories in the gospels that points to this practice.

In Luke 19:1-10, the gospel writer provides the reader with a model of Jesus' hospitality and openness. Jesus welcomes someone who is already despised by his own society and has grievously wronged those dear to Jesus. Jesus' hospitality elicits from this "enemy" a conversion of spirit, a radical change that allows him to begin to repair what he has broken, or to attempt reparations for what he cannot repair. Zacchaeus is a tax collector (sometimes called "toll collector"), and not only a tax collector, but also the chief tax collector for that region of Judea under Roman control. He is a Jew; his name tells us that. Luke tells the reader that he is also wealthy; to write that someone is a tax collector, chief tax collector at that, and wealthy is redundant. All tax collectors were wealthy in comparison to the people of the land, chief tax collectors even more so. The Romans would have put the contract for collecting tolls and tariffs on persons and goods, which crossed the borders into and out of Roman-controlled Judea, up for bid among Jews willing to work for the Romans. Whoever placed the highest bid would have received the contract. It was expected, as a matter of course, that whoever "won" the contract would significantly increase the amount he would collect from the people in order to cover the cost of the contract (in tribute to Rome) and "compensate" himself. But such an increase did not stop there.

As chief tax collector, Zacchaeus would have been responsible for the collection of taxes within the province under direct Roman control; he would have needed many hands to help him collect what was due him and his Roman masters. To do so, he would have "farmed out" smaller contracts to local or regional Jewish tax collectors who, in turn, would have increased the amount they needed to collect for Zacchaeus so that they might pay themselves handsomely, too, almost as handsomely as the chief tax collector would himself. Tax collectors became extortionists of their own people, and the chief tax collector the biggest extortionist of them all. They sinned daily against the statutes and commandments of the Torah, and by doing so they oppressed their own people, helping to drive them into penury, slavery, and even suicide.

The gospel writer sets the stage carefully for readers, making sure we know within the first two sentences of the story (vv. 2-3) that Zacchaeus is chief tax collector, seeking to see Jesus, and so short he cannot see over the heads and shoulders of the gathered crowd. Luke does not yet verbally express the hostility of the gathered crowd toward Zacchaeus, but the word picture he forms of a short man running behind a densely packed row of people lining the sides of the road (vv. 2-3) suggests there is something more at work here than a short man's inability to see over the heads and shoulders of those taller than he. Why could Zacchaeus not find an opening, a small gap, through which he could worm his way into a clear view of the prophet-miracle worker soon to pass by? It is likely the people would not let the chief tax collector through; out of animus for him, they would have tried to thwart his attempt to see Jesus. Why? Perhaps the only way they would have been able to express their anger and deep resentment toward a fellow Jew, whom they saw as responsible for so much pain and suffering in their community, was to prevent him, at least this once, from getting what he wanted.

Zacchaeus, not to be thwarted by the inhospitality of his coreligionists, threw his official's dignity aside and raced ahead to climb a tree from which he would have a view of Jesus as he passed by on the road beneath his perch (v. 4). Jesus did not pass by, but stopped at Zacchaeus's spot, knowing who he was, even calling him by name (v. 5). Zacchaeus was the person on the margins of this community, a wealthy pariah amidst his own people, and treated by them as such—but not by Jesus. By inviting himself to become a guest of Zacchaeus in Zacchaeus's own home (v. 5), a known sinner, hated oppressor of his own people, and despised collaborator with the Roman occupiers, Jesus made possible the repair and restoration of two relationships. Through announcing his imminent visit to all assembled, Jesus offered Zacchaeus the hospitality he had been denied by those in the crowd and, by extension, by all the inhabitants of Judea, and his own acceptance of him as a full human being. Jesus created a physical and psychic space of welcome for Zacchaeus that he had not known for a very long time, if ever. The effect of this hospitality on both the crowd of people (v. 7) and Zacchaeus (vv. 6, 8) is instructive for our topic of restorative justice.

Members of the crowd "grumbled," murmuring against Jesus' decision to spend time under the roof of a known sinner—and an oppressor of his own people at that (v. 7). Jesus, a popular and respected figure (by some, anyway), was going to honor the equivalent of a criminal (in their eyes) by visiting him at his house. Can you imagine the barely suppressed anger toward Jesus bubbling up in the crowd's angry muttering? His own disciples likely joined in. Perhaps you hear something like, "Sure, he's just like all the other so-called 'prophets' and 'miracle workers'; as soon as they smell money, they head right for it and forget about us"; or "There he goes, sucking up to the powerful; I knew this guy was too good to be true"; or still even, "It just goes to show you—there is no justice for us." But wait; listen to Zacchaeus's response to Jesus' hospitality and the crowd's hostility. He says, "Behold, half of my possessions, Lord, I shall give to the poor, and if I have extorted anything from anyone I shall repay it four times over" (v. 8).

In Jewish law anyone who has committed an offense is duty bound to confess the trespass, to pay full restitution to the person he has harmed, and to include an additional compensation worth a fifth of the restitution (Num 5:7). When someone has defrauded, cheated, or extorted goods or money from another, he is required to return its value fourfold to the victim (Exod 21:37). Zacchaeus announces to the whole village not only that he will follow the Torah prescription by returning to his victims four-fold the amount he has defrauded them, but he will turn over half of all he owns to the poor. The Law and the Prophets demand that Israelites, and so Jews, care for the poor (e.g., Deut 15:11; Jer 22:16), consider their needs when making agricultural and business policy (Exod 23:11; Lev 23:22; Deut 24:12, 14-15), and never take advantage of them, financially or otherwise (Isa 3:15; Jer 22:16; Amos 8:4-6), but not that they give away half of their possessions to care for the poor. Yet, this is what Zacchaeus proclaimed he would do.

What made it possible for Zacchaeus to respond differently this time? What had changed that allowed Zacchaeus to begin to repair his broken relationship with God and his own people, this double axis of being in right relationship with God and other human beings that lays the groundwork for the practice of justice? Yet Jesus knew who Zacchaeus was, a sinner and oppressor of his own people, and still extended the hospitality of God to him, even in his sinfulness. In one sense, Jesus' words and actions opened up for him the possibility of "a future of hope" (Jer 29:11). Jesus gave Zacchaeus a "taste," an experience of what living in right relationship with God and other humans could be like, and Zacchaeus grabbed for it, reversing his life's direction 180 degrees. He experienced the kingdom of God in his interaction with Jesus, and it changed him (v. 8). Zacchaeus's return to the practice of Torah allowed Jesus to announce that "salvation [had] come to this house" and that "this man too [was] a descendant of Abraham" (v. 9).

Jesus restored Zacchaeus to his life in God and to his life in the local Jewish community. Jesus opened up to him salvation that was both spiritual and physical, from which his previous actions and way of life had excluded him. Zacchaeus, in his declaration to give half of what he possessed to the poor and return four times over whatever he may have extorted from the people, moved to repair what he had broken in the past. Luke does not tell us how the crowd may have responded to Zacchaeus's declaration, perhaps because he wants us to attend further to the "main event," in which the hospitality of Jesus to one so often refused hospitality by his own people provides the emotional and spiritual "space" to choose another way of life. This account makes me wonder where or when in my own life I have offered another person, someone with whom I had some reason to distrust, dislike, even despise, the kind of space to become a different person that Jesus offered to Zacchaeus. It is so very difficult to do, especially when the hurt runs deep. Yet the kingdom of God that Jesus preached and enacted in the tale of Zacchaeus is the same kingdom of God to which Jesus invited disciples—then and now—to join him in preaching, enacting, and living. Can it be that the practice of restorative justice is a way to join with Jesus in preaching, enacting, and living some part of the kingdom of God, God's vision of *shalom*?

In this story from Luke's gospel, we have encountered one example that seems to support the contemporary approach to crime or injustice we have called "restorative justice." The four gospels abound with such examples of Jesus who, by word and deed, repairs what the practice of injustice (crime) has broken. In the story of the woman caught in adultery in John's gospel (8:1-11), we find Jesus confronted with a situation rife with criminal intent and injustice.

Jesus had been teaching in the temple and a group of men hostile to him and his teaching brought before him a woman for judgment, who had been caught in adultery, hoping to catch him in a faulty application of what the law required for one caught in adultery—death by stoning (vv. 2-6). These men asked him for his reading of the law. Rather than pronounce judgment, Jesus suggested that whoever had not sinned should throw the first stone. When all her accusers had slunk away in response to him, he asked the woman who condemned her (vv. 9-10). Finding no one left to condemn her, Jesus did not condemn her but rather charged her "not [to] sin any more" (v. 11). What principle of biblical justice—or of restorative justice—did Jesus draw on in this story?

According to Leviticus 20:10, when a married woman is caught in adultery with a man, they both are to be stoned to death. Although Deuteronomy 22:22 does stipulate death for such a couple, it does not specify stoning. If in a city a woman who is betrothed is found having sex with a man, both man and woman are to be stoned (Deut 22:23-24). If this should happen out in a field, it is presumed no one could have heard the woman's cries, so she is not held culpable, although no punishment for the man is mentioned in this case (Deut 22:25-27). The law also stipulates that no one may be put to death without the testimony of two or three witnesses, and then the witnesses themselves must be the first to enact the sentence of death (Deut 17:6-7).

In the case presented to Jesus, no man has been accused of adultery along with the woman, and then no witnesses have come forward to press the charge, only the collection of scribes and Pharisees mentioned in John 8:3, and none of these claims to be a witness. Jesus' response to her accusers, "Let the one among you who is without sin be the first to throw a stone at her" (John 8:7), cuts to the heart of the law. Bypassing the men's twisted desire to use the law against the woman in order to get at Jesus, he reminds them that they are also under the law and also guilty of sin. In the give-and-take between the men and Jesus, he appears to be writing on the ground (vv. 6, 8). Some have tried to claim that the men leave because he is writing their sins down, which they recognize when they crowd around him, but this interpretation reads into the text something that is not there. He is writing; that is all the text indicates.

What is he writing? He looks like a man trying to communicate his total disinterest in what the deceitful accusers are trying to do to him through the woman, coolly ignoring them as he doodles in the dirt, much the same way a person today may patiently doodle on a pad of paper while waiting for those trying to entangle him in some kind of intrigue to become bored and wander away.

Is the woman guilty of adultery? Jesus' response to her answer that no one had condemned her, "Neither do I condemn you. Go, [and] from now on do not sin any more" (John 8:11), suggests that she is likely to have been guilty in some way of this sin. Yet, Jesus' focus does not rest there on her guilt or on any condemnation of her for it. Jesus corrects her (v. 11), and sends her on into a future those men would have denied her. As I watch the story unfold in my mind's eye, I wonder where my own focus would have rested were I to have been a bystander listening to this dialogue between Jesus and the men. I wonder, too, where my focus rests today when I encounter stories about crimes in newspapers, radio, and television.

Jesus restores the woman to her life, repairs her accusers' misapplication of the law, and, in doing so, makes present the reign of God, which is a way of naming God's vision of *shalom* for all creation that we first encountered in Genesis 1–3. John has had Jesus model for his followers, both then and now, how God imagines the practice of justice: action that will repair people broken by another's sin, restore the network of relationships making up the community in which both sinner and those sinned against live, and accomplish this without violence. In Matthew's Sermon on the Mount (5:1–7:29) and Luke's Sermon on the Plain (6:17-49), Jesus offers a series of instructions for how to live justly in relationship with God and one another to a crowd of people who have followed him across the Galilean countryside.[8]

Among these instructions, and the parables that illustrate them, Jesus includes a succession of commands that seem to bear directly on the contemporary practice of restorative justice, and may well be the most difficult to follow. They surely are for me. From Matthew we read,

> You have heard that it was said, "You shall love your neighbor and hate your enemy." But I say to you, love your enemies, and pray for those who persecute you, that you may be children of your heavenly Father, for he makes his sun rise on the bad and the good, and causes rain to fall on the just and the unjust. For if you love those who love you, what recompense will you have? Do not the tax collectors do the same? (Matt 5:43-46)

Jesus repeats the biblical command "You shall love your neighbor" (Lev 19:18) with the nonbiblical command "hate your enemy" (Matt 5:43) that popular practice had likely been combined with the biblical injunction from Leviticus. Jesus knows that a society with one foot resting on love of neighbor and the other on hatred of enemies cannot build the kingdom of God, let alone live in it. He challenges his followers to do what is hard, perhaps the hardest thing any human being can do, to love one's enemies and even to pray for one's persecutors (v. 44). He reminds them that not only does God care for them, but he also cares for those whom they themselves would hate and vilify because of their treatment of them

---

[8] Matthew almost always wrote the phrase "kingdom of heaven" whenever Mark and Luke would have written "kingdom of God." As a pious Jew, writing to other pious Jews of the first century AD Mediterranean world, Matthew employed a "circumlocution" for the name of God; here the word "heaven" was his stand-in for the name of God as was the word "Power" for the name of God in 26:64.

or their loved ones—for the enemy and the criminal belong to God, too. When Jesus says, "[F]or he makes his sun rise on the bad and the good, and causes rain to fall on the just and the unjust" (v. 45), he reveals the substance of God's original vision for creation (cf. Gen 1:1–2:4; 2:5–3:24). God desires everyone to live in the vision of *shalom*, in the kingdom of God.

We read a similar series of commands in Luke that also contains the "golden rule" in which Jesus charges his audience to treat every other person in the way they would want themselves treated (Luke 6:31):

> But to you who hear I say, love your enemies, do good to those who hate you, bless those who curse you, pray for those who mistreat you. To the person who strikes you on one cheek, offer the other one as well, and from the person who takes your cloak, do not withhold even your tunic. Give to everyone who asks of you, and from the one who takes what is yours do not demand it back. Do to others as you would have them do to you. For if you love those who love you, what credit is that to you?" (Luke 6:27-32)

Behind this command lies the same reason that God sends the sun and rain to "the bad and the good" (Matt 6:45). Because they follow Jesus, they will learn to see as Jesus does, to act as Jesus does. To learn anything entails practice, so Jesus commands those who would be his followers to practice seeing the very people they would reject, hate, or curse as they already see themselves, to practice acting toward the other as they already do toward themselves. He commands them to see others and to act toward others, including those hateful to themselves, in order to create the experience of hospitality that enabled Zacchaeus to embrace a new kind of life, which would lead him toward the kingdom of God. He directs them to act toward those who are guilty of sin and crime so that, like the woman caught in adultery, having been judged and corrected, they may continue on into a future God has hoped for them.

In his mission on earth Jesus preached about the kingdom of God and then enacted it right in front of his audience's eyes. He did the very hard, but not impossible, work of building and beginning to model a society based on biblical justice. He invited those who would follow him to join him in this work. After his death and his resurrection, these first followers recognized that Jesus had left them to continue his "kingdom work" until his return, and they took up this work, as have their religious descendants throughout the millennia. None of the gospel writers calls any of Jesus' work "restorative justice." Yet, from working through several stories and sayings of Jesus left to us by these very gospel writers, it seems that he did work to restore justice within his society and called his followers to do the same. That call to his followers to pick up the work of restoring relationships based on justice that he had done does not remain in the past. It continues to call those who would follow Jesus today to the same work. One name, today, for this work is "restorative justice."

Review and Looking Forward

Editors

Combatants for Peace (established in 2006) was founded by a group of Israelis and Palestinians "who had taken an active role in the conflict [and] laid down their weapons . . . on the belief that the cycle of violence can only be broken when Israelis and Palestinians join forces."[9] One of the organization's founders, Bassam Aramin, started along the path of reconciliation and peace when he was drawn to a surprising openness to his enemies, the kind of hospitality that, according to Sr. Mary Kate in this chapter, builds the kingdom of God.

Bassam was involved, at a young age, in the Palestinian struggle and started a seven-year prison sentence at the age of seventeen—for planning an attack on Israeli troops.

> At the age of 12 I joined a demonstration where a boy was shot by a soldier. I watched him die in front of me.
> From that moment I developed a deep need for revenge. I became part of a group whose mission was to get rid of the catastrophe that had come to our town. We called ourselves freedom fighters, but the outside world called us terrorists.[10]

He and other freedom fighters were considered heroes among the Palestinian prisoners, but they received rough and often brutal treatment from soldiers. During one particular beating, Bassam recalled a movie that he had seen about the Holocaust several years before. He started to yell at the guards, calling them Nazis and oppressors. At the same time, he remembered how he felt when he saw the film; he had pity and compassion for the Jews under the Nazis. He recalls, "The incident with the soldiers made

---

[9] "Who We Are," Combatants for Peace, http://cfpeace.org/about-us/our-vision/.

[10] "Bassam Aramin (Palestine)," The Forgiveness Project, http://theforgivenessproject .com/stories/bassam-aramin-palestine/.

me realize that we had to preserve our humanity—our right to laugh and our right to cry—in order to save ourselves."[11]

After this beating, accusations, and fighting back, Bassam began to talk with some of the soldiers. He learned to see them as human beings. The experience had a lasting effect. A few years after he was released from prison, his ten-year-old daughter "was killed in cold blood by a member of the Israeli border police while standing outside her school with some classmates." Still, Bassam held to the lessons he learned in prison, through his debate and dialogue with Israelis.

> We discovered many similarities and . . . [one soldier] even became a supporter of the Palestinian struggle. From then on he always treated us with respect. Seeing how this transformation happened through dialogue and without force made me realize that the only way to peace was through non-violence. Our dialogue enabled us both to see each other's purity of heart and good intent.[12]

This experience of sharing and listening to an enemy formed the seed for the establishment of Combatants for Peace. The experience forms the core of restorative justice. Looking forward to the next chapters, we will see that community and restorative relationships like Bassam's are at the heart of Catholic social teaching.

Questions for Discussion

1. At the center of Jesus' ministry is his announcement of the kingdom of God. Consider the Lord's Prayer, Matthew 6:9-13, in reference to this chapter on restorative justice in the New Testament. "Our Father in heaven, / hallowed be your name" (v. 9) is a petition that God "manifest his glory by an act of power . . . in this case, by the establishment of his kingdom."[13] Likewise, "Give us today our daily bread" (v. 11) is a petition for a "speedy coming of the kingdom (today), which is often portrayed in both the Old Testament and the New under the image of a feast."[14] Reflect on the next petition, Matthew 6:12, on forgiveness, as well as Jesus' own reflections on

---

[11] Ibid.

[12] Ibid.

[13] Donald Senior, ed., *Catholic Study Bible*, 2nd ed. (New York: Oxford University Press, 2011), Matt 6:9 note.

[14] Senior, *Catholic Study Bible*, Matt 6:11 note.

forgiveness after the prayer is given (vv. 14-15). What role does forgiveness play in bringing forth the kingdom of God?

2. Consider the Beatitudes in Matthew 5:3-12 in terms of restorative justice and the coming kingdom of God. It is common to think about the blessedness of the poor in spirit, the meek, and the clean of heart as a reward that these lowly people will be given after death. Approach them now in a different way—as actual ways of living that will bring restoration and peace. For example, in relationship to Matthew 5:5, Bassam found that the meek (the temperate and peaceful) will be the ones (rather than the aggressive and violent) who will "inherit the land." Consider the other Beatitudes in a similar way. Make a connection between the Beatitudes and the call from Jesus that immediately follows to "the salt of the earth" (v. 13) and "the light of the world" (v. 14).

Chapter 7

Catholic Social Thought

Editors

In chapter 10, Fr. James Donohue will discuss the hard teaching of forgiveness in Matthew 18:16-27, which includes the parable of the Unforgiving Servant. The parable is prompted by Peter's question, "Lord, if my brother sins against me, how often must I forgive him? As many as seven times?" Jesus replies, "[N]ot seven times but seventy-seven times" (Matt 18:21, 22). A key theme in Jesus' teaching on forgiveness (and as Fr. Jim will show) is restoration of community. In other words, forgiveness is not about wiping the slate clean as much as it is about welcoming the coming of the kingdom of God, restoring relationships, and sustaining hospitality to the outcast and the enemy. It is no mistake that just prior to the parable of the Unforgiving Servant, Jesus tells the parable of the Lost Sheep—where the shepherd leaves the ninety-nine (who did not go astray) in order to find and then rejoice over finding the one who was lost (Matt 18:10-14). The parables of the Lost Sheep and the Unforgiving Servant are difficult for the ones who have not gone astray: Jesus seems to put all the work on the side of the good and dutiful ones and give all the benefit to the wayward. The shepherd "rejoices more over it [the finding of the lost one] than over the ninety-nine that did not stray" (Matt 18:13).

Consider, however, that this opposition between the one and the ninety-nine, forgiver and forgiven, leads to a misinterpretation of Jesus' teaching. The power and jolt of the parables come from this opposition— "forgive someone who has wronged me seventy-seven times?" or "let ninety-nine sheep go unprotected and risk losing more in order to find one?" But we should not confuse the shock factor with the actual point of the parables. Consider that the "one hundred" is a family out on a holiday excursion, and along the way, one is lost. If their guide says to those who have not gone astray, "stay here and fend for yourselves while I try to find the lost one," few would argue—or see an opposition between their own good and the finding of the lost. The family would certainly join the guide in a celebration when the lost was found. All would take more joy in the presence of that one than those who had not gone astray. If this interpretation is correct, the point is not the opposition between lost and not-lost, forgiver and forgiven, but the unity and community that is restored. The parables are lessons in how to see the lost and unforgiven as our brothers and sisters, who we hope will return to us.

One more biblical illustration is unavoidable: Between the parable of the Lost Sheep and the parable of the Unforgiving Servant, Jesus gives instruction on what to do with an unrepentant brother (Matt 18:15-20). If he sins against you, talk with him one-on-one. If he refuses to take you seriously, take one or two others with you next time. If he still refuses to repent, bring him before the whole community of the church. After this attempt fails, Jesus' teachings appear to be far more harsh and definitive: "If he refuses to listen even to the church, then treat him as you would a Gentile or a tax collector" (Matt 18:17). However, we have seen in chapter 6, Sr. Mary Kate's discussion of restoration in the New Testament, that Jesus showed hospitality to Zacchaeus, who was the equivalent to a mob-boss of tax collectors (insofar as tax collecting for Rome took the form of extortion). Likewise, the Gentile—the Roman centurion—in Matthew 8:5-13 becomes an example of faith for Israel: "Lord, I am not worthy to have you enter under my roof; only say the word and my servant will be healed" (Matt 8:8). Treating another as a Gentile and tax collector is treating your brother as someone who is lost and needs to be found. All will rejoice, if after the seventy-seventh time, he recognizes his wrong for what it is and returns to you.

We are brothers and sisters bound together by God's grace and enlivened when we set our lives by God's hospitality and good company. As stated by the Compendium of the Social Doctrine of the Church, "God, in Christ, redeems not only the individual person but also the social relations existing between men."[1] At a very human level, redemption and restoration of relationships are at the heart of Catholic social thought—in regard to economic exchange, work, political life, religious liberty, and a whole

---

[1] Pontifical Council for Justice and Peace, Compendium of the Social Doctrine of the Church (Vatican City: Libreria Editrice Vaticana, 2004) 52, www.vatican.va/roman_curia/pontifical_councils/justpeace/documents/rc_pc_justpeace_doc_20060526_compendio-dott-soc_en.html.

host of other areas related to our lives at various levels of community.[2] For example, John Paul II, in his *Centesimus Annus* (1991), proposes that businesses and companies ought to form a "community of work."[3] On this basis, St. John Paul shows that healthy economies and business enterprises foster mutual dependence and care, as well as work that provides for a good life for the worker and those who are served by the work. Along this line of thought, William Collinge will review, in this chapter, a document by the US bishops on criminal and restorative justice—*Responsibility, Rehabilitation, and Restoration* (2000). Community and restoration are the underlining themes of the document. A justice system ought to foster a community of good relationships, first by restoring the victim and then by calling the offender to responsibility to the community. Restoration of the victims and community and responsibility for criminal acts are the best means to welcome and restore offenders back into common life.

Responsibility, Rehabilitation, and Restoration: The US Bishops' Statement on Criminal Justice (2000)

William J. Collinge

In the gospels, Jesus expresses concern for prisoners, as when the declaration "I was . . . in prison and you visited me" is one of the criteria used in the Last Judgment (Matt 25:35-36), as well as concern for the victims of crime, as in the parable of the Good Samaritan (Luke 10:29-37). Likewise, *Responsibility, Rehabilitation, and Restoration: A Catholic Perspective on Crime and Criminal Justice*, issued in 2000, the United States Catholic bishops' most comprehensive statement on its subject, combines these two concerns. This article will discuss the process that led to the statement, the contents of the statement, and the impact of the statement.

The Road to the 2000 Statement

Responsibility, Rehabilitation, and Restoration has antecedents in a 1978 statement by the bishops' Committee on Social Development and World

---

[2] See David Matzko McCarthy, "Catholic Social Teaching," in *Oxford Handbook of Catholic Theology*, ed. Lewis Ayres (Oxford: Oxford University Press, 2015); and "Modern Economy and Social Order," in *The Heart of Catholic Social Teaching*, ed. David Matzko McCarthy, 129–40 (Grand Rapids, MI: Brazos Press, 2009).

[3] *Centesimus Annus* (Vatican City: Libreria Editrice Vaticana, 1991) 32.

Peace, "Community and Crime," to which is appended "A Formal Statement of the United States Catholic Conference on the Reform of Correctional Institutions in the 1970s," issued by the bishops in 1973.[4]

The 1978 statement begins with expressions of concern about the rising levels of crime in the United States. The bishops base their recommendations in values of the Christian tradition, such as compassion for those rejected by society, and American values, such as equal justice under law. They call for greater community involvement in dealing with problems such as drugs, rather than exclusive reliance upon the criminal justice system. Among causes of crime, they highlight false values (such as materialism and lack of respect for human life), social injustice, family and neighborhood breakdown, and lack of moral leadership among those in government, business, the media, and the churches.[5] They proceed to consider eleven "criminal justice issues," of which prisons receive the most attention: "Prisons are dehumanizing and depersonalizing" (598). Imprisonment must simultaneously make clear society's disapproval of offenders' crimes and make it easier to reintegrate offenders into society as contributing members. The bishops endorse alternatives to prison, including restitution and community mediation programs. They criticize disparity in sentencing and oppose capital punishment. They call for gun control, criticize plea bargaining, and urge grand jury reform. Next they turn to "the responsibility of the local church" and call for twenty-two actions, from organizing discussion groups, to sponsoring crisis intervention and family counseling projects, to forming block patrols, to aiding parolees, to celebrating Dismas Sunday (the second Sunday in October). Finally, they urge churches to support public policy initiatives, including community-based alternatives to incarceration that match the criminal justice issues they have earlier listed.

Between 1978 and 2000, the rate of incarceration skyrocketed in the United States. While the rate of violent crime increased by about 50 percent and then declined back to near-1978 levels,[6] the number of sentenced

---

[4] "A Community Response to Crime" (later titled *Community and Crime*), *Origins* 7, no. 38 (March 9, 1978): 593, 595–604; the "Formal Statement" of 1973 can be found as "Prison Reform Statement of the U.S. Bishops," *Origins* 3, no. 22 (November 22, 1973).

[5] Notice that, as church leaders, they do not exempt themselves from criticism. See "A Community Response to Crime," 597.

[6] According to the FBI's Uniform Crime Reporting Statistics, the rate of violent crime per 100,000 people rose from 497.8 in 1978 to 758.2 in 1991 and then fell to 506.5 in 2000 (www.ucrdatatool.gov/index.cfm). In 2014, according to FBI, "Crime in the United States 2014," it was 365.5 (https://www.fbi.gov/about-us/cjis/ucr/crime-in-the-u.s/2014/crime-in-the-u.s.-2014/offenses-known-to-law-enforcement/violent-crime). These FBI statistics count only crimes reported to law enforcement authorities.

prisoners in state and federal facilities rose nearly fourfold, from 294,396 in 1978 to 1,391,892 in 2000, according to the Bureau of Justice Statistics.[7] (The US population increased by about 27 percent during that time.) The primary cause of the increase in incarceration was changed sentencing policies resulting from the "war on drugs," government initiatives against the trade in, and use of, illegal drugs. In the 1980s, especially, sentences for drug offenses were increased and mandatory minimums imposed, with the result that drug offenders came to form about half of federal prisoners and a substantial minority of prisoners on the state level.[8] Along with the increased incarceration rate came increased racial disparity among prisoners. In 1978, 51.7 percent of state and federal inmates were white, 47.2 black (Hispanics were not counted separately); in 2000, 55.3 percent of non-Hispanic inmates were black, 42.7 percent white.[9]

A development of a different kind was the rise of restorative justice. The term "restorative justice" was not in wide use until Howard Zehr's *Changing Lenses: A New Focus for Crime and Justice* was published in 1990.[10] Zehr defined restorative justice as "a process to involve, to the extent possible, those who have a stake in a specific offense to collectively identify and address harms, needs and obligations in order to heal and put things as right as possible."[11] By the late 1990s, restorative justice had become a movement.

At its 1987 meeting in Las Cruces, New Mexico, the National Convocation of Jail and Prison Ministries (NCJPM), which began as an organization of Catholic jail and prison chaplains and had by then developed into an interfaith advocate of restorative justice, urged the bishops to issue an

---

[7] Bureau of Justice Statistics (BJS), U.S. Department of Justice, "Prisoners 1925–81," https://www.bjs.gov/content/pub/pdf/p2581.pdf; and Allen J. Beck and Paige M. Harrison, "Prisoners in 2000," https://www.bjs.gov/content/pub/pdf/p00.pdf. In 2000, another 621,149 were in the custody of local jails; I do not have a figure for local jail inmates in 1978.

[8] Michelle Alexander, *The New Jim Crow: Mass Incarceration in the Age of Colorblindness*, rev. ed. (New York: New Press, 2012), 92–93.

[9] See sources cited in n. 7. In the 1980 census, 11.7 percent of the US population were black or African American, and 80.3 percent were white. In the 2000 census, in which Hispanic origin was counted but not as a race, 12.3 percent of the population were black or African American, and 75.1 percent were white, while 2.4 percent claimed more than one race (a new category). See https://www.census.gov/newsroom/cspan/1940census/CSPAN_1940slides.pdf.

[10] *Changing Lenses: A New Focus for Crime and Justice* (Scottdale, PA: Herald Press, 1990).

[11] *The Little Book of Restorative Justice* (Intercourse, PA: Good Books, 2002), 37.

updated statement. "The following year, the bishops of Region XIII, the region to which the Diocese of Las Cruces belongs, presented the *varium*, or motion, before the body of the U.S. Bishops to write a statement addressing pastoral issues of inmates and needed reform of our criminal justice system."[12] Pressure also came from National CURE (Citizens United for the Rehabilitation of Errants), which was founded in Texas in 1972 by Charles Sullivan, a former priest, and his wife, Pauline Sullivan, a former religious sister, as an organization for service to prisoners and their families but which developed into a national advocacy organization whose goals were "that prisons should be used only for those who absolutely must be incarcerated and that those who are incarcerated should have all of the resources they need to turn their lives around."[13] Charles Sullivan had the ear of a number of bishops.[14]

In 1999, the Institute on the Common Good at Regis University in Denver hosted a private meeting on criminal justice for the US bishops' Committee on Domestic Policy. Those in attendance included John Carr, director of the Department of Justice, Peace and Human Development at what was then the United States Catholic Conference (USCC) and is now the United States Conference of Catholic Bishops (USCCB), and Dan Misleh, the USCC staff member in charge of drafting the criminal justice document. Father Michael Bryant of the NCJPM presented a paper that brought the work of Howard Zehr to the attention of the committee.[15] As a result, restorative justice assumed a central position in the developing document.

A draft appeared in the spring of 2000. The bishops approved it with only minor corrections. But it did not satisfy the NCJPM. It was "very Pollyannaish," according to Fr. Bryant, and "would offend no one. It was lacking in the prophetic voice of the 1978 statement." He believed that the draft

---

[12] Ricardo Ramírez, bishop emeritus of Las Cruces, "Responsibility, Rehabilitation, and Restoration: A Bishop Looks Back," talk given to Summer Institute on Social Action, St. Louis (July 22, 2014), https://www.dioceseoflascruces.org/documents/2016/1/bp_sp_68.pdf.

[13] See www.curenational.org. For a history of CURE, see Pauline and Charles Sullivan, "Thirty Years of CURE: The Struggle is its Own Reward," in *Criminal Justice: Retribution vs. Restoration*, ed. Eleanor Hannon Judah and Rev. Michael Bryant, 233–44 (New York: Haworth, 2004).

[14] Rev. Michael Bryant, personal interview (April 23, 2016). Father Bryant is chaplain of the DC Detention Facility and a past chairman of the National Convocation of Jail and Prison Ministries.

[15] Ibid.

was out of balance in its focus on the needs of victims of crime, reversing the emphasis of the 1978 statement. In particular, there was nothing on prison conditions. Father Bryant sent a letter to Cardinal Roger Mahony of Los Angeles, then-chairman of the Domestic Policy Committee of the USCC, expressing his concerns. He intended to copy it to the Executive Committee of the USCC, but it was accidentally copied to the Conference's much larger Administrative Committee, giving it greater exposure than intended. After a tense "standoff" during the summer of 2000, the committee agreed to revise the statement to accommodate the NCJPM's concerns and to incorporate more balance between concern for victims of crime and concern for those in prison. The section on restorative justice was strengthened and became the key to harmonizing the two concerns. The revised document was passed without difficulty on November 15, 2000, at the USCC's fall meeting in Washington.[16]

Responsibility, Rehabilitation, and Restoration—*What Does It Say?*

Responsibility, Rehabilitation, and Restoration is published as a booklet of sixty-nine pages (plus front matter).[17] It comprises an introduction, three main sections, a conclusion, and an appendix. Ten text boxes are interspersed throughout the document. Nine of them are quotations from people involved in the criminal justice system in some way, from a prisoner and a crime victim to two wardens and a judge; the other reprises the bishops' case against capital punishment. The following four sections of this chapter will review the document's introduction and main sections.

Introduction

The bishops begin by noting the prevalence of crime and the fear of crime and calling for "a new national dialogue on crime and corrections, justice and mercy, responsibility and treatment" (1). They preview their

---

[16] Most of the information in this paragraph, including all of the quotations, comes from my interview with Fr. Bryant.

[17] United States Conference of Catholic Bishops, *Responsibility, Rehabilitation, and Restoration: A Catholic Perspective on Crime and Criminal Justice* (Washington, DC: USCCB, 2000); used by permission. My in-text citations will be to the booklet. It also appears in *Origins* 30, no. 25 (November 30, 2000): 389, 391–404; and on the USCCB website: www.usccb.org/issues-and-action/human-life-and-dignity/criminal-justice-restorative -justice/crime-and-criminal-justice.cfm.

argument, establishing its grounding in Catholic teaching on human dignity, in this paragraph:

> A Catholic approach begins with the recognition that the dignity of the human person applies to both victim and offender. As bishops, we believe that the current trend of more prisons and more executions, with too little education and drug treatment, does not truly reflect Christian values and will not really leave our communities safer. We are convinced that our tradition and our faith offer better alternatives that can hold offenders accountable *and* challenge them to change their lives; reach out to victims *and* reject vengeance; restore a sense of community *and* resist the violence that has engulfed so much of our culture. (2)

The bishops proceed to describe the process of consultation "with Catholics who are involved in every aspect of the criminal justice system" (4) that they followed in preparing this document—a last echo, perhaps, of the consultative process followed in the two great pastoral letters of the 1980s, The Challenge of Peace (1983) and Economic Justice for All (1986). They summarize, "All those whom we consulted seemed to agree on one thing: the status quo is not really working—victims are often ignored, offenders are often not rehabilitated, and many communities have lost their sense of security" (6).

Next comes a statistical overview, "Some Dimensions of Crime and Punishment in the United States." While the bishops' statistics are now out of date, the general picture they furnish remains broadly accurate. I will provide a sample of the statistics in the document and update them as near to the present as I can:

- "In 1998, about one out of every twenty-seven Americans over the age of twelve was the victim of a violent crime" (7). In 2014, the figure was about one out of every forty.[18]

---

[18] The document's 1998 figure is from the Bureau of Justice Statistics (BJS), Callie Marie Rennison, *Criminal Victimization 1998*, https://www.bjs.gov/content/pub/pdf/cv98.pdf. It includes homicides. To obtain a comparable figure for 2014, I had to combine BJS data (Jennifer L. Truman and Lynn Langton, *Crime Victimization, 2014*, https://www.bjs.gov/content/pub/pdf/cv14.pdf), which does not include homicides, with FBI data ("Crime in the United States 2014"; see n. 6 above) on homicides. The two sets of data are not entirely commensurable, since the FBI enumerates only crimes reported to police, while the BJS data, based on a survey of victims, excludes homicide victims for obvious reasons and includes crimes not reported to police. Homicides, of course, are almost always reported to police.

- "One and one-half million children under the age of eighteen (or 2.1 percent) have a parent in state or federal prison." By 2007, the number had risen to about 1,700,000. Other data in *Responsibility, Rehabilitation, and Restoration* remained more or less current in 2007: about 92 percent of imprisoned parents were fathers, and they were disproportionately African American (49.4 percent in 2000, 42.9 percent in 2007).[19]

- "In 1998, the imprisonment rate in America was 668 per 100,000 offenders" (8). "Per 100,000 offenders" is clearly an error; BJS statistics for 1998 show 672 inmates in federal and state prisons and local jails *per 100,000 population*.[20] The figure for 2014 was 705.[21] The bishops add, "This is six to twelve times higher than the rate of other Western countries" (8). It remains the case that the rate of imprisonment in the US is far higher than that of other Western nations.[22]

- "The inmate population has risen from 250,000 in 1972 to a record two million inmates in 2000" (9). The figure for 2014 was 2,306,100,[23] representing a slightly higher rate of increase from 2000 than that of the population as a whole.

- "African Americans make up 12 percent of the U.S. population but represent more than 49 percent of prisoners in state and federal prisons. . . . Hispanic Americans make up 9 percent of the U.S. population but 19 percent of prisoners in state and federal prisons" (10).[24] In 2014, African Americans were close to 13 percent of the

[19] 2007 figures are from Bureau of Justice Statistics Special Report, Lauren E. Glaze and Laura M. Maruschak, *Parents in Prison and Their Minor Children* (August 2008), https://www.bjs.gov/content/pub/pdf/pptmc.pdf.

[20] Allen J. Beck and Christopher J. Mumola, *Prisoners in 1998*, Bureau of Justice Statistics Bulletin, https://www.bjs.gov/content/pub/pdf/p98.pdf.

[21] Combining the numbers in E. Ann Carson, *Prisoners in 2014*, BJS, https://www.bjs .gov/content/pub/pdf/p14.pdf, table 5 (471 inmates), with those in *Jail Inmates at Midyear 2014*, https://www.bjs.gov/content/pub/pdf/jim14_sum.pdf (234 inmates).

[22] Comparative statistics for 2013 are available at Roy Walmsley, International Centre for Prison Studies, "World Prison Population List," 10th ed., www.apcca.org/uploads /10th_Edition_2013.pdf. The rate for Canada was 118 per 100,000 population; for England and Wales, 148. Only two small island nations (Seychelles and St. Kitts and Nevis) had rates comparable to that of the US.

[23] This figure is from Truman and Langton, *Crime Victimization, 2014*.

[24] The bishops cite BJS, *Prison and Jail Inmates 1999* (NCJ no. 183476), but the actual title is *Prisoners in 1999*. This report, by Allen J. Beck, is now available at www.bjs.gov/content /pub/pdf/p99.pdf. From that report, I derive a figure of 45.7 percent for inmates who

population, and Hispanics were up to 17.4 percent. Prisoners were 35.7 percent African American and 21.6 percent Hispanic.[25]

- "The United States spends more than $35 billion annually on corrections" (9). This figure, for which the bishops do not cite a source, appears to be low for 2000. A study by the Hamilton Project cites a figure of $65 billion for 2000 and $80 billion for 2010 for spending on corrections at the federal, state, and local levels.[26] For 2010, this amounted to $260 for each US resident.

In short, the bishops' figures continue to portray the general shape of crime and punishment in the United States, although there are some differences in detail today. Crime rates have gone down; incarceration rates have remained fairly stable at a high level; and the prison population remains disproportionately African American, though somewhat less so than in 2000.

The bishops close their introduction by remarking on two areas of special concern. One is the great increase in the detention of immigrants, sometimes in conditions that are "clearly inappropriate" (11). The second is treatment for drug and alcohol abuse, which they argue can be effective in reducing recidivism (12). Both remain current issues. Human rights groups continue to be critical of conditions in facilities supervised by the

---

are African American (non-Hispanic), and 17.9 who are Hispanic (there is another BJS report, also by Beck, *Prison and Jail Inmates at Midyear 1999*, NCJ no. 181643, now available at http://bjs.gov/content/pub/pdf/pjim99.pdf, from which the same percentages may be derived). The bishops appear to be using 1990 census figures for percentages of the general population; U.S. Census Bureau estimates for 1999 are 12.8 percent African American and 11.5 percent Hispanic. See *Population Profile of the United States 1999*, available at https://www.census.gov/prod/2001pubs/p23-205.pdf, 12.

[25] In 2014, but not 1999, "persons of two or more races" (but not Hispanic) were classified as "other," along with Native Americans, Alaskan Natives, Asians, Native Hawaiians, and Pacific Islanders; the percent of prisoners classified as "other" rose from 3.4 in 1999 to 8.6 in 2014. Figures on prisoners are derived from *Prisoners in 1999*, 9 (see n. 24), and *Prisoners in 2014*, 15 (see n. 21).

[26] Melissa S. Kearney and others, *Ten Economic Facts about Crime and Incarceration in the United States* (Washington, DC: The Hamilton Project, 2014), 13, http://www.hamiltonproject.org/assets/legacy/files/downloads_and_links/v8_THP_10CrimeFacts.pdf. Federal sources confirm this study's numbers for federal and state expenditures in 2010 ($6.2 billion and $48.5 billion, respectively): "Federal Prison Systems (BOP) 2011 Budget Request at a Glance," https://www.justice.gov/sites/default/files/jmd/legacy/2013/12/30/fy11-bop-bud-summary.pdf; Tracey Kyckelhahn, "State Corrections Expenditures, 1982-2010," BJS, www.bjs.gov/content/pub/pdf/scefy8210.pdf.

Immigration and Customs Enforcement agency,[27] while government data support the cost-effectiveness of drug and alcohol treatment for offenders, at the same time confirming that far too little treatment is available.[28]

First Main Section: "Scriptural, Theological, and Sacramental Heritage"

An affirmation that we are both guilty of sin and forgiven by God keynotes this section. Offenders must acknowledge their responsibility for their crimes, but at the same time the community should seek to rehabilitate them and reintegrate them into communal life. Restorative justice is the hallmark of a Catholic approach: "A Catholic approach leads us to encourage models of restorative justice that seek to address crime in terms of the harm done to victims and communities, not simply as a violation of law" (17).

Two pages of "Scriptural Foundations" follow, and then the bishops note the four traditional elements of the sacrament of penance—contrition, confession, satisfaction, absolution—and observe that they "teach us about taking responsibility, making amends, and reintegrating into community" (19). Next they select six themes of Catholic social teaching that guide Catholic approaches to criminal justice, in most cases viewing them through the lenses of concern for offenders and concern for victims, side by side:

1. *Human Life and Dignity.* Every person is created in the image of God and therefore has an inherent dignity that is not lost by crime or incarceration. Penal systems must respect this dignity by providing for the basic needs of inmates, including food, clothing, personal safety, and education. Victims should not be excluded, ignored, or degraded in criminal proceedings.

2. *Human Rights and Responsibilities.* "Those who commit crimes violate the rights of others and disregard their responsibilities. But the test for the rest of us is whether we will exercise our responsibility to hold the offender accountable without violating his or her basic rights" (23).

---

[27] See Molly Hennessy-Fiske, "Immigrant Family Detention Centers are Prison-Like, Critics Say, Despite Order to Improve," *Los Angeles Times*, October 23, 2015, www.latimes .com/nation/nationnow/la-na-immigration-family-detention-20151020-story.html.

[28] National Institute on Drug Abuse, "Is Providing Drug Abuse Treatment to Offenders Worth the Financial Investment?," https://www.drugabuse.gov/publications/principles -drug-abuse-treatment-criminal-justice-populations/providing-drug-abuse-treatment -to-offenders-worth-f.

3. *Family, Community, Participation.* The disintegration of family and community life is a cause of crime. Offenders' connections with their families and home communities should in most (but not all) cases be preserved and can help in their reintegration. Victims are often excluded from participation in criminal processes; their needs "to be heard and to be healed" must be acknowledged and addressed (24).

4. *The Common Good.* This term refers not to a sum of individuals' goods but to the good of a whole society, including the conditions in which individuals can flourish as individuals and in their relationships with one another. Crime violates the common good. "Redress"—repair of harm done to victims and to society, often through restitution—can help restore the common good.

5. *The Option for the Poor and Vulnerable.* The failure to provide for the basic needs of individuals due to poverty, neglect, and abuse can turn them toward crime. The church should address those needs through "pastoral care, charity, and advocacy" (25). (The bishops might have mentioned that the poor are disproportionately the victims of crime.)

6. *Subsidiarity and Solidarity.* Subsidiarity calls on us to strengthen families and local communities and deal with social problems first on those levels, while recognizing that larger, systemic approaches may also be needed. Solidarity calls on each person to take responsibility for the well-being of our communities and of all who make up those communities.

Two themes of Catholic social teaching that appear in the standard list that is posted on the US bishops' website[29] but are not considered in *Responsibility, Rehabilitation, and Restoration* are "The Dignity of Work and the Rights of Workers" and "Care for God's Creation." Their exclusion reveals one of the limits of the document. Serious crimes against labor and the environment are ordinarily committed by collective bodies such as corporations, though individuals are complicit, and often dealt with through administrative and civil law (e.g., regulations, fines, and class-action lawsuits) rather than criminal law. But the document has little to say about social sin and the systemic crimes that result from it.

---

[29] "Seven Themes of Catholic Social Teaching," www.usccb.org/beliefs-and-teachings /what-we-believe/catholic-social-teaching/seven-themes-of-catholic-social-teaching .cfm. The list originates in US Catholic bishops, *Sharing Catholic Social Teaching: Challenges and Directions* (Washington, DC: United States Catholic Conference, 1998), 4–6.

Second Main Section: "Policy Foundations and Directions"

This is the longest section in the document and the heart of its argument. It comprises recommendations for eleven "foundations" for new approaches to criminal justice. The bishops preface their recommendations with a broad statement that reflects the basic orientation of the restorative justice movement: "We seek approaches that understand crime as a threat to community, not just a violation of law; that demand new efforts to rebuild lives, not just build more prisons; and that demonstrate a commitment to re-weave a broader social fabric of respect for life, civility, responsibility, and reconciliation" (27). I will quote the eleven "foundations" and summarize some subordinate points:

1. "Protecting society from those who threaten life, inflict harm, take property, and destroy the bonds of community" (27). Punishment is not to be done for its own sake but in order to protect and strengthen communities.

2. "Rejecting simplistic solutions such as 'three strikes and you're out' and rigid mandatory sentencing" (28). Penalties should be adapted to the circumstances of the offenders. "For those who are trying to change their lives, a combination of accountability and flexibility works best." The bishops recommend community-based approaches, especially for nonviolent offenders. Juvenile offenders, even the most violent, should not be treated as if they were adults and should not be placed in adult jails.

3. "Promoting serious efforts toward crime prevention and poverty reduction" (29). While poverty and family breakdown are not sufficient to cause crimes, they are "significant risk factors for criminal activity." In addition, quality education is necessary to prepare children for responsible citizenship.

4. "Challenging the culture of violence and encouraging a culture of life" (29). The bishops call for measures to end domestic violence and to assist its victims and to curb the sale and use of firearms and increase firearm safety. They deplore social and cultural values that can license or encourage violence, and they especially challenge the media "to stop glorifying violence and exploiting sexuality" (31). They reiterate their call[30] to end the death penalty. It is a sign of disrespect for human life, and it is no longer necessary in order to protect society. A long text box expands

---

[30] Administrative Board, US Catholic Conference, A Good Friday Appeal to End the Death Penalty (Washington, DC: United States Catholic Conference, 1999).

the case against the death penalty: "It is cruel, unnecessary, and arbitrary; it often has racial overtones; and it fails to live up to our deep conviction that all human life is sacred" (32). Moreover, "there is evidence of wrongful convictions and poor representation in death penalty cases" (34).

5. "Offering victims the opportunity to participate more fully in the criminal justice process" (31). Victims have a right to be kept informed throughout criminal processes that result from crimes committed against them. They should be offered opportunities to express the pain and loss they have suffered. "If they wish, they should be able to confront the offender and ask for reparation for their losses" (35).

6. "Encouraging programs of restorative justice that provide the opportunity for mediation between victims and offenders and offer restitution for crimes committed" (36). "Restorative justice," they say, "is a model of justice that "focuses first on the victim and the community harmed by the crime, rather than on the dominant state-against-the-perpetrator model" (36). They encourage voluntary "victim-offender mediation" programs or, when those are not possible or not advisable, "impact panels" composed of victims and perpetrators of similar crimes. Such panels "can assist the victim's healing, the community's understanding of the crime, and the offender's sense of responsibility" (39).

7. "Insisting that punishment has a constructive and rehabilitative purpose" (39). Prisons should aim at leading offenders to "change their behaviors and attitudes," and to teach them skills for life and work in the community. Parole and probation as alternatives to incarceration should be given new emphasis. Prisons should not be located in remote areas, far from the families and home communities of offenders. Effective substance abuse treatment programs should be available not only in prisons but in communities. The bishops question whether prisons can be run by private, profit-seeking corporations.[31] They discourage the use of isolation units. Finally, they call for society to welcome ex-offenders back as full participating members, including, when possible, restoring their right to vote.

8. "Encouraging spiritual healing and renewal for those who commit crime" (41). Prisoners' religious freedom should not be restricted, and they should have access to chaplains. "Every indication is that genuine religious

---

[31] Their suspicions are confirmed in an exposé by Shane Bauer, "My Four Months as a Private Prison Guard," *Mother Jones* (July-August 2016), www.motherjones.com/politics/2016/06 /cca-private-prisons-corrections-corporation-inmates-investigation-bauer.

participation and formation is a road to renewal and rehabilitation for those who have committed crimes" (41).

9. "Making a serious commitment to confront the pervasive role of addiction and mental illness in crime" (41). The bishops reiterate their call for drug and alcohol treatment facilities inside and outside of prisons. They add that American society needs to address the underlying problems that drive people into the sale and use of drugs. They observe that mental illness often goes undiagnosed and untreated among offenders, and that "many in our prison system would do better in other settings" suitable to their conditions (43).

10. "Treating immigrants justly" (43). Although they are not citizens, migrants too deserve due process, fair treatment, and freedom to practice their religions.

11. "Placing crime in a community context and building on promising alternatives that empower neighborhoods and towns to restore a sense of security" (44). The bishops describe community as a "web of relationships and resources" (44). Crime and fear of crime damage communities, but community groups—sometimes funded by the bishops' Catholic Campaign for Human Development—can partner with police to reduce crime and deal with potential crime situations. The bishops commend "broken window[s]" policing, by which police focus on disorder and less serious crimes (e.g., broken windows and subway turnstile jumping) in an effort to create an environment less conducive to serious crimes.[32]

Third Main Section: "The Church's Mission"

The recommendations of the preceding section were addressed to the makers of public policy. This section turns to the Catholic Church, identifying what parishes and dioceses ought to do in response to "the challenge of curbing crime and reshaping the criminal justice system" (47). They enumerate seven ways in which the church is called to responsibility and action, expanding each one and making more specific observations. More detailed

---

[32] "Broken windows" has come to refer to many types of programs, including policies of "zero tolerance" for lesser crimes and widespread "stop and frisk" practices, which are often perceived as harassment of minority communities. A recent negative report on "broken windows" policing, as practiced in New York City, is summarized in Greg B. Smith, "Department of Investigation Report Suggests 'Broken Windows' Policing Strategy Doesn't Work," *New York Daily News* (June 23, 2016), www.nydailynews.com/new-york/report-suggests-nypd-broken-windows-policing-doesn-work-article-1.2683516.

ways of implementing the first six responsibilities are noted in an appendix titled "Suggestions for Action" (57–62). I will quote and expand the seven tasks to which the church is called, drawing on the appendix as needed.

1. "Teach right from wrong, respect for life and the law, forgiveness and mercy" (47). An adequate approach to crime requires "a moral revolution in our society," which involves "a renewed emphasis on the traditional values of family and community, respect and responsibility, mercy and justice, and teaching right from wrong" (48). The church teaches these values in churches and schools, and through advocacy and witness. The bishops call for alternatives to abortion, for curbing violent and sexual content in media, for character-building activities for young people such as athletics and Scouting, for conflict resolution education, and for opposition to the death penalty.

2. "Stand with victims and their families" (49). In particular, the bishops call for programs to educate pastors and pastoral ministers in ministry to victims and for greater awareness in parishes of services available through Catholic Charities and other agencies.

3. "Reach out to offenders and their families, advocate for more treatment, and provide for the pastoral needs of all involved" (49). The bishops reiterate calls already made for prison ministry programs, outreach to families of inmates, and prisoner reentry programs (60).

4. "Build community" (50). "Catholics are encouraged to promote all of those things that support family life and lift up the community" (61). In reference to crime, these include "neighborhood watch groups, community-oriented policing, and partnerships between law enforcement and the local faith community" (61). They urge financial support for their Catholic Campaign for Human Development, which gives grants "to support organizing projects that bring people together to work on community needs, including crime and criminal justice" (61).[33]

---

[33] Examples of CCHD-funded programs in criminal justice, some of which predate the 2000 document, can be found in Daniel J. Misleh and Evelyn U. Hanneman, "Emerging Issues: The Faith Communities and the Criminal Justice System," in Judah and Bryant, ed., *Criminal Justice: Retribution vs. Restoration* (see n. 13), 123–30. Ironically, a number of dioceses, including the one in which I live, have withdrawn support from CCHD. One reason given is concern that CCHD gives grants to organizations that join coalitions that include organizations that oppose Catholic positions on abortion and same-sex marriage. CCHD defends itself at www.usccb.org/about/catholic-campaign -for-human-development/Who-We-Are/truth-about-cchd.cfm.

5. "Advocate policies that help reduce violence, protect the innocent, involve the victims, and offer real alternatives to crime" (52). This section provides a brief summary of the types of policies supported in the document. On the other hand, "We should resist policies that simply call for more prisons, harsher sentences, and increased reliance on the death penalty" (52).

6. "Organize diocesan and state consultations" (52), similar to those that the bishops conducted in preparing this document.

7. "Work for new approaches" (53), such as those advocated in the document.

Conclusion of the Statement

The main text of *Responsibility, Rehabilitation, and Restoration* ends with a one-page conclusion, affirming, "We believe a Catholic ethic of responsibility, rehabilitation, and restoration can become the foundation for the necessary reform of our broken criminal justice system" (55).

Reception and Impact of the Statement: Belatedly Timely?

Upon its publication, *Responsibility, Rehabilitation, and Restoration* evoked minimal response from scholars and only a limited response from Catholic Church leaders.[34] But there are movements both within the larger society and within church circles that indicate people may now be ready to pay attention to its message. The influential, conservative Charles Koch Foundation has begun a project for "Criminal Justice and Policing Reform," with the aim of bringing about "reforms to the criminal justice system that promote human dignity, reduce costs, enhance public safety, and make

---

[34] See Joseph L. Falvey Jr., "Crime and Punishment: A Catholic Perspective," *The Catholic Lawyer* 43, no. 1 (Spring 2004); Robert DeFina and Lance Hannon, "Engaging the U.S. Bishops' Pastoral on Crime and Criminal Justice: From Atomism to Community Justice," *Journal of Catholic Social Thought* 8, no. 1 (2011). See also DeFina and Hannon, "Cruel & Unusual: The True Costs of Our Prison System," *Commonweal* (January 28, 2011):, 11–14.

Jim Consedine, "Crime and Punishment: Cautious Bishops Miss the Mark in Pastoral on Crime," *National Catholic Reporter* (March 9, 2001), http://natcath.org/NCR_online/archives2/2001a/030901/030901n.htm.

victims whole." The Foundation's first specific aim of this project is to bring about an end to "Excessive & Disproportionate Sentencing."[35] Every one of these aims echoes *Responsibility, Rehabilitation, and Restoration.* From the other side of the political spectrum, the civil rights lawyer Michelle Alexander, through her book *The New Jim Crow,* has brought about widespread public awareness of how the system of mass incarceration has produced a racial caste system in this country that resembles those of slavery and segregation. Recently, and despite the present climate of political polarization, legislation for reforming mental health care along the lines that the bishops recommend has begun to receive bipartisan support in both houses of Congress.[36] Restorative justice is receiving increasing attention by educators and criminologists.

Pope Francis, without using the words "restorative justice," endorses the substance of restorative justice in a letter to two conferences of criminologists, urging a "higher justice" that seeks

> to reestablish relationships and reintegrate people into society. To me, this seems to be the great challenge that we all must face together, so that the measures adopted against evil are not satisfied by restraining, dissuading and isolating the many who have caused it, but also help them to reflect, to travel the paths of good, to be authentic persons who, removed from their own hardships, become merciful themselves. The Church, therefore, proposes a humanizing, genuinely reconciling justice, a justice that leads the criminal, through educational development and brave atonement, to rehabilitation and reintegration into the community.[37]

In the United States, the Catholic Mobilizing Network (CMN) has broadened its focus from opposing the death penalty to include also promoting restorative justice. The group sponsored two conferences, "Restore Justice! Encounter and Mercy: A Conference on Restorative Justice" (2014) and "A New Path to Justice: A Conference on Criminal Justice Reform in the Year of Mercy" (2015), both at The Catholic University of America. CMN also

---

[35] Charles Koch Institute, "Criminal Justice & Policing Reform," https://www.charles kochinstitute.org/issues/criminal-justice-policing-reform/#.

[36] Editorial, "Hope for Reforming Mental Health Care," *The Washington Post* (June 25, 2016), A18.

[37] "Letter to Participants in the 19th International Congress of the International Association of Penal Law and the 3rd Congress of the Latin-American Association of Penal Law and Criminology" (May 30, 2014), http://w2.vatican.va/content /francesco/en/letters/2014/documents/papa-francesco_20140530_lettera-diritto-penale -criminologia.html.

encouraged *Journal of Moral Theology* editor David McCarthy to produce a scholarly treatment of restorative justice, which appeared as *Restorative Justice* in the journal.[38] And, of course, the CMN and especially Vicki Schieber have been a vital part of the production of the book you now have in your hands. So much of the work done in restorative justice has been foreshadowed by *Responsibility, Rehabilitation, and Restoration*. Sixteen years after its appearance, might the USCCB's statement have belatedly become timely?

Review and Looking Forward

Editors

The words of Pope Francis will serve well to summarize the approach of the US bishops and look forward to the treatment of restorative justice by Judge Janine Geske in the next chapter. In the excerpt below, the pope is addressing the International Association of Penal Law and the Latin American Association of Penal Law and Criminology (2014). First, Francis notes that focus needs to be on harm done to the victim:

> The Lord has gradually taught his people that there is a necessary asymmetry between crime and punishment, that one cannot apply the remedy: an eye for an eye or a tooth for a broken tooth, by breaking that of another. Justice is to be rendered to the victim, not by executing the aggressor.

Then he turns to the needs of the community as a whole:

> In our communities, we tend to think that crimes are resolved when the criminal is caught and condemned. . . . However, it would be error to model compensation only on punishment, to confuse justice with revenge, which would contribute only to increasing violence, even if it is institutionalized.

Pope Francis turns to the nature of God's justice and mercy. In God, the demands of justice and the offer of forgiveness are united (even though we tend to keep them apart):

> [That God] is there even before the human sinner, waiting and offering him his forgiveness, thus reveals a higher justice which is, at the same time impartial and compassionate, without

---

[38] David M. McCarthy, ed., *Restorative Justice, Journal of Moral Theology* 5, no. 2 (June 2016). The journal is sponsored by Mount St. Mary's University and the issue can be accessed through the journal website: www.msmary.edu/jmt.

contradiction in these two aspects. Forgiveness, in fact, neither eliminates nor diminishes the need for correction, precisely that of justice, nor does it overlook the need for personal conversion, instead it goes further, seeking to reestablish relationships and reintegrate people into society.

Finally, Francis calls us to develop practices of "a humanizing, genuinely reconciling justice":

> To me, this seems to be the great challenge that we all must face together, so that the measures adopted against evil are not satisfied by restraining, dissuading and isolating the many who have caused it, but also helps them to reflect, to travel the paths of good, to be authentic persons who, removed from their own hardships, become merciful themselves. The Church, therefore, proposes a humanizing, genuinely reconciling justice, a justice that leads the criminal, through educational development and brave atonement, to rehabilitation and reintegration into the community.[39]

Questions for Discussion

1. Teach right from wrong. Stand with victims and their families. Reach out to offenders and offer them ways to change and set things right. Build community. These are the first steps, outlined by the US bishops, on what parishes and church communities can do. Consider what could be done in your community.

2. This book has and will provide many examples of people—victims and offenders—whose lives have been served by a restorative justice approach. Restorative justice programs and other approaches that emphasize the good of community have success in meeting the needs of victims and changing the lives of offenders. Consider why retributive and "tough on crime" approaches continue to be celebrated as more effective and better for victims—when there is plenty of evidence that they are not.

---

[39] Letter of Pope Francis to Participants in the 19th International Congress of the International Association of Penal Law and of the 3rd Congress of the Latin-American Association of Penal Law and Criminology (May 30, 2014), https://w2.vatican.va /content/francesco/en/letters/2014/documents/papa-francesco_20140530_lettera -diritto-penale-criminologia.html.

Chapter 8

The Judicial System

Editors

The previous chapter outlined the linkage between Catholic social teaching and restorative justice. Many persons come to their understanding of restorative justice through formation in a religious tradition. Some persons reach this understanding through reflection on their work in our justice system. Justice Janine Geske initially was far from a restorative justice enthusiast. She tended to dismiss restorative justice as a problematic practice that risks revictimizing victims. A serendipitous invitation brought this Wisconsin law professor, circuit court and Supreme Court judge to change her mind. Liz Oyer, a federal public defender practicing in Baltimore City, valued a restorative justice approach early in her career. She welcomed opportunities to take such a restorative approach and regretted that few such opportunities are available on the federal level. One such opportunity arose, however, in 2016.

Tensions had been rising in numerous cities over the treatment of African Americans by some police departments and officers. Cell phone and police body camera videos captured incidents that escalated these tensions. The April 2016 death of Freddie Gray, a twenty-five-year-old African American living in Baltimore City, from injuries suffered during his transport in a police van after his arrest triggered citywide protests. Continuing protests remained peaceful until violent incidents directed against police officers occurred during a march from city hall resulting in injuries and arrests. On the day of Freddie Gray's funeral, full-scale riots broke out, with violence and looting spreading to different sections of the city. By early evening, following looting, a CVS pharmacy was set ablaze, resulting in the governor declaring a state of emergency. More buildings and vehicles were set on fire as the city descended into a state of violent confrontation and chaos. Police began arresting people and by the end of the rioting 235 people had been arrested.[1]

Friends, coaches, and teachers who knew Gregory Butler could not believe that the twenty-two-year-old got caught up in the riots and made a decision he would so deeply regret. A video of the area near the CVS pharmacy captured firefighters struggling to stop the blazing fire engulfing the building. It also captured Greg riding a bicycle and stopping to puncture the fire hose being used by firefighters to extinguish the fire. A number of persons involved in the fire were federally convicted of arson and sentenced to between four and fifteen years in prison. Greg was the only person federally charged who was not involved in an act of arson. Initially the US attorney charged him with the very serious crime of aiding and abetting an arson. Greg Butler's life would have turned out quite differently if he had not had the good fortune of having Liz Oyer as his federal public defender. The more Liz learned about him, the more she was convinced this was a young man worth fighting for. She was also convinced the best way to address his case was through a restorative justice approach, and she recognized the challenge in trying to do this in response to a federal charge.

Members of the Baltimore community knew that once these cases were charged federally rather than on a state level, they would carry heavier punishments and be prosecuted by federal attorneys who were not members of their local community. Being external to their community, these attorneys likely would not understand the growing frustrations and tensions that led to the rioting and would view the participants as mere thugs intent on violating the law and disrupting the peace. Liz understood the uphill battle she faced. Contentious meetings ensued in which she built a strong, passionately presented case for both dismissing the aiding and abetting arson charge and allowing Greg to plea to a lesser charge. The prosecution resisted but finally was open to this proposal but only on the condition that Greg serve two years in prison. At the motions hearing, in response to Liz's persuasive reasoning, the judge dropped the more serious charge that carried mandatory prison time, maintaining that Greg's conduct did not constitute involvement in the arson. Greg then pled guilty to the federal crime of obstructing

---

[1] An analysis of the situation in Baltimore in relation to restorative justice can be found in V. McGovern and L. Field's "Restorative Justice in Baltimore," *The Journal of Moral Theology* 5, no. 2 (June 2016): 143–57.

firefighters during a state of civil disorder. The US attorney sought a sentence of thirty-three months in prison. Most likely Greg would be serving that prison sentence now if the firefighters, who were the victims, had not had the gracious willingness to accept Liz's invitation to take a restorative justice approach to the case.

The US attorney never contacted the fire department members who were the victims in this case. He never inquired about how they wished to see this case resolved. Liz recognized the importance of reaching out to them. Her outreach brought them to understand what she had learned about Greg. Initially, the firefighters were not prepared to take the position she eventually proposed (which would result in Greg being placed on probation and doing community service). But Liz knew how important it was for them to understand Greg's life, character, current situation, and response to what he had done that day. She proactively asked them to read and discuss with her the materials about Greg she had prepared. Surprised by their willingness, she soon learned that she was dealing with good and thoughtful people who sought to understand what brought this young man to do this action.

The firefighters welcomed the opportunity to learn about Greg. They learned that he grew up in a rough neighborhood plagued by drugs, crime, and urban plight. He was raised by a heroin-addicted mother who often left her children unattended and fending for themselves, especially when she was in jail. Greg did all he could to oversee the care of his two sisters. He never got into trouble with the law as his brothers did. His early life entailed a series of highly traumatic experiences, the details of which Liz shared. Greg's father also struggled with drug addiction and imprisonment. After being released from prison and while still facing numerous personal challenges, his father focused on raising his children, working hard as a mechanic, and trying to do his best to help his children succeed. Fortunately, he enrolled them in the Franciscan Youth Center, a youth development program in East Baltimore that played a major role in Greg's development.[2]

Throughout his youth, Greg was actively involved in the Center, taking full advantage of its academic enrichment, mentoring, and leadership programs. He assumed positions of responsibility, mentoring some of the most troubled children at the Center and becoming known as the

---

[2] The Center is an over-twenty-five-year-old community youth development program that provides after-school and summer opportunities for youth in East Baltimore. Its programming focuses on cultural awareness, academic excellence, recreation, and leadership-career development. Its motto "Where youth can go to grow" captures its mission.

"peacemaker." To this day he remains actively involved with the Center. People who knew Greg through the Center admired his integrity, fine character, and the ways in which he dealt with the hardships of his personal life. Teachers spoke highly of him as a bright and engaged student, even as his home life was in turmoil. He was awarded a scholarship for outstanding academic achievement and was eventually admitted to a selective magnet school with a demanding curriculum in STEM studies. Greg also showed impressive athletic talents, eventually becoming the captain of the varsity basketball team. His balancing of the demands of his studies, sports, and employment, while dealing with the challenges of his personal life and local community, was nothing short of amazing. He worked as an apprentice in a home improvement company, mastering technical and business skills. His basketball coaches were understanding when he had to take on increasing responsibilities after his father lost his job. They had ample good reason for admiring his work ethic, sense of responsibility, and devotion to his family. While carrying so many responsibilities, he struggled to take as many honor classes as possible, even when this proved overly ambitious. His teachers knew the family burdens and challenges Greg faced. With good reason, they were immensely proud when he graduated, becoming the first member of his family to finish high school. He planned to attend St. Leo University in Florida on an NCAA basketball scholarship, but was devastated when he learned that he did not meet the scholarship's GPA requirements because his school weighted honor classes differently than schools in other districts. A *Baltimore Sun* article referenced him in its discussion of the problems that arose from such an unfair weighting system.[3] Refusing to let this disappointment stop him, he began taking classes at a community college until the financial costs became too burdensome. Fortunately, he was able to continue his employment at the home improvement company, eventually being promoted to project manager. He also was caring for his own family, raising a son to whom he was devoted.

Greg had never gotten into trouble in his neighborhood or school and had never been arrested. He was well respected by everyone who knew him. People were shocked that he had gotten caught up in the anger of the volatile rioting and had made a terrible split-second decision in the heat of the emotion that carried the crowd. He never planned to do the action he committed. He was especially ashamed of his harming firefighters since he had long admired the Baltimore City firefighters who had tried to save his childhood friends as their adjoining house burned.

---

[3] Erica L. Green, "Baltimore Student GPAs To Get Boost Under New Policy," *The Baltimore Sun* (August 16, 2015), http://www.baltimoresun.com/news/maryland/education /bs-md-ci-gpa-policy-change-20150816-story.html.

Greg already recognized the harm he had done to the firefighters and his community. Through the restorative dialogue, the firefighters were able to recognize the remorseful young man who committed an action so deeply contrary to his character. Once the firefighters understood the young man, his journey, positive contributions to the community, and remorse, they were willing to forgive and support something positive coming out of this regrettable situation. They also understood the importance of healing this local community. They recognized that a federal prison sentence would not improve Greg's life or the situation of his local community. His coach, employer, fellow staff member of the Franciscan Youth Center, and teachers spoke of the continuing good Greg could do in Baltimore City. The local community, including the firefighters, were convinced a young man like Greg Butler definitely deserved a second chance. After consulting with his firefighters, the fire department chief, who had been the incident commander the night of the fire, expressed support for what Liz Oyer proposed. In her letter to the judge before the sentencing hearing, she argued that Greg, who had already served thirty-seven days in jail, should not serve more time in jail. She persuasively laid out the negative effects of incarceration, the collateral consequences of a felony conviction, and support for a merciful second chance within the community. She requested that the judge sentence Greg to time served and a period of probation with community service. Persuaded by her reasoning, the judge sentenced him to three years of probation and 250 hours of community service. He also ordered Greg to pay one million dollars in restitution related to the damage that had been done to the CVS pharmacy. He will be making restitution payments to the end of his life.

Greg continues to interact with the firefighters who are committed to seeing him succeed and make positive contributions to the life of the local community. They are supportive of his finishing his community college studies. He welcomes the service he can do for his city to make up for a moment's bad decision and hopes to do it through the fire department. Rick Hoffman, president of the Baltimore firefighters union, said he thought it was good that Greg was given a second chance. He recognized that the riot was "an absolutely horrible time for everybody, in uniform and out. Now moving forward, if everyone's decided that the best way to handle this is to try and make something positive out of this kid, I'm all for it."[4]

---

[4] Justin Fenton, "Man Who Punctured Fire Hose during Baltimore Riot Gets 3 Years Federal Probation," *The Baltimore Sun* (November 3, 2016), http://www.baltimoresun .com/news/maryland/freddie-gray/bs-md-ci-butler-gas-mask-plea-20161103-story.html.

Liz Oyer also keeps in touch with Greg Butler. She knows through this experience the transformative power of restorative justice dialogues that bring victims and offenders to understand each other and collaboratively repair the harm that has been done. Working in a federal system that is all too often driven by mandatory minimum sentencing, Liz knows how rewarding this case was for herself and all her colleagues who do what they can to orient our judicial system toward restorative justice. It is not at all surprising that this talented defense attorney found this case to be one of the most heartening experiences in her career. Far too often the outcomes of cases strike public defenders as unfair and not productive of what is good. This was different, and now Liz Oyer can hope for more such rewarding experiences.

The Transformative Power of Restorative Justice

Janine Geske

I'm passionate about restorative justice. But I wasn't always such an advocate. I know very well the criminal justice system described in the chapters of this book. I served as a trial court judge for almost twenty years in Wisconsin; for nine of those years I served in criminal court, presiding over homicide and sexual assault cases before serving for ten years on the Wisconsin Supreme Court. Through this experience I have seen the successes of our criminal justice system as well as its failures. I taught classes in Wisconsin prisons for over twenty-three years because I wanted to be sure I understood what happened to the persons I sent to prison. I also spent time with neighborhood and crime survivor groups so I could hear their voices and learn from their experiences in our criminal justice system. My enthusiasm for restorative justice is traceable to a serendipitous observation of restorative justice programming.

In 1997 I was invited by some of the teachers in the Green Bay Correctional Institution, one of Wisconsin's maximum-security prisons, to observe a three-day restorative justice program facilitated by a lawyer. That invitation played a pivotal role in my own development and was the impetus for my ongoing involvement in restorative justice. My journey is an unusual one. Many people start by working on restorative justice projects in schools or cases involving juveniles with the goal of turning these young people around before they run the risk of getting involved in serious crimes. I started at the other end of the spectrum, working with persons convicted of homicide, rape, and armed robbery, and then later became involved in smaller projects and programs involving juveniles. Before my initial experience, the thought of victims dialoguing with offenders was unfathomable to me. I dismissed restorative justice as a crazy practice that risked revictimizing victims. Little did I know of the transformative power of restorative justice to address harms and heal persons impacted by crime. As I learned through that initial experience, once someone experiences restorative justice he or she is not the same person. Given the impact of my first exposure, it was not surprising that I began facilitating restorative justice programs and continue to do so today. I have become convinced that restorative justice is an effective means of addressing the needs of persons harmed by crime and some of the weaknesses, even failures, of our criminal justice system.

That initial experience introduced me to the philosophy and practice of restorative justice. Restorative justice is commonly conceived through the image of a triangle. The foremost point, the top of the triangle, is the victim, or survivor as many victims prefer to be called. The second point is the community that has been negatively impacted by crime and can come to play a role in repairing its harm. The third point is the offender or person who chose to commit the action that impacted the victim and community. Howard Zehr articulates well the three fundamental questions that underlie restorative justice in regard to these three triangle points:

1. *Who is harmed by what happened?* This is a very different question from the one raised in our criminal justice system. Our system asks, was there a crime and who did it; do we have enough evidence to convict that person; and, if we do, what should we do with that person? Here, the focus is clearly on the offenders. Can this suspect be charged; is there sufficient proof of guilt; have the constitutional rights of the accused been protected; and, if found guilty, what constitutes a just punishment? With restorative justice, the focus shifts to who was harmed by what happened—all persons harmed by the crime. Clearly, the victim or survivor was harmed, but we need to draw circles around each of those three points of the restorative justice triangle. If we look at the survivors of crimes, those persons don't stand alone as persons impacted by crimes. Victims' families, friends, neighbors, colleagues, communities—all of these are impacted in different ways. I conceive "community" as those persons who do not directly know the victim of the crime. A few years ago four home-invasion burglaries occurred in my neighborhood. I didn't know the victims or the homes that had been broken into, but I definitely felt the impact of those burglaries. They influenced how I locked my door, made sure the dog was out, closed the

garage door before exiting my car, and looked suspiciously at people on the street. People started profiling, questioning whether people they saw belonged in our neighborhood. We recognized the ripple effect of crime moving throughout our neighborhood. We often see such ripples in our even larger community. We know the blitz of media coverage when a child is abducted, and how children across the country are afraid in their beds even though they live nowhere near the crime scene. Parents restrict their play and become vigilant about their comings and goings. 9/11 illustrates best the wide-ranging impact of crime. That day's criminal acts affected the entire world, which would never again be the same. The impact of crime is wide and far reaching. The same is true when we look at the crime through the angle of the perpetrator, who is also surrounded by a circle. The offender's children, parents, neighbors, friends, teachers, mentors, coaches, and colleagues—all of these people are impacted. So when we ask who is harmed by what happened, we need to think of this wide circle of victims and the depth of the crime's impact, which increases with the degree of the offense.

2. *How can we understand the harm caused by the crime?* This requires us to consider all points on the triangle, for crime has an impact on the victim, the community, and the offender. For the courts, the question regarding the burglaries in my neighborhood focuses on whether this person did this crime and the worth of what was stolen. Evidence is presented and value calculated. But if you ask burglary victims about the impact of the crime, their responses don't zero in on the monetary cost of the stolen objects. Its impact is the invasion of their privacy, the fact that they no longer feel safe in their home and neighborhood, and the daily ripple effects on all of those around them. Such impact, mentioned perhaps in passing reference at sentencing, cannot be measured in a courtroom. How do we begin to understand and repair such harm? Many of the restorative justice processes draw on the traditions of First Nation Native Americans and indigenous peoples of Canada and New Zealand. At the center of these traditions is the deep conviction that persons are always part of a larger community. Since we all are intermeshed in communal life, our actions affect others. When harm is done within the community, the community can play a role in understanding both the harm and the ways in which persons can repair the harm and heal the relationships affected by the harm that has been done.

3. *How do we, as a community, go about repairing the harm caused by this crime?* Survivors of crime often emphasize that repairing is one of those "ing" words. Every time a victim hears comments about "closure," the event that promises to close the door on this crime, they know "closure" is not

the right word. There is no closure on a homicide, on a sexual assault, and on some lesser crimes. *Repairing* and *restoring* are not events on a checklist. There is no boilerplate listing of things to be done in response to crime. Restorative justice focuses on the complex task of recognizing and repairing the harm crimes have done to particular persons. The challenge is to recognize the nature of the harm, deliberate about possible ways to repair it, and envision positive ways of moving forward in response to what has been done and the harm it has caused.

These questions frame the context of restorative justice and help us begin to think about both the principles and processes of restorative justice. A good way to begin to understand both of these is to think about two specific kinds of restorative justice programs, Restorative Justice Circles and Victim-Offender Dialogues, which I have been involved with for seventeen years. I love working in these programs as part of my pro bono work. I have seen in myself the spiritual renewal that affects other aspects of my life, which participants commonly describe. Often the response to involvement in restorative justice programming is one of gratitude and hope.

My involvement in Restorative Justice Circles at Green Bay Correctional Institute has convinced me of their power in transforming lives. We have about twenty-five male offenders who have been convicted of serious crimes participating in our program; probably at least half of them will never get out of prison. Some of them have let me know that I am the judge who sentenced them to life in prison. In addition to these serious offenders, we bring in about twenty-five community members—volunteers, church members, prosecutors, media professionals, judges, and district attorneys. This group varies every time. We also include at least three surrogate survivors of violent crimes, meaning that they are survivors of crime, but their offenders are not in the room. In this way, these circles are different from direct Victim-Offender Dialogues, in which the victim meets with the person who committed the crime.

On the first day of the program I try to build a sense of community that makes all the participants feel comfortable by asking them to talk about persons who impacted their lives. The focus is on people telling their stories, our sharing and listening to each other, similar to the ministry of presence that Pope Francis so often emphasizes. We then break into groups, who select representatives to lead an exercise based upon my presentation of a crime, the impact of which they explore together. Together we generate a list of persons impacted by the crime, which the smaller groups then discuss in light of their understanding of restorative justice.

On the second day, we have the survivors talk, and these are often survivors who return again and again to participate in these circles. Often they share things they never shared with family members or even me as a judge. Their stories help us truly understand the impact of crime. To give a sense of the power of their stories, I'll share a few accounts. One survivor named Lynn has participated for years and become a good friend. She is the widow of a police officer killed in the line of duty while responding to a domestic violence call. Lynn was a young twenty-three-year-old mother of two small children when her husband, Bob, was killed when struck by the bullet intended for the woman's son. Lynn takes us through that night—how she kissed her husband as he went out the door, telling him to be careful, to which he responded, "Don't worry, God and I are like that," gesturing with his fingers to show their closeness. She takes us through her bathing the children, going to bed, hearing sirens during the night while she prayed that her husband would be safe, and then falling back to sleep, only to hear the loud knocking on the door. She knew immediately the meaning of such pounding at 2:00 a.m., as she pulled the covers over her head, hoping she would wake from a nightmare. She walks us through the officers taking her children as she was rushed to the hospital, her bursting into the ER to find the doctors holding her husband's heart by his cut-open, blood-soaked chest, as they try to save him. Kissing him on the head, she walks out, knowing so vividly what is happening, as her attention is riveted on the squeaking sound of her sneakers as they trek his blood down the hospital hallway. Now thirty years later, she thinks of that moment anytime she walks across a gym floor with wet tennis shoes as if that day was just yesterday.

We sit conversing in that circle over three days together, and when we hear the sound of a man's shoes squeaking as he comes in from walking across the wet grass, we all hear the silence in the room. Every member of the circle feels it. Lynn goes on to talk about what it was like to tell her children and what happened to them. And she describes the terrible way she was treated by the criminal justice system—how they let the person who killed her husband out on bail and how he called her, leading her to flee the community so her children would be safe. She talks about how many months later as she prayed the Our Father with her children, she stopped at the line about God forgiving our trespasses as we forgive those who trespass against us and thought, "You don't mean *this* guy—that I forgive the guy who murdered my husband and the father of these children?" She humorously tells us how she got up and went to her Bible to check if this was really what it said, crying out, "If you want me to do this, God, you better show me how to do this!"

Kim, a schoolteacher, describes how she was sexually assaulted many years ago. She was a schoolteacher, a mother of a little girl, and three months pregnant at the time. She was jogging at six o'clock in the morning when suddenly a man came out of the bushes and held a gun to her head. She takes us through every step of being pushed into his car, trying to focus on what he wanted, and talking to him as he threatened to blow off her head at any second. She describes what it was like to be at the end of that gun, thinking the next moment will be her last, and how he takes her into the woods, ordering her to strip naked and lie down on the ground to be raped. She explains how her rape was different from other rapes due to the threat of that gun. After raping her he tells her to turn her head and, putting the gun to her head, says, "When I brought you here I was going to leave you dead, so what am I going to do?" We hear what it was like for her to think, "this is the last moment of my life," and how in that moment she recalls that she did not say good-bye to her husband and daughter and that this will be their lasting memory of her for the rest of their lives.

We listen as these survivors take us through their stories and then all of us in the circle—survivors, offenders, community members—talk together for over three hours about what we've just heard. We share how we reacted to what we heard, how the stories affected us, and what they brought us to think about and understand. I've seen the reactions of the offenders follow two tracks, which doesn't surprise those who work with incarcerated men. Some are thinking about their own victims and in ways they never previously thought about them. They had never thought about the victims' children, their spouses, mothers, or relatives. And they also had not thought previously about their own mothers or children as victims of their crimes. Many of these men were victims themselves, so they also speak of being able to identify with these survivor stories. Many speak of how they almost took their lives, the depression they faced, and the anger of these victims with which they can identify. This emotionally charged discussion can last for hours. Following that I have the participants do artwork and we also do intermittent skits over the three days that can at times be humorous (e.g., key points on how to be a good drug dealer), which bring everyone to share belly laughs. We end the circle with talk about what each of us will do with what we have experienced. Afterward the men in prison describe how very deeply the circle affected them as far as their feelings and thoughts.

These circle conversations show how transformational restorative justice can be and how it has the power to move people in a new direction. The impact is felt by all the participants, not only those remaining in prison. Whether or not we live behind bars, we all have at times been offenders and victims, and the question is how we can learn to move forward in a positive way. I have learned so much from these circles about relationships I have had and the people I have hurt. The offenders in the circle talk about the deep effects of the circles. Often they emphasize how they came to think differently about the ways in which their actions harmed people. The circle puts a human face on the victims, making them think about what they don't want to think about—the harm done to that wider circle of victims, all the persons affected by the crimes, including their own families and communities. Many continue to participate in circles, recognizing how they have grown and changed due to these encounters. The sharing of such stories is healing. These circles give us a sense of the humanity of each of us, and the recognition and acknowledgment of everything discussed helps us find moments of being understood, cared for, and connected as persons.

I am also involved in Victim-Offender Dialogues, which involve direct face-to-face meetings between an offender and his or her actual victim, facilitated by a mediator who works to create a safe environment for the dialogue. These can also include the family members of both if they wish. In cases of homicides, family members of the victim participate in the dialogue. These are victim-initiated dialogues that often occur ten to twenty years after the offender has been convicted. Having an offender initiate the dialogue risks revictimizing the survivor. Offenders choose whether or not to participate. Much preparatory work goes into these dialogues; it takes six months of facilitated preparation for each participant to be ready for such an encounter. Many people wonder why victims would ever decide to sit down to dialogue directly with their offenders. Survivors commonly explain that they want the opportunity to look offenders in the eye and say, "This is what you did to me and what happened afterward to me and those close to me." They want offenders to understand that they did far more than just violate the law, that they did grievous harm to persons. Families of murder victims want offenders to know about the loved ones they have lost; many also want to finally know the details of what exactly happened to their loved ones. Survivors also seek to understand who this person is and how he or she got to the point of doing such harmful action. Very difficult, intense conversations follow, and that is why such careful preparation is required. Many people across the world have seen video clips from South Africa's Truth and Reconciliation Commission's encounters between victims and offenders. These show how painful these encounters can be, but they also disclose what I have seen directly—how incredibly healing these dialogues can be. This is clearly shown in the videotaped victim-offender dialogue between Linda White, her granddaughter Ami, and Gary Brown, one of the two men who raped and murdered Cathy O'Daniel, their daughter and mother.[5]

Much reflecting and soul-searching had gone on within Linda, Ami, and Gary before they began their four-hour restorative justice dialogue approved by the Texas Department of Corrections and led by Ellen Halbert, a victim services director, who trained them for the encounter. After the passage of fourteen years since Cathy's murder, Linda and Ami wanted to understand who the offender was, what happened that day, and what Cathy's last moments were like. They especially wanted to know what her last words were. Gary said that he could never forget her words, as she looked at her two assailants. As she lay dying, Cathy said, "I forgive you and God will too." Hearing these words, Cathy's mother and daughter collapsed into each other's arms. Knowing that her daughter had such peace at the moment of her death brought Linda great peace. Experiencing such an encounter, Linda, who had gone on to become a psychologist and a teacher of classes in prisons, became trained as a mediation counselor who facilitates victim-offender dialogues. Decades later she is still in touch with Gary, who works hard to fulfill his promise to Linda to turn his life around in positive ways.

There are numerous accounts of how such encounters can be life changing for offenders. Kris Miner, a friend of mine, facilitated a dialogue between a teenager who spray-painted graffiti on a gravestone and the mother whose son was buried beneath the stone. When she met the offender, who was the same age as her son, she put a picture of her child on the table, explaining that this was the person she visits whose stone he had defaced. How different this exchange was than what would have occurred in a court proceeding focused on delinquency charges. In the victim-offender dialogue, both parties learn about themselves and each other and explore ways that they can move forward in positive ways in their lives.

---

[5] This dialogue is captured on the video *Meeting with a Killer: One Family's Journey*, which can be accessed in four parts on YouTube. An account of their encounter can be found in "Beyond Retribution," a chapter in Rachel King's *Don't Kill in Our Names: Families of Murder Victims Speak Out Against the Death Penalty* (New Brunswick, NJ: Rutgers University Press, 2003); and in this article: Mark Obbie, "He Killed Her Daughter. She Forgave Him," *Slate* (June 30, 2015), http://www.slate.com/articles/news_and_politics/crime/2015/06/gary _brown_and_linda_white_he_killed_her_daughter_she_found_a_way_to_forgive.html.

Such dialogues, which can last for hours, are extremely difficult and yet can be powerfully transformative. Surprisingly, they often move into a discussion of what the victims or murder-victim family members and the offender have in common. The participants begin to disclose who they are and often find shared connections, associations, and roots. This is truly amazing for the silent facilitator to observe! In one such dialogue the participants realized that they shared Native American backgrounds and common traditions regarding nature—their shared love of the earth, especially its sunrises and sunsets. At one point the survivor, who had been brutally raped, asked to speak privately with the facilitator, explaining that she had hoped to be able to tell her offender that she forgave him, but was not able to forgive him at this point. She decided to share these thoughts with the offender. He explained that this was all right, for he never expected to be forgiven, but then added that if she ever decided to forgive him, she need not tell him. She could just go to the top of a hill and watch the sun rise for both of them. He understood that the essence of forgiveness was about *her*—how she felt and whether she could find peace and healing. He added that if ever she told him that would be her gift of forgiveness to him.

This raises an important point since people often link forgiveness and restorative justice, but they are not necessarily linked. Many people go through restorative justice processes without wanting to forgive. As explored in a subsequent chapter, there is a complexity in defining forgiveness, and different people conceive it in differing ways. Victims often grow weary of people telling them they just need to forgive. For some people forgiveness entails wiping the slate clean; others express concern that it can be interpreted as meaning that what happened did not really matter. Some say they want to forgive and yet still feel justified anger toward their assailant, as if the intellect is telling them one thing, but the heart another. I always tell people during the restorative justice process that they do not have to decide right now whether they want to forgive. As Mark Umbreit emphasizes in his book and video *The Energy of Forgiveness*, the biggest acts of forgiveness are often done without words. I know one victim whose act of forgiveness in response to her father's murder entailed hugging the offender and then putting her father's picture back up on the wall that night. She never said the words "I forgive you" but her gestures spoke powerfully. In another program I met a woman whose sister had been killed in a terrible drunk-driving accident. She did not want to even look at the offender, and yet as she saw him weeping while he watched the video about her sister's life, she gently pushed a box of Kleenex toward him. For me these are acts of healing. This woman hugged this man at the end, telling him, "You just saved my life today." She never had to say the words "I forgive you."

Through these encounters, I have learned that people walk this journey as best as they can and label it as they choose to label it. Each encounter is unique, yet they share commonalities. I have never met a victim or an offender who regretted going through a restorative justice dialogue. In fact, offenders often tell me the dialogue is the best thing they have done in their lives. One offender in a videotaped discussion of his experience said, "Restorative justice gave me a chance to see myself not just as a convicted felon anymore, but also as a human being, you know, that still has some, maybe some type of redeemable value to me." What becomes clear through all these experiences is that they are always locally situated. Restorative justice entails a philosophical approach to harm that involves certain principles. But restorative justice programs always must be practiced in culturally and community-specific ways. What works in Milwaukee may not work in Baltimore. This is not surprising since at the very center of restorative justice is the encounter between persons in particular communities whose lives have intersected due to a range of differing factors and choices.

I have briefly discussed the two major restorative justice programs in which I have been engaged. Restorative justice is practiced in many different settings, and more settings will arise as we come to better understand the power of restorative justice. One thing I am strongly convinced of is that the restorative justice focus has to be always on the victims and the harm done to victims. This is not denying the great importance of the rehabilitation of offenders in which I strongly believe. But rehabilitation, however defined, is different from restorative justice. They are related, but the focus of restorative justice is not "fixing" the offender, but rather repairing the harm that has been done to persons. This is not denying the great importance of giving offenders opportunities for education and professional training. But what must remain the core of restorative justice is the fundamental understanding that we are all brothers and sisters in community. We must recognize that harm to persons happens in multiple ways, whether it be through neglect, racial profiling, and numerous injustices. We harm persons when we fail to treat persons justly, as persons deserve to be treated. We harm persons when we fail to recognize that they are capable of reflecting on and understanding the impact of their actions and their capacity for positive change. Anyone familiar with our criminal justice system knows the extent of harm that is done to persons. But as members of our own communities, we need to recognize the harm that is being done in our community by each of us in varying ways and work on repairing the harm done to persons.

When I speak with prison ministers and other people working with offenders, I often ask them, what programs do you have for victims? Do you have support systems in your communities and parishes for victims of crime? I ask this because very often these offenders have suffered much harm in their lives—they too have been victims. They are often survivors of great physical and psychological violence done earlier in their lives, and perhaps if we had intervened much earlier, they would not be now sitting in maximum-security prisons.

We definitely have major problems in our criminal justice system, especially in light of the severe problem of mass incarceration. And these problems must be addressed. But too often there is little talk of victims. We need to make sure that we begin to address the complex, interrelated problems faced by both victims and offenders in our communities. Victims need the support of their communities and, in fact, offenders benefit from such support. I think it is also very important that offenders understand the harm caused by their acts. They need to understand that they did much more than break a law or just "catch a crime," to use their common language, as if it were a cold. But rather they made choices, for lots of personal and societal reasons, which caused harm and hurt people around them, including their own families. We need to transform our orientation so that we call them to be part of our human family and together seek to find solutions to these problems.

Due to my witnessing the tremendous healing power of restorative justice processes and the powerful transformational experiences it offers offenders and survivors, in 2002, I asked Marquette Law School Dean Joseph Kearney about the possibility of starting the Restorative Justice Initiative at Marquette, which would train law students in how to use restorative justice practices in healing victims and communities. His strong support led to the law school's restorative justice program, which facilitated circles in a range of cases, including homicides, sexual assaults, and armed robberies. I welcomed the opportunity to teach a course on restorative justice and to run a clinical program focused on victims, offenders, and communities as part of this program. Our work has also led to Marquette law students running restorative justice circles in middle schools to address bullying issues. We also saw Marquette University introduce restorative justice practices into its own disciplinary programming. Through this we all learned of the deep resources offered by restorative justice to address harm that is done to persons and communities. Hopefully other law schools, especially those at Catholic universities, will begin similar restorative justice initiatives.

Knowing the tremendous healing power of restorative justice programs, I am always attentive to the ways through which we can harness its power to address in positive ways the harm done to persons in our communities. Milwaukee provides a number of examples. Restorative justice talking circles are held in Milwaukee, which, like most American cities, experiences violent crime on a daily basis. Wisconsin has one of the highest incarceration rates for African American males in our country; its prisons are overcrowded, and the effects of mass incarceration have taken a heavy toll in local communities. Milwaukee has developed a number of collaborative efforts to decrease and address crime. It implemented the Safe Streets Initiative, which emphasized ways of helping offenders lead productive lives when they reenter their communities. This program incorporates restorative justice circles for offenders returning from prison and as an alternative to prosecution or incarceration for first-time offenders. Supported by funds from the US Department of Justice, the project seeks to decrease crime by providing alternative means of law enforcement, enhanced community engagement, and new creative practices within the Department of Corrections. Its success is tied to its being a community-wide, collaborative initiative engaging civic leaders and local institutions.

The Marquette University Law School's Restorative Justice Initiative draws on a restorative justice model to lead the community engagement component of the program. Shifting from the traditional retributive model in which resources, efforts, and time are spent on offenders—arresting, charging, investigating, prosecuting, convicting, sentencing, and incarcerating them—emphasis is now placed on restorative justice programming. The law school's community coordinators focus on developing relationships, strengthening community ties, and holding restorative justice circles for a range of constituencies, all of which have borne positive effects. One of the most significant challenges faced by the project is the long, negative history of relations between the police and communities of color. Restorative circles have brought together those who otherwise might never have had the possibility to speak and listen to each other. Such dialogue has been transformative as participants come to understand the tragic impact of violence on police and neighbors in the community. The Safe Street Initiative also effectively uses circles to engage offenders returning from prison to their communities. Through the circles, they learn how the community members deeply suffer the impact of criminal behavior, will not tolerate violence in their neighborhoods, and pledge their support in helping them reenter and lead productive lives in their community. They provide them with information about education, job training, employment, alcohol and drug treatment, the recovery of driver's licenses, and other helpful information and resources. Many offenders recount the positive effect of this community support, and victims and community members speak of the healing aspects of the dialogue. One former gang member spoke of how powerful it was for a police officer in the circle to hand him his card with the words, "If there's ever anything I can do to help you, give me a call." And this young man did.

Restorative justice circles have also been conducted with offenders who, following their arrest, had their prosecution deferred based on the hope that community resources might be used effectively to avoid their ever committing another crime. There are also nonprofit agencies offering restorative justice programming outside the criminal justice system. Our Marquette Law School program facilitates restorative circles in high-crime neighborhoods. These gather reentering offenders, gang members, police, community members, and crime victims with the aim of rebuilding and strengthening local communities. The schools in Milwaukee have also incorporated such circles in response to bullying, gang violence, disrespectful treatment of teachers, and poor sportsmanship. Participation in such circles brings members of the school community—teachers, students, administrators—to understand the impact of disruptive behavior that causes harm. Milwaukee shows us the many ways in which a city can begin to incorporate restorative justice in creative ways. Much of the impact of such programming rests in persons coming to understand the impact of their behavior on themselves and others. Rather than creating greater distance, resentment, and alienation among people in a community, restorative justice programs have the power to transform participants in ways that promote healing and strengthening of relationships.

Our criminal justice system focuses on righting wrongs through the application of retributive justice to offenders. Too often justice is seen as a matter of a judgment handed down by judges and juries following set rules and procedures in response to violations of laws by offenders. I believe the notion of "justice" has to be expanded beyond the ways it is conceived and practiced by judges, prosecutors, and defense attorneys. I am convinced the fundamental activity of justice must always be that of *listening to and responding to persons*. We need to become better listeners to those who have been harmed by crime and better practitioners of healing for all persons wounded by crime. I do believe herein lies the most fundamental way of addressing the violence and dysfunction found in our communities, the growing tensions between many of our communities and the police, and the failings of our criminal justice system. Restorative justice can provide a way of hope for all of us to heal and move forward.

Review and Looking Forward

Editors

Justice Janine Geske is convinced the most fundamental way to address the violence and dysfunction found in many communities, the tensions between police and community members, and the failings of our criminal justice system is through the foundational activities of restorative justice, which are *listening to and responding to persons.* Liz Oyer's handling of Greg Butler's case models well these activities. Judges and attorneys who seek to reorient our justice system from a narrowly retributive approach to a more restorative approach face a daily uphill battle. They deeply value victims who are open to and even proactively seek restorative solutions to the harms done to them and their communities. Judge Janine Geske and defense attorney Liz Oyer experience deep satisfaction and respite when they encounter such victims. Lucius Outlaw, Liz's cocounsel in the Greg Butler case, captures well the daily experience of such restorative justice advocates:

> Often I feel as if I am sitting in a small boat resting on the sea of human despair, and my job is to negotiate with the government what size weight to affix to the ankle of my clients who are already flailing in the water. On November 3, 2016, due to the efforts of some extraordinary people—the firefighters, public defender, judge and those persons who spoke well of this young man—Greg Butler was thrown a lifeline instead. It was a lifeline built from Greg's life prior to his mistake on that fateful day, and the recognition that sending Greg to prison would not serve the greater good, but offer only brief and fleeting feelings of justice for some, and not heal the problems that divide the city. On that day, empathy triumphed over anger, hope surpassed fear, and the knee-jerk reaction to imprison was subordinated by the recognition that Greg Butler is more, and better, than his actions on one day—a recognition that not sending Greg to prison is a worthy investment in the community and its future. That is the power and promise of restorative justice.[6]

[6] Lucius Outlaw, interview with Trudy Conway (January 30, 2017).

This book pays tribute to the principles of restorative justice shaped by persons in communities across the world. It also pays tribute to the exemplary efforts of victims of crime who seek better ways of responding to harm-doing in their communities than simply returning harm to those who harmed them. This book also honors the too often unrecognized hard work and valor of judges and public defenders who maintain, in the most difficult circumstances, the hope that our system can become a more just system promoting the common good.

Questions for Discussion

1. Janine Geske explains that the challenge of restorative justice is "to recognize the nature of the harm, deliberate about possible ways to repair it, and envision positive ways of moving forward in response to what has been done and the harm it has caused." Discuss how and to what extent Liz Oyer's handling of Greg Butler's case met this challenge.

2. This chapter discusses victims whose religious beliefs played a significant role in transforming their initial response to the crimes affecting them. Discuss the extent to which you think we bring our religious convictions to bear on how we approach crime and punishment. How might the New Testament passages analyzed by Sr. Mary Kate Birge in chapter 6 encourage us to reflect more thoughtfully on our criminal justice system? To what extent do persons tend to separate our religious convictions and views on criminal justice?

3. Janine Geske says she has never met a victim or offender who regretted participating in a restorative justice dialogue. Discuss the reasons why you think both victims and offenders value these encounters.

4. Local communities and churches should be encouraged to develop programs that support crime victims. Such programming has an impact on offenders who often were victims themselves. Discuss whether your local community offers such programming and how you might support or strengthen its development.

Chapter 9

Harm and Healing

Editors

Justice Janine Geske ended the last chapter with words that speak to our daily life in our families, neighborhoods, and society. After decades of judicial experience, she concludes that the fundamental activity of justice must be the activity of listening and responding to persons. And for this reason, we all need to work on becoming better listeners and responders through practice and self-examination. Having spent all of her professional life interacting with offenders and victims, she asks each of us to become especially attentive to persons harmed by crime and to respond to them in ways that help heal their wounds. What families in our parishes and local communities need such attention? On a national level, Janine Geske is convinced we must orient our society more toward restorative justice, if we are to address the violence and tension that recently have been brought to the surface across our country. Otherwise we will just avoid or tinker with lingering problems that so need attention.

Restorative justice is focused on repairing and healing. Although it does not necessarily entail forgiveness, the dialogues it promotes often lead to forgiveness. This chapter helps us think through what forgiveness is and the role it plays in relation to restorative justice. Many of us are amazed by individuals who choose to forgive those who have done them and their loved ones deep harm. In his General Audience of November 25, 2013, Pope Francis mentions such persons who pardon those who injure them. He prays,

> Let us ask the Lord, grant that we be more and more united, never to be instruments of division. Enable us to commit ourselves, as

the beautiful Franciscan prayer says, to sowing love where this is hatred; where there is injury, pardon; and union where there is discord.[1]

We are especially amazed when such victims or their family members actively reach out to those who caused them grave suffering. How often do we do this in response to those who injure us? Pope Francis often speaks of each of us fostering a "culture of encounter"—of our becoming "servants of communion and of the culture of encounter."[2] At the same time he recognizes the demands of this distinctly Christian response extended even to enemies, whom we could easily curse and reject for doing us harm. As he said in his General Audience of October 2, 2013, "The Church, which is holy, does not reject sinners . . . because she calls everyone to allow themselves to be enfolded by the Mercy, the tenderness, and the forgiveness of the Father, who offers everyone the possibility of meeting him, of journeying toward sanctity."[3] How radical a notion—evildoers being called to sanctity!

In our work on restorative justice we have met murder-victim family members who have reached out to offenders. Each encounter deeply affected us. These stories are numerous. We share a special story about two sets of Catholic parents who traveled together on their journey of merciful forgiveness. Andy and Kate Grosmaire and Michael and Julie McBride were devastated to learn that a distraught nineteen-year-old Conor McBride had walked into the Tallahassee, Florida, police station to tell them he should be arrested for having just shot his fiancée, Ann Margaret Grosmaire, with his father's shotgun in her parents' home.[4] A day and a half of fighting on the phone, by text, and in person climaxed in this violent moment. Community members could not believe the news of the tragic interaction between two deeply loved and admired high school students.

Conor assumed the single shot had killed Ann, but the police found her alive and unconscious. At the hospital Ann's parents learned that her recovery was unlikely. As her father Andy held vigil by her bedside, he held onto the slenderest of hopes one particular night. Although she never regained consciousness, Andy felt her saying to him, "Forgive him; forgive him"—a response he could not begin to fathom. His response, "You're ask-

---

[1] *The Church of Mercy: A Vision for the Church* (Chicago: Loyola, 2014), 29.

[2] Ibid., 61.

[3] Ibid., 31.

[4] In telling this story, we draw on Paul Tullis, "Can Forgiveness Play a Role in Criminal Justice?," *The New York Times Magazine* (January 4, 2013), http://www.nytimes.com/2013 /01/06/magazine/can-forgiveness-play-a-role-in-criminal-justice.html.

ing too much," captured his incredulity. The Grosmaires had been deeply fond of Conor, who often stayed at their home when conflicts arose in his life. They looked forward to his being the father of their grandchildren someday. A hundred miles away, Conor's parents vacationed with their teenage daughter. After the devastating call from the police, they agreed that Michael should drive to Tallahassee alone and Julie would stay with Conor's sister, who had developmental disabilities. As he drove off, Julie called to him, "Go to the hospital. Go to the hospital." Michael was so shaken that he became ill six times on the side of the road. Michael was sickened by the thought of seeing Ann's parents. What could he say to them? Never did he expect Andy's immediate reaction to him. Hugging him, Andy thanked him for coming to them, adding that he might hate him by the end of the week. At that moment Andy realized the four of them were on this painful journey together.

Ann's parents prepared themselves for turning off their daughter's life support. As he sat with his daughter, Andy kept thinking of the likeness of Ann and Christ. Like Christ, Ann had wounds on her head and her hand from trying to block the gunshot. He wondered if the voice he had heard might be the voice of Christ, not Ann, calling him to forgive. Since he and his wife had tried always to model their lives on the life of Christ, he was filled with joy as he now told his daughter he forgave Conor.

Conor could list five people who would be allowed to visit him in the jail after being booked. Ann's mother Kate was on his list. At first Kate resisted going; then she became willing, and finally she felt she needed to visit him. She refused to reduce this young man she had loved to that one horrific act that ended her daughter's life. She wanted neither to define Conor as a killer nor her daughter as a murder victim. Kate had an emotional visit with a deeply remorseful Conor, before heading to the hospital to remove Ann from life support. Andy then joined Kate in visiting Conor.

Due to the pending first-degree murder charge, Conor faced a mandatory life sentence or a death sentence. Since there were no aggravating circumstances, the prosecutor decided not to pursue a capital sentence. While meeting with the Grosmaires, he explained that the state attorney is given broad discretion, so he could reduce the charges, resulting in a lesser sentence. The Grosmaires were not typical murder-victim family members who knew little about the workings of the judicial system. They had learned about restorative justice programming from Allison DeFoor, an Episcopal priest who served as a prison chaplain after having served in a number of professional positions in the judicial system. Andy also learned of restorative justice while studying to become a deacon.

The Grosmaires wanted a restorative justice handling of their daughter's case but thought a state like Florida would never cooperate. They reached out to the McBrides, knowing they too were suffering. Soon all their conversations focused on restorative justice. Julie McBride was in touch with Sujatha Baliga, a former public defender who directed a restorative justice program in Oakland, California. Sujatha, herself a crime victim, had had an experience similar to Andy's experience at his daughter's deathbed. She too doubted a restorative approach would be permitted in this state. But sustained by their shared hope, the two sets of parents persisted with their request as they met with Conor's lawyer, Sujatha, and Allison. They concluded that the best route was to propose a pre-plea conference at which the prosecutor and defense attorney could work out a plea arrangement. The conference would take the form of a restorative justice conference. Now only one challenge remained—convincing the prosecutor to agree to their plan. After a hard press, the prosecutor finally agreed to this novel proposal, reserving the right to make his own subsequent sentencing decision.

The conference was held inside the jail. The four parents, Conor's attorney, the prosecutor, a victim's advocate, and Rev. Foley, the Grosmaires' parish priest who represented the local community, were present when Conor joined the conference. The Grosmaires spoke at length of Ann's character and life and the deep suffering her death caused them. It was excruciatingly painful for everyone to hear, but most especially Conor. Conor spoke of Ann, their relationship, his love for her, and the fighting that began to define the most recent stage of their relationship. He recalled the brutal details of their last fight up to the moment of his shooting Ann. Conor made no excuses for his horrific, deeply regretted action in the heat of a vicious argument. At the end of this emotionally exhausting exchange, Sujatha asked the Grosmaires what attempted restitution they sought. With a depth of emotion, Kate told Conor that he would have to do the good works of two persons since Ann could no longer do her part. Witnessing the exchange, Sujatha proposed a sentence of five to fifteen years. Andy Grosmaire proposed ten to fifteen years, to which the McBrides agreed. Conor felt he should have no say. As the conference came to a close, the prosecutor said he would need to deliberate more about what had just happened. The prosecutor had gone into the conference thinking he would not agree to anything less than a forty-year sentence. He eventually offered Conor the choice of a twenty-five-year sentence or a twenty-year sentence plus ten years of probation. Conor chose the latter.

The Grosmaires explained that they forgave Conor primarily for their own sake. By forgiving him, they now could feel again, could speak of Ann, and could hear others speak of her as the person she was. They no longer felt pulled into a black hole of anger over this awful murderous act. In forgiving, they did not feel pitted against an enemy. Their forgiveness made possible their self-preservation. Conor has upheld his promise to do what Kate asked, by doing good work in the prison, working to understand and address what brought him to such a horrific choice, taking anger-management classes, and preparing for talking to local groups about teen-dating violence when he is on probation. His parents continue to visit, and so do Ann's parents. Ann's parents find peace in talking at church and community gatherings about how their experience of restorative justice and forgiveness helped them begin to heal as persons.

Forgiveness

Trudy D. Conway

Forgiveness, like restorative justice, is about harms done to persons. We all grapple with forgiveness, whether it be our forgiving or being forgiven for acts that on some level cause harm and evoke hurt and anger. We know what it is like to be preoccupied with and lose sleep over forgiveness. At times as we struggle with issues tied to forgiveness, relationships already have been severed; at other times the relationships continue with painful recollection simmering below the surface. I once taught a college course on forgiveness and mercy, and it became obvious that all our class members were applying our readings and discussions to our own lives. All of us connected the readings to situations involving family members, friends, neighbors, and colleagues; some members related them to situations involving egregious criminal acts that caused grave suffering to their families. When we explore forgiveness, we take our bearings in relation to personal reflections that matter deeply to us.

Issues of forgiveness touch our personal lives. But in recent years attention has been drawn to dramatic political and social situations involving forgiveness. People across the world continue to be deeply affected by how the South African Truth and Reconciliation Commission grappled with healing a community after the horrific harms perpetuated during apartheid. Once we begin to study forgiveness, we become aware of numerous examples of communities facing the challenge of responding to grievous wrongdoing that inflicts suffering. Our own nation has not been spared such experiences, as we faced and continue to face the legacy of slavery and the related civil war that required magnanimous efforts to heal and restore our nation. Today we still live in the aftermath of the tragic events of September 11 that so deeply affected families and our entire nation. In many such cases, as in criminal cases, the offenders inflicting the harm and the victims suffering it did not know each other prior to the offenses. The harmful actions are what brought these persons into relationship.

As any crime victim knows, criminal justice situations raise very complex questions about forgiveness. Given the gravity of some crimes, we wonder, how could anyone forgive persons who had done such grievous harm to them or their loved ones? We question whether it is possible to forgive someone who feels no remorse or has not even acknowledged the harm done. Family members and friends question whether it is right for them to forgive someone who so harmed their loved one. We worry that forgiveness risks diminishing the gravity of the wrong done, as if in some way forgiving cancels the burden or debt carried by the offender. All the major religious traditions—Jewish, Christian, Muslim, Buddhist, Hindu—call for and offer powerful models of forgiveness. The Catholic tradition, in both its Scriptures and practices, places great emphasis on forgiveness—both the acts of forgiving and being forgiven. Christ calls all Christians to forgive seventy times seven without end and to realize that our wrongs will be forgiven as we forgive those who have wronged us. And yet we all struggle to understand what forgiveness means and entails.

I turned to philosophers, especially Glen Pettigrove and Martha Nussbaum, and theologians, especially Henri Nouwen, as I tried to understand forgiveness. But my deepest insights came from persons who have been on long and difficult journeys of forgiveness—persons such as Nelson Mandela and Desmond Tutu; the Amish community of Nickel Mines, Pennsylvania; and all the amazing murder-victim family members, like Marietta Jaeger, Vicki Schieber, Bill Pelke, and Bud Welch, from whom I continue to learn so much about forgiveness. I have found that reflection on the most challenging cases of forgiveness in response to the most horrific human wrongdoing helps us understand and practice forgiveness in our daily lives. The journeys of these persons illuminate and grace our own journeys.

Our discussions of criminal justice in American society focus on retributive justice, and considerations of forgiveness rarely surface in such discussions. Wrongs are seen as being righted by officers of courts and corrections administering punishment to criminal wrongdoers. Many of us presume our institutions and procedures mete out just punishments according to just procedures to ensure that offenders get what they deserve for what they did in the past. Restorative justice shifts the emphasis to responding to harms done to all persons affected by crime so as to right wrongs in a future-focused sense of restoration. As previous chapters have developed, this involves much more than meting out just punishments. It entails offenders taking responsibility for their actions and seeking ways of righting these wrongs; communities acknowledging and addressing factors that contribute to crime; and participants taking steps to advance the healing of all persons, most especially victims, affected by these crimes. Often forgiveness surfaces with such a shift to restorative justice. Why is this so?

Restorative justice neither entails nor expects acts of forgiveness. But restorative justice practices often create interactions that open and facilitate their possibility. Given that restorative justice focuses on personal encounters of persons affected by crime, this is not surprising. In the preceding chapter Justice Janine Geske brought us to see how this happens. Operating from a restorative justice model, she emphasized,

> The fundamental activity of justice must always be that of *listening to and responding to persons.* We need to become better listeners to those who have been harmed by crime and better practitioners of healing for all persons wounded by crime. I do believe herein lies the most fundamental way of addressing the violence and dysfunction found in our communities, the growing tensions between many of our communities and the police, and the failings of our criminal justice system. Restorative justice can provide a way of hope for all of us to heal and move forward.

In his book on the Truth and Reconciliation Commission (TRC) in South Africa, Desmond Tutu stresses, in agreement with Janine Geske, that communities can begin to heal only if restorative justice is emphasized.[5] He is convinced that forgiveness, rather than anger, plays an important part in such healing. Anger is a natural human response to harms done to persons and can manifest our respect and care for persons, especially those who have not been treated justly. But anger can grow and fester in a debilitating way that obstructs healing. When we feed our anger, it can destroy the seeds of other, positive human responses. When ten Amish schoolchildren of Nickel Mines, Pennsylvania, were murdered and severely wounded by Charles Roberts (who then committed suicide), the Amish community immediately sought to reach out compassionately to his widow, recognizing she too was suffering. They visited his widow, parents, and in-laws and sought ways to continue supporting his family. Marie Roberts, his widow, wrote an open letter to the community, explaining

---

[5] See Desmond Tutu, *No Future Without Forgiveness* (New York: Image, 2000).

how their loving response provided the healing her family so needed. In response to the shock many felt regarding their unexpected response, the Amish community explained that their way of life encourages them to let go of anger and to forgo vengeance in response to those who do evil. They knew that moving beyond their anger would also help each of them begin to heal.

In a similar way, Nelson Mandela and Desmond Tutu were attentive to the effects of anger in both experiencing and observing the suffering tied to apartheid. They knew that anger transformed into rage precludes reflection and hope. In videos of the TRC hearings, we witness, to our utter amazement, the capacious generosity and mercy of victims toward their offenders. They believed that only such a response would enable them to reclaim their lives and begin to build something better for all South Africans. They recognized that anger transformed into rage, resentment, and retaliation would draw them into an endless cycle of suffering. Transitional anger would have to give way to more affirmative responses if there was to be any hope for building a society focused on the common good. Tutu drew on the insight of his own Xhosa language in which a person asks for forgiveness with the words *Ndicel'uxolo* ("I ask for peace"). Forgiveness is not an invitation to forgetting or denying the suffering and harm, but rather an invitation to healing and its peace.[6] In heading the TRC hearings, Tutu remained convinced that there could be no future for South Africa based on the spiraling of debilitating anger. Only forgiveness and mercy over time could restore this society and offer hope for a shared future.

But what is forgiveness and what does it entail? Often we address such questions by looking at paradigm cases of forgiveness, which seem to embody the essential characteristics of forgiveness. We also think of situations in which a bare minimum of characteristics is present, resulting in our being unsure about whether this is or isn't a case of forgiveness. In this sense we explore robust and minimal instances of forgiveness.[7] I conceive of this thinking in terms of a spectrum of instances embodying traits associated with forgiveness, some of which we think minimally qualify a state as forgiveness and others that clearly identify very robust embodiments of

---

[6] Desmond Tutu and Mpho Tutu, *The Book of Forgiving* (New York: HarperOne, 2014), 24.

[7] This discussion of forgiveness draws heavily on the excellent book *Forgiveness and Love* by Glen Pettigrove (Oxford: Oxford University Press, 2012). I am deeply indebted to his insights in helping me better understand forgiveness.

forgiveness. Rather than identifying the essential trait defining forgiveness, we find, to use the philosopher Ludwig Wittgenstein's phrase, a cluster of family resemblances. We can pretty easily identify and disqualify some responses in regard to forgiveness, but other cases are more complicated and unclear. Forgiveness is tied to the particularity of human situations and circumstances, so it does not lend to the conceptual clarity philosophers so often desire. Our lives, as lived, often don't reveal such crystal-sharp clarity and precision.

Forgiveness as Transforming Anger

I think we can all agree that forgiveness occurs in response to a perceived action of morally blameworthy wrongdoing to oneself or someone about whom one cares. In some cases this action is also judged to be legally blameworthy. Wrongdoing naturally evokes a negative emotional and attitudinal response; we assume something is wrong when anger is not evoked in response to harmful actions, for it is our way of registering our awareness of their being wrong. But when unchecked or sustained, festering anger can develop into corrosive hostility, resentment, and contempt. We experience and observe how anger negatively affects our bodies; we speak of our "blood boiling"; we flush; we feel our heart racing; we see muscles contracting. Numerous studies evidence how sustained anger exacts a heavy toll and can influence the development of depression, insomnia, anxiety, and related physical disorders.[8] Aristotle offers an interesting discussion of nuanced states of anger in Book IV of his *Nicomachean Ethics* and cautions that the virtuous person feels anger when appropriate but not to an excessive degree and tends more toward pardon than retaliation.

Thus, forgiveness in a minimum sense entails a reduction in our negative emotions and attitudes in response to wrongdoing. Through an act of forgiveness, something in us changes; we can recognize a before and an after. Forgiveness does not necessarily entail the elimination of all negative emotions and attitudes, but a noticeable reduction in them. In forgiving, some persons may never again have negative feelings toward the person who harmed them or those they care about; and for a range of reasons others may feel less anger, and it may surface only periodically. But persons

---

[8] Everett Worthington, professor of psychology at Virginia Commonwealth University, has published numerous studies of the relationship of anger and forgiveness to health (http://www.evworthington-forgiveness.com/journal-articles-forgiveness-and-reconciliation/).

who forgive are no longer held captive by negative responses that can be exhausting and debilitating on both emotional and physical levels. Crime victims and their loved ones know all too well the painful dimensions of sustained intense anger. Bill Pelke, a murder-victim family member, often throws people by describing forgiveness as fundamentally a *selfish* act. I believe he is referencing this debilitating effect of anger. Persons who forgive no longer suffer the intense pain of strong negative feelings toward the person(s) who harmed them or their loved one. In this sense they free themselves. There is a palpable lessening of negative emotional states in response to harmful actions. In some cases this lessening follows dialogue between the persons harming and being harmed. In Bill Pelke's case this occurred through his interactions with Paula Cooper, who murdered his grandmother when Paula was fifteen years old, and her grandfather. In some cases, depending on the relationships and circumstances, these negative emotional states may be replaced with more positive responses, be they compassion, empathy, concern, or goodwill toward the other who harmed them or their loved one. It is quite amazing to learn of these responses from crime victims who have undergone deep pain and suffering. Restorative justice dialogues preserved on videotapes clearly manifest this transformative power of forgiveness as tied to this lessening of anger. (A very powerful example is the videotaped dialogue between Linda and Ami White [the mother and daughter of Cathy O'Daniel] and Gary Brown [one of the two men who raped and murdered Cathy].)[9]

Forgiveness as Forswearing Ill Will and Hostility

Such change in emotion also has an impact on how persons respond and act toward the persons who caused the harm and suffering. Many persons respond to wrongdoing by initially desiring a form of retaliatory reaction. We can see this embedded in our desire for retributive justice. A person's wrongdoing deserves payback; suffering must be inflicted on the offender in some way because of the suffering caused to others. For this

---

[9] Rachel King's *Don't Kill in Our Names* (New Brunswick, NJ: Rutgers University Press, 2003) recounts Bill Pelke's and Ami and Linda White's journeys of forgiveness in chapters 4 and 9. The video of the White-Brown restorative dialogue is found at https://mvcc-video.mvcc.edu/app/plugin/plugin.aspx?insideIFrame=true&styleSheet Url=http%3A%2F%2Fmvcc-video.mvcc.edu%2Fapp%2Fplugin%2Fcss%2Fensemble Plugin.css&q=www.mvcc.edu&destinationID=no0t7hZkV0eZoP1_7oMeIw&contentI D=LJxp71c3NkWl8m3wsXAiQw&pageIndex=91&pageSize=10give.

reason persons may gain a sense of satisfaction through the infliction of punishment. Aristotle acknowledges that some persons suffer the pain of anger until the offender suffers deserved punishment, allowing the pain to be replaced by the pleasure accompanying just retribution. But such pleasure runs the risk of revealing what might be a desire for retaliatory vengeance. This concern hovers over the meting out of retributive justice. Is justice being sought or vengeance? Forgiveness involves more than a changed emotional response—a lessening or eliminating of our anger. Forgiveness involves changes in how we act. Desmond Tutu speaks of the shift from a retributive to a more restorative response to wrongdoing, when he says, "Forgiving means abandoning your right to pay back the perpetrator in his own coin."[10] Herein persons do not wish to inflict suffering in response to suffering; they do not seek to retaliate in kind. In forgiving, they do not will that the harm-doer be harmed.

This nonwilling of harm does not exclude affirming the need for punishment for wrongs done, when punishment serves some positive goal(s). As parents we punish children in response to their wrongdoing, believing the punishment will do some good to the child and the family. But here punishment is not rooted in a vindictive ill-wishing toward the other. A person who forgives an offender can acknowledge the need for and good of punishment (be it deterrence, safety, positive change, symbolic sacrifice). Some victims of crime participating in restorative justice practices make comments disclosing this understanding. Prior to or through the encounter, their anger has diminished; they feel no desire for retaliatory revenge, and they seek for some good to come out of the suffering the wrongdoer has caused and the offender's sentence. Glen Pettigrove speaks of this characteristic of forgiveness as being a matter of one's forswearing hostile reactive attitudes and emotions and committing oneself to some degree of willing the other person's well-being. Even if their anger surfaces again intermittently, they stand committed to not acting on such resurfaced negative feelings. Victims often speak of their desire to move past what has happened, not in the sense of "closure," but in the liberating sense of no longer being held hostage to the wrong done to them. They want lives not consumed by anger, resentment, and ill will about what happened in the past. For this reason, forgiveness is often spoken of as allowing a new beginning. And not surprisingly, forgiveness is often disclosed in actions rather than words. Janine Geske describes such powerful gestures by victims toward offenders during restorative justice dialogues. Those who

---

[10] Tutu, *No Future Without Forgiveness*, 272.

forgive choose a different course of action that shows the diminishing of their anger and relinquishing of ill will, even if words of forgiveness are never uttered. In this sense forgiveness entails and reveals a change in how persons feel, respond, and act.

It is important to note that forgiveness does not necessarily entail reconciliation. In forgiving, one can reconcile or release oneself from the relationship, choosing not to interact with the forgiven person, be it in periodic encounters or in programs like restorative justice dialogues. In forgiving, one's anger is diminished; one forswears hostile responses to the person; one harbors no ill will; and one may even wish the person well. Forgiveness and reconciliation are distinct states, and persons who forgive may have good reasons for not interacting with the persons they have forgiven. In some cases, the persons who have been forgiven may not even be aware that the persons they harmed have forgiven them. On the other hand, people debate another issue—can one forgive persons who fail to show remorse or even acknowledge their wrongdoing? It seems that the act of forgiving is dependent on the person deciding whether or not to forgive, not on the state of the person being forgiven. During his lengthy prison term, Nelson Mandela viewed himself as the master of his own fate. He realized he had the inner strength to treat his guards differently than they treated him. And his kind and respectful treatment of them, over time, affected their own transformation, which he celebrated by inviting them as VIPs to his presidential inauguration. He was willing to respond graciously and respectfully to them even while their wrongdoing continued and long before they understood their need to be forgiven. His forswearing of hostility toward them was an unmerited gift he freely chose to give them. Not surprisingly, direct encounters, such as those that occur through restorative justice dialogues, often bring about changes within both the offending and offended persons. In numerous such cases, many previously nonremorseful offenders come to understand and take responsibility for their actions. Many offenders undergo change due to the transformative power of forgiveness, which affects the persons forgiving and forgiven.

Forgiveness as Seeing Oneself in the Other

Glen Pettigrove describes the fullness of forgiveness as the type of forgiveness each of us hopes for ourselves. In this case, we forgive as we wish that we would be forgiven. Aware of our own brokenness, we treat the wrongdoer as we hope to be treated when we are the wrongdoer. This "forgiveness for which we hope" evokes a benevolent response on our part. We hope the other person is not driven by anger or hatred toward us because of what we have done. We hope the other will not wish to retaliate in kind. We hope the other will view us as people capable of transformation. We hope the other, while acknowledging the wrong we have done, will not reduce us to what we have done in this single past action. If anger about what we have done surfaces again within the other, we hope he or she will resist acting on those negative feelings, feel some positive regard toward us, and act on such a benevolent response. We hope that the person might even be open to reconciliation. This is what we hope for ourselves, and realizing this helps us view the other as we wish to be viewed.

This raises another related issue tied to restorative justice practices. Often when we are the wrongdoer, we hope the person whom we have wronged might come to understand our actions, not in the sense of excusing or justifying them, but in the sense of understanding what was at play in them. So too victims and offenders may learn more about each other and the action that brought their lives together. Victims may feel more anger upon learning more about the crime. But at other times their anger may diminish as they learn more about the offender and the action. Sometimes there are significant mitigating factors that, when known, influence their responses.

The courts consider not only the actions done by convicted offenders but also any mitigating factors that should influence sentencing. But this is done by professionals representing victims and offenders in settings governed by very strict procedures and according to circumscribed roles. One of the reasons I so enjoy and learn so much from reading good novels is that they bring us deeply into the lives of a range of characters. We often reassess our initial judgments about events and characters as the novel brings us deeper and deeper into understanding. Prosecutors and defense attorneys also build narratives about the accused, but their closing narratives must be brief and selective. Novels give us a better bird's-eye view of a story, developing our moral imagination that enables us to understand and reassess characters, the circumstances of their lives, and unfolding events. For this reason they can play a role in our own moral development, enabling us to be better perceivers, judges, and agents. It is not surprising that restorative justice dialogues often commence with the participants sharing their life stories.

The Buddhist monk Thich Nhat Hanh stresses that in our judgments about persons who cause harm, it is not surprising that we often very quickly condemn them. But he cautions that before we can condemn, we must judge what was done; before we can judge, we must understand; and, at times, when we understand, we end up not condemning the person. We distinguish the person and the act. In not conflating the person with a singular wrong act, we better understand the person and, in turn, the action. We've all experienced the impact of better understanding in our lives. I continue to find it amazing that some victims of crime seek to learn about the lives of the offenders who so harmed them. This is the case with family members of murder victims who seek to know the details of what happened to their loved one and to understand why the offender committed this horrific act. Many of them value restorative justice dialogues because they lend to such understanding. Bud Welch, whose twenty-three-year-old daughter Julie was killed in the Oklahoma City bombing, visited Timothy McVeigh's father and sister to better understand his actions. Bill Pelke contacted Paula Cooper, the teenager who murdered his grandmother, and her grandfather, and then began to visit Paula. Coming to understand the circumstances of her life and the depth of her remorse, he became a passionate and successful advocate for the commutation of her death sentence to a sixty-year sentence. Vicki Schieber, one of our coeditors, knew she wanted to understand what brought a seemingly respectable family man with security clearances, allowing him to work on missile silos at an Air Force base, to become a serial rapist who murdered her daughter, Shannon. Vicki sought opportunities to meet with his family and any other avenues that might deepen her understanding. As she often explains, using the phrasing of Native Americans, she seeks to walk in this man's shoes as far as possible so that she might understand better what brought him to do the action that so shattered the Schiebers' lives. She also often wonders whether her own children's lives would have turned out very differently had they lived the childhood of Shannon's assailant. Such an amazing generosity of spirit forces us to rethink how we have responded to people who caused us far less pain. At times this desire for understanding opens the door to attaining the peaceful state of forgiveness many of these family members desire.[11] But they also emphasize that each journey is the individual's own, and no one can dictate the process or the timing of each individual's response to such pain and suffering. For this important reason, forgiveness should never be mandated or expected. To do so risks deepening the suffering of those who have been harmed.

---

[11] The Forgiveness Project gives accounts of numerous persons who chose the path of forgiveness in response to grave harm done to themselves or their loved ones. See http://theforgivenessproject.com for these accounts.

Built into this seeking of understanding is a powerful assumption, operative in restorative justice programming. Participants seek to understand the *person* who harmed them or their loved one—the person's choices, life circumstances, relationships, background, and personal story. They also want the offender to understand the *person* who was the victim of the crime. Participants describe how restorative justice encounters humanize both offenders and victims, who begin to see each other as persons. The victim-offender dialogues described by Janine Geske become possible only if restorative justice facilitators can create safe spaces for such encounters. In such spaces, victims can ask questions that only offenders can answer. Offenders can come to understand the impact of their actions on the lives of victims and their loved ones, coming to see how their actions inflicted harm on persons rather than merely violating laws. Such restorative justice contexts make possible dialogues that facilitate better mutual understanding of crimes and what led to them, their impact on the lives of survivors and their loved ones, and offenders and their loved ones. Such dialogues deeply influence all participants, including facilitators. Our judicial system is set up from charges through appeals in ways that discourage guilty offenders from admitting and addressing their responsibility for their actions and their human impact. And this is exacerbated by their consciousness that our system is deeply flawed by racial and economic inequities. In contrast, restorative justice practices bring the humanity of all participants to the center, creating conditions that can lead to encounter, dialogue, and greater mutual understanding.

Often, such dialogues deeply transform participants and, in some cases, make forgiveness possible. Offenders describe how such dialogues bring them to see the human impact of their actions, bringing them, often for the first time, to face their own actions, hold themselves accountable, and feel remorse for what they have done to their victims—now encountered as persons. At times these encounters evoke explicit expressions of remorse and forgiveness, gestures that express forgiveness, or explanations of why victims cannot forgive. The journeys of persons through restorative justice programming is as varied as the participating individuals and their lives. Some participants describe their reaching a merciful state of peace, and others speak of their continuing journey that has not yet brought them, or may never bring them, to forgive their offenders. Restorative justice neither requires nor expects forgiveness; it simply opens spaces for encounter and dialogue.

Most simply put, restorative justice is always *about persons* and *for persons*. It may be the case that the failure to truly see and be present to another person enables both the committing of crimes and vengeance in response to crimes. Whereas crime depersonalizes, restorative justice repersonalizes, for restorative justice begins with and remains always centered on persons. For this reason, it respects the individuality of persons on journeys in the aftermath of crimes. Janine Geske describes common elements found in many such restorative justice encounters. And yet her experiences have taught her that no two encounters are the same, for at the center of each lies the profound recognition that this is an encounter of persons in their irreplaceable individuality and uniqueness. This reciprocity of human recognition and response defines and makes possible restorative justice.

Forgiveness entails a diminishing or eliminating of anger, a forswearing of responding in a retaliatory way, and some level of goodwill toward the other. These traits might be minimally present; in some cases one of these characteristics might strongly overshadow the others. In other cases a trait may be lacking, resulting in our debating whether this is or isn't a state or act of forgiving. As phrased earlier, one can think of forgiveness along a spectrum from a bare minimum to a robust form. I think when powerful examples of forgiving persons come to mind, they embody this robust sense. For me, Nelson Mandela and Desmond Tutu are such well-known examples. Tutu speaks and writes extensively about forgiveness. And Mandela was clearly not consumed by anger. He condemned retaliatory actions, even those of his own wife, despite his understanding of their motivational sources. As president he welcomed opportunities to model his fundamental commitment to sharing and promoting a vision of the common good of South Africa, based on the traditional notion of *Ubuntu* or our shared humanity and human condition.

Traces of this robust conception of forgiveness are found in many narratives about persons in a range of cultural settings. It has struck me through my reflections on forgiveness that the most robust conceptions of forgiveness are grounded in a spiritual understanding and commitment. We often are able to forgive those we love due to our valuing their many good traits, good actions, and our shared positive experiences. These transcend the negative traits and actions of the person we love and forgive. Forgiveness comes more easily to those with whom we have relations and especially good relations. But how can we respond so to persons with whom we have no relation and no basis for admiration? As we have considered, our suffering lessens when our anger diminishes or ends. At times through restorative justice encounters, persons come to understand better the strangers who harmed them, and in ways that lessen their negative or hostile responses. They may learn that these persons cannot be reduced to one harmful act and have positive, even redeeming, traits that help them form better views of such persons. Forgiveness entails some level of goodwill—be it simply forswearing hostile reactions to the other, not wishing them ill, or even actively wishing them well. But does there exist an even more robust form of this response? On some level in some way, can persons who have been deeply harmed paradoxically feel *love* for those who have harmed them, and even when they have not come to know any of their redeemable traits?

We can envision such possibilities again through the powerful witness of examples. Christ asks the Father to forgive those who do him harm because they do not know what they do. Perhaps we can feel a type of love for persons when we see their deep flaws, failings, and suffering, which bring them to inflict harm on others, and in turn themselves. Henry Wadsworth Longfellow makes us wonder, "If we could read the secret history of our enemies, we should find in each man's life sorrow and suffering enough to disarm all hostility."[12] André Trocmé, a French Huguenot pastor who helped hide Jewish refugees in Nazi-occupied France, spoke of feeling sympathy for those he called "the limited," who failed to think through the horrific implications of Nazism and its toll of suffering. At times individuals can empathically see the deficiencies and, in some cases, the suffering of those who inflict grave harm. Marietta Jaeger was tormented by calls from her young daughter Susie's abductor and killer. She prayed one single prayer—that she might come to respond to him in a Christlike way rooted in Christian love. She understood the challenge of such love. During one call, she genuinely expressed compassion for this man, telling him she understood the suffering he must be going through in killing such a lovely child. Her compassion overpowered him, in ways that led to his arrest and cooperation in disclosing information about other children he had killed, before he hung himself in his cell in remorse. Marietta took a restorative approach. Although Susie's killer was unable to respond to her invitation, most restorative justice encounters result in participants very actively intending the good of each other and their mutually seeking of ways to make each other's lives better. These accounts fill us with amazement and awe. They humble and inspire us.

Forgiveness and Christian Love

Pope Francis often speaks of Christian love as excluding no one, not even criminals who have done grievous harm to persons. It seems the theological virtues of faith, hope, and charity make possible this most

---

[12] "Table-Talk," in *Drift-Wood, The Prose Works of Henry Wadsworth Longfellow*, vol. 1 (Boston: Houghton, Mifflin, 1883), 173–74.

robust form of forgiveness. Faith in a creator God yet unseen leads to a love of one's Creator, which transforms all human relationships and a hope in the possibility of human community grounded in such love and manifest in peaceful relations among persons. Such faith, hope, and love open the possibility of limitless forgiveness since it calls for the love of even enemies who have harmed us. Despite the failings and wrongs of these persons, there is a dignity and worth intrinsic to each person that is worthy of respect and loving goodwill. In light of this, it seems that we are called to forgiveness, but always as a gracious, freely chosen act—a generous act of benevolence. Independent of what persons have done, they, on a very fundamental level, are worthy of our love. Such love is not won through their actions and character traits, but through their inherent worth as persons. They have not earned this gracious response, but rather as brothers and sisters we deem them worthy.

With this understanding, we do not forgive primarily to free ourselves from our own suffering, but rather in gratitude for our shared existence as persons beloved by God. Henri Nouwen speaks of gratitude as a way of acknowledging that what each of us is and has is given as a gift of love, which is to be appreciated and joyfully celebrated.[13] Forgiveness, in this sense, is a gift given in gratitude for our gift received and in hope of the community for which we yearn. And this may help us understand the joy and peace we experience in forgiving others. Here, we are not focused on retributive justice, for we treat others better than their actions deserve. Here, we truly are concerned with restorative justice—with healing broken, suffering persons and restoring community among persons. This is what we hope for—for ourselves and those we love. Forgiveness, in this context, is invitational—it seeks to be transformative of relations based on hope for community that is grounded in love. This is what Pope St. John Paul II modeled in his visiting Mehmet Ali Ağca, his would-be assassin, in his prison cell, and saying afterward, "What we said to each other is a secret between him and me . . . I spoke to him as a brother whom I have forgiven."[14] This is what we saw Pope Francis model in his visit to prisoners and their families in Philadelphia. Declaring 2016 a Jubilee Year of Mercy, Pope Francis called on Catholics throughout the world to open wide the doors of their hearts to forgive others and to work against all forms of so-

---

[13] *The Return of the Prodigal Son: A Story of Homecoming* (New York: Doubleday, 1992).

[14] Henry Kamm, "Pope Meets in Jail with His Attacker," *The New York Times* (December 28, 1983), http://www.nytimes.com/1983/12/28/world/pope-meets-in-jail-with-his-attacker.html.

cial exclusion, including those who have caused us suffering. In the chapel of the Basilica in Assisi later that year, he emphasized, "The world needs forgiveness; too many people are caught up in resentment and harbour hatred, because they are incapable of forgiving. They ruin their own lives and the lives of those around them rather than finding the joy of serenity and peace." And he compassionately stressed, "How hard it is to pardon! How much effort it takes for us to forgive others!"[15]

Martin Luther King Jr. repeatedly stated and showed in his actions such an understanding of Christian love. He believed that "love is the only force capable of transforming an enemy." In his sermon "Loving Your Enemies," he emphasized, "We never get rid of an enemy by meeting hate with hate; we get rid of an enemy by getting rid of enmity. By its very nature, hate destroys and tears down; by its very nature, love creates and builds up. Love transforms with redemptive power."[16] Crime and forgiveness meet as polar opposites; one depersonalizes and the other repersonalizes. Crime involves refusing to see and value the persons being harmed; forgiveness involves seeing and valuing persons on a most fundamental human level.

Recently, so many intersecting issues have surfaced in our society: do *all* lives truly matter; is our criminal justice system truly *just*; is the imprisonment of persons with severe mental disorders evidence of social *neglect*; does our mass incarceration serve the *common good*; does our preoccupation with punishment truly address the *causes* and *effects* of crime? Perhaps as our society begins to grapple with the depth of challenges we face in reforming our criminal justice system, we need to bring to the forefront this radical shift from *criminal* justice to *restorative* justice. Through my reflections on and encounters with persons caught up in our criminal justice system, both victims and offenders, I am convinced the holistic approach of restorative justice—that affirms human dignity and worth, addresses the harm crime does to persons, and focuses on healing and restoring persons—is the only way we can truly address these challenges. Only through such a fundamental recentering can we hope to reform our system and begin to build our shared future together. Hopefully, this slowly emerging national dialogue about our justice system can also shed light on our response to those who cause us pain and our need to practice

---

[15] Francis, Meditation, Visit to Basilica of St. Mary of the Angels, Assisi (August 4, 2016), https://w2.vatican.va/content/francesco/en/speeches/2016/august/documents/papa-francesco_20160804_assisi-santamariadegliangeli.html.

[16] Martin Luther King Jr., *A Gift of Love: Sermons from* Strength to Love *and Other Preachings* (Boston: Beacon Press, 2012).

forgiveness in our daily lives. Hopefully, this needed discourse will be sustained and seed bountiful insight and wisdom.

Review and Looking Forward

Editors

Restorative justice focuses on persons inextricably embedded in relationships within communities. Crime disrupts these relationships; restorative justice seeks to repair them. Restoration, reconciliation, rehabilitation, reintegration, and reparation all hinge on this fundamental core. As Kate Grosmaire knew all too well, anger, hostility, and contempt pit one against an enemy. Forgiveness entails the magnanimous willingness to see oneself in the other. The Grosmaires knew the suffering of the McBrides as they struggled to forgive their son Conor. Glen Pettigrove speaks of the fullness of forgiveness as the type of forgiveness each of us hopes for ourselves. Here, as echoed in the Lord's Prayer, one forgives as one wishes to be forgiven. One treats the other as one wishes to be treated. One hopes the other will not be driven by rage and retaliation, reducing all of me to this one action I have done. Another way of conceiving this is understood by parents who love their children even when they do grievous wrong. Parents condemn their child's action while continuing lovingly to hope for what is best for their child. This is what we hope for ourselves; this is what we hope for our children. The Grosmaires and McBrides were able to collaborate in a restorative justice dialogue to discern the best course of action in response to Conor's conviction. The path of forgiveness was opened to them because they could envision the deep pain and loss each of them, as parents, suffered. Each could see a vision of the self in the other. Perhaps the path of forgiveness was opened to the Grosmaires and McBrides because their daily lives had been lived following the words and actions of the Gospel. They had been raised in a community with words and practices centered on forgiveness and reconciliation. Their community prepared them for the choices they faced together. We now turn to Fr. Jim Donohue's reflection on the transformative power of the sacrament of reconciliation.

Questions for Discussion

1. Restorative justice is practiced in communities. Discuss the role of communities in bringing persons to understand forgiveness and the role it plays in our lives. In light of these discussions, consider why Pope Francis thought it was so important to declare an Extraordinary Jubilee Year of Mercy and what Catholics were encouraged to do during this year.

2. Consider situations in which you found it extremely difficult to forgive. Discuss whether any particular aspect of this chapter helped you better understand such situations. Discuss which points from the chapter you judged most salient and which points you took issue with, as you considered these situations.

3. Desmond Tutu says forgiving means "abandoning your right to pay back the perpetrator in his own coin." Retributive justice focuses on that right to payback by the victim. Discuss why individuals freely choose to abandon that right and seek to find a different way of moving forward.

Chapter 10

Reconciliation

Editors

Over a three-month period in 1994, about 800,000 Rwandans—mostly Tutsis—were murdered by Hutu citizens who were organized and armed by the military.[1] On April 6, 1994, the president of Rwanda, Juvénal Habyarimana, was assassinated; his plane was shot down as it returned to Kigali. The president represented the Hutu ruling majority, so that blame for the assassination immediately fell upon the Rwandan Patriotic Front, a rival political party and rebel group consisting mainly of Tutsi exiles (along with some moderate Hutus). Decades later, evidence points toward the fact that extremist Hutus were responsible for the assassination—in hope it would be a catalyst for the genocide of the Tutsi minority. The mass killings began on April 7 and continued until July, when the Rwandan Patriotic Front gained control of the capital city and the Hutu leadership fled to Zaire.

Immaculée Ilibagiza, a Tutsi, survived the one-hundred-day massacre but lost everything and nearly everyone—every neighbor, loved one, and family member (except a brother who was studying abroad).[2] When the killing began, when villages and towns were searched, house by house, and Tutsis executed, Immaculée's father sent her to a local Hutu minister, who hid her in his house, in a "closet-sized" bathroom, with seven other

---

[1] "Rwanda: How the genocide happened," *BBC News* (May 17, 2011), http://www.bbc.com/news/world-africa-13431486.

[2] "About Immaculée," https://www.immaculee.com/pages/about.

women. The eight women spent ninety-one days cramped in that small space. Gangs of assassins searched the house several times. Each time Immaculée prayed to be saved. In her book, *Left to Tell*, she recounts her spiritual as well as her physical trials:

> I believe that God had spared my life, but I'd learn during the 91 days I spent trembling in fear . . . that being spared is much different from being saved . . . and this lesson forever changed me. It is a lesson that, in the midst of mass murder, taught me how to love those who hated and hunted me—and how to forgive those who slaughtered my family.[3]

Immaculée would find redemption through love and forgiveness. Eventually she would confront the leader of the gang who murdered her mother and one of her brothers. Face-to-face with the killer, she wept for him and forgave him (much to the consternation of the town's new Tutsi burgomaster):

> I wept at the sight of his suffering. [He] had let the devil enter his heart, and the evil had ruined his life like a cancer in his soul. He was now the victim of his victims, destined to live in torment and regret. . . . I reached out, touched his hands lightly, and quietly said what I'd come to say. "I forgive you."[4]

Immaculée's commitment to and acts of forgiveness did not come easy (which probably is needless to say). She attributes the gift of forgiveness to God's grace and many, many long days of prayer—in a twelve-foot-square room, with seven other women, a Bible, and her rosary. During these long days, she continually battled with anger, resentment, and hatred. As she remembers those ninety-one days in captivity, "In my mind and heart I cried out to Him for help: *Yes, I am nothing, but You are forgiving. I am human and I am weak, but please, God, give me Your forgiveness. Forgive my trespasses.*"[5]

Immaculée's prayer for the ability and gift of forgiveness goes to the heart of Fr. Jim Donohue's chapter on forgiveness and reconciliation in the church. He shows that the plea of the disciples—for Jesus to give them faith—is inextricably connected to the seemingly impossible requirement of the gospel to forgive all offenses: to forgive seven times a day for wrongs done seven times a day (Luke 17:1-4). Father Jim explores the riches of the sacraments and the liturgy that offer a grace-filled pathway for our

---

[3] Immaculée Ilibagiza, with Steve Erwin, *Left to Tell: Discovering God Amidst the Rwandan Holocaust* (Carlsbad, CA: Hay House Books, 2007), xx.

[4] Ibid., 203–4.

[5] Ibid., 78 (italics original).

own forgiveness and learning to forgive others. In his study of the rites of penance and through his experiences as a priest, he notes that we—parishes and the contemporary church in general—have not taken full advantage of the communal nature of repentance and forgiveness, that too often we focus on penance as a private affair. He brings to mind people (most notably Martin Luther King Jr.) who have endured great trials, not despite but through their openness to follow Jesus' way of forgiveness as God's good work of creating and healing community. Like Immaculée, the saints among us who have taken on the risky promises of compassion and mercy have experienced great joy and grace.

Forgiveness and Reconciliation in the Church

Rev. James M. Donohue, CR

The preceding chapter on forgiveness references a number of persons, Bud Welch and Bill Pelke, for example, who understood the transformative power of forgiveness. For most of us there is a huge difference between our ability to understand the power of forgiveness and actually forgiving a person who has done grave harm to someone we deeply love. Both Bud and Bill felt the natural impulse of anger and a desire for retaliation, but they also experienced the inner destructiveness of these impulses. Deep within the brokenness of anger, Bill prayed for the ability to forgive. At the time (the 1980s), he would not have characterized his response of forgiveness and love in terms of "restorative justice." Yet, this phrasing clearly captures what he sought—the righting of the wrongs done to persons he loved (his murdered grandmother), in a restorative way that did no further harm, brought forth good, and honored the goodness of his grandmother, Ruth Elizabeth Pelke. Restoration was his focus, and he believed that the goodness of restoration might bring the peace of merciful forgiveness over time. (Trudy Conway notes, in the previous chapter, that Bill calls forgiveness a "selfish act.") Not surprisingly he sought a personal encounter with Paula Cooper, Ruth's killer. Personal encounters, like Bill's, seed the possibility of forgiveness. His Christian faith had already opened him to redemptive possibilities and prepared him for the challenging journey of forgiveness. These deeply personal journeys, like Bill's, are sustained by a shared community life rooted in Christian faith, hope, and love.[6]

---

[6] See Bill Pelke, *Journey of Hope: From Violence to Healing* (Bloomington, IN: Xlibris, 2003).

This chapter locates forgiveness and reconciliation within the context of the church's social and ecclesial actions. Forgiveness is difficult at the best of times, and it is the ecclesial community of the church, with its emphasis on word and sacrament, that calls us again and again to die to our sinful and selfish tendencies so that we can conform ourselves more closely to Christ. Growing in our awareness of God's love and forgiveness throughout our life journey, we can enter more deeply into the paschal mystery of dying to all that is sinful and evil so that we might rise to new life with Christ. Experiencing the love and forgiveness of God in its myriad ways offered by the church, the goal is for us to become more loving and forgiving in our own lives, to become "reconciled to God" so we can join St. Paul as "ambassadors for Christ" (2 Cor 5:20).

Forgiveness Demands an Increase in Faith

There is an abrupt cry that begins the gospel reading for the Twenty-Seventh Sunday in Ordinary Time (Year C) in the Roman Catholic Lectionary. In the reading taken from the Gospel of Luke (17:5-10), the disciples say to the Lord, "Increase our faith." There is nothing new about such a request in the gospels, especially coming from the group of followers whom Jesus had chosen, for they seem to struggle with having faith in Jesus throughout the whole of Jesus' public ministry. But, as I prepared my homily on this text, I thought I should look at the previous Sunday's reading to see why it was that the disciples were making such a request at this moment in the gospel. It turns out that the previous Sunday contained the gospel story of the rich man, Dives, and the poor man, Lazarus (Luke 16:19-31). I was a bit puzzled with this discovery and began to think that the disciples were making such a request because the reversal of fortune for the rich man had left them quite uncomfortable. But, then I thought I should look at a Bible, since the Lectionary does not always follow story upon story. What I discovered absolutely amazed me.

It turns out that the Lectionary left out four verses between the gospel selections of the twenty-sixth and twenty-seventh Sundays in Year C (the year in which Luke's gospel is read). Here are the omitted verses:

> He said to his disciples, "Things that cause sin will inevitably occur, but woe to the person through whom they occur. It would be better for him if a millstone were put around his neck and he be thrown into the sea than for him to cause one of these little ones to sin. Be on your guard! If your brother sins, rebuke him;

and if he repents, forgive him. And if he wrongs you seven times in one day and returns to you seven times saying, 'I am sorry,' you should forgive him." (Luke 17:1-4)

No wonder the disciples asked for an increase in faith! Jesus had just indicated that they were to forgive people who have repented seven times in one day! Seriously, I have a hard time forgiving anyone once a day, even if the person is really sorry. Imagine something small, such as someone forgetting your name several times at a conference or a party. Even if he were sincere in his apologies, I would find it difficult to forgive him and would probably carry that with me, not only in my thoughts, but probably also by talking badly about this person to others until I got it out of my system. Forgive him? Okay, once, maybe twice, but not seven times. As an indication that Jesus knows the challenging nature of this teaching, he begins by stating, "Be on your guard!"[7]

This emphasis on what might be called the ridiculousness of the call to forgive is found throughout the gospels, but perhaps none so clearly as in Matthew 18:6-35, which, at the beginning of its section on forgiveness, parallels our Lukan story. Here, Matthew 18:6-7 contains the material about it being better to be thrown into the sea with a millstone about one's neck than to cause one of these little ones who believe in Jesus to sin. Matthew 18:8-9 then includes some hyperbole about the drastic measures that one should take to avoid sin: "If your hand or foot causes you to sin, cut it off and throw it away. . . ." Next comes the parable of the Lost Sheep (Matt 18:10-14), which is really about the irrational nature of God's love for the sinner—after all, would you really leave ninety-nine sheep in search of a lost one, or would you not simply cut your losses? But, the parable reminds us that God's ways are not our ways, and that "it is not the will of your heavenly Father that one of these little ones be lost."

Matthew now picks up a slightly different version of what we saw above in Luke's gospel:

> If your brother sins [against you], go and tell him his fault between you and him alone. If he listens to you, you have won over your brother. If he does not listen, take one or two others along with you, so that "every fact may be established on the testimony of two

---

[7] The footnote in the *Catholic Study Bible*, ed. Donald Senior and others (New York: Oxford University Press, 1990), indicates that while verse 3a is often taken as the conclusion to the saying on scandal, it could be taken as the beginning of the saying on forgiveness (131).

or three witnesses." If he refuses to listen to them, tell the church.
If he refuses to listen even to the church, then treat him as you
would a Gentile or a tax collector. (Matt 18:15-17)

Here, we see that Matthew's version elaborates on the steps that one must
take to win over the sinner. He also concludes with Jesus' words about
what happens if the sinner refuses to repent after all the steps have been
taken: the person is to be treated like a Gentile or a tax collector. To understand what this means, however, we must remember that these are the very
people to whom Jesus reached out, receiving the constant criticism of the
religious authorities of the day: "Why does he eat with tax collectors and
sinners?" (Mark 2:16). His response is a pointed one: "Those who are
well do not need a physician, but the sick do. I did not come to call the
righteous but sinners" (Mark 2:17). So, one must conclude that even if the
sinner remains unrepentant, the sinner should continue to be the object
of concern and even love, for as we just read in the previous story, "It is
not the will of your heavenly Father that one of these little ones be lost."

In response to all that Jesus has said, Peter, in Matthew's gospel, asks
how many times one must forgive a brother . . . seven times? Jesus responds to this seemingly generous view on the part of Peter with the words,
"I say to you, not seven times but seventy-seven times" (Matt 18:22). He
then tells a parable about the unforgiving servant who was forgiven a
very large debt and later refused to forgive a much smaller debt that was
owed to him. This is truly a remarkable parable that maintains that there
are, according to Jesus, lasting consequences to our decision to forgive or
not forgive.[8] As repulsive as it might seem to us today, the master in the
parable who was owed the great debt was completely within his rights to
have the servant, as well as his wife and children, sold in payment of the
debt. How else would he recoup his loss? As repulsive as this seems to us
today, this would be the just solution for him to be repaid. Realizing what
was to happen, the debtor pleads for more time, assuring the man that he
will pay him back fully. In a striking gesture, the master abandons the just
solution and is moved with compassion, releasing the servant, and forgiving him the loan! But, when the newly released servant is confronted with
a similar situation—except the debt was of a much smaller amount—he
ignores the pleading of his fellow servant and has him thrown into prison.

---

[8] My understanding of this parable grew remarkably through the insights of Fr.
Fred Scinto, CR, at a Congregation of the Resurrection summer retreat in Waterloo,
Ontario, in 2012.

The other servants are appalled at the actions of the servant who had so recently been forgiven his debt, so they report this to their master. The master is shocked that the servant has chosen to use the standard of justice for this small debt, when he earlier had begged for and received the standard of compassion for his large debt. If we could rephrase the biblical words, the master says, "Oh, I thought you wanted to use the standard of compassion, for after all, that is what *your words* asked of me. But, I see from *your actions* with your fellow servant that you want to use the standard of justice, and so that is what I will use with you as well." Jesus concludes with words that should shock us all when we think about our tendency to use the standard of justice and to avoid the standard of compassion: "So will my heavenly Father do to you, unless each of you forgives his brother from his heart" (Matt 18:35).

This brings us back to our Lukan passage where the disciples cry out for an increase in faith! The revelation by Jesus about God's compassion and forgiveness seems impossible to us. No wonder, then, that Jesus responds to their request for more faith by saying, "If you have faith the size of a mustard seed, you would say to [this] mulberry tree, 'Be uprooted and planted in the sea,' and it would obey you" (Luke 17:6). From our perspective, forgiving someone seven times in one day, even if she is sorry, is no more possible than telling a mulberry tree to be uprooted and planted in the sea. Both actions are equally impossible in our eyes. What Jesus is trying to teach us, however, is that a little faith can do the impossible. With a little faith, we can stop loving in the flawed and narrow way of a human being, and start loving as God loves. With a little faith, we can conform ourselves to Christ, allowing God to work within us, discovering, as St. Paul did, that "I live, no longer I, but Christ lives in me" (Gal 2:20).

Lessons in Forgiveness by a Minister of the Church: Martin Luther King Jr.

Recognizing the seeming impossibility of forgiveness, Martin Luther King Jr. gave a wonderful sermon on this subject on November 17, 1957, at Dexter Avenue Baptist Church in Montgomery, Alabama.[9] The title of the sermon is "Loving Your Enemies"; Dr. King recognized that relationships in

---

[9] "Loving Your Enemies," Dexter Avenue Baptist Church, Montgomery, Alabama (November 17, 1957), http://kingencyclopedia.stanford.edu/encyclopedia/documentsentry/doc_loving_your_enemies/.

need of forgiveness and healing most often see the "other" as the "enemy." While the context of his sermon is the history of racism and segregation, his insights apply to any situation where someone has been harmed by another. This sermon provides some very thoughtful reflections on two aspects of forgiveness and the love that we should have toward those who have done harm against us: how we should go about forgiving and loving, and why we should forgive and love.

The good preacher that he was, King suggested three ways in which we might go about forgiving and loving one who has done us harm. First, if we are to begin to love one who has harmed us, we must first begin with ourselves. King quoted Jesus' question, "Why do you notice the splinter in your brother's eye, but do not perceive the wooden beam in your own eye?" (Matt 7:3). Jesus recognizes how easy it is for us to see the faults in another and not our own faults. A careful analysis of our own shortcomings has the effect of making us more understanding of the faults of others. But, the opposite is true as well. Not taking ownership of our own sinfulness can make us a harsh judge of others. This is what Jesus frequently confronted in the religious authorities of his day, and he constantly reproached them for their hardness of heart.

A second thing that King believed would help us to forgive and love those who have harmed us is to try to discover an element of good in them. He recognized that within the best of us, there is some evil, and within the worst of us, there is some good. When we come to see this, we will take a different attitude toward others. If we can see deeply within each person and perceive within "the image of God," we will begin to forgive and love despite the evil the person has committed.

Thirdly, King thought that another way to forgive and love those who have harmed us is to avoid defeating them when the opportunity presents itself. Here, he referred to those moments when a person—maybe even someone we have deeply hated—has become most vulnerable. Our tendency might be to deliver the "death blow" at this moment, but King believed that this is precisely the moment when we are called to love in the specific manner of *agape*—that love that seeks nothing in return. He described *agape* as "an overflowing love . . . the love of God working in the lives of men." *Agape* is elevating. When we love with the love of God, we love others not because of who they are or what they do for us, but because "God loves them." In people whom we do not see much worth, we start to see the invaluable love of God. King was very clear that the issue is not about liking people or what they have done. We may not like their attitudes or what they have done, but Jesus calls us to love them. In this light, we choose to love others because God loves them. When we find ourselves capable of loving like God does, we will be able to love the person who does an evil deed, while hating the deed that the person has committed.

In his sermon, King moved from the practical aspects of how to love and forgive to the more theoretical reasons as to why we should do this. First, he insisted that forgiveness alone can stop the cycle that hurt and violence begin: "Men must see that force begets force, hate begets hate, toughness begets toughness. And it is all a descending spiral, ultimately ending in destruction for all and everybody. Somebody must have sense enough and morality enough to cut off the chain of hate and the chain of evil in the universe. And you do that by love."

Second, without forgiveness, the person who has been hurt becomes further distorted and harmed. He noted that we tend to focus on the harm done to those who are on the receiving end of hatred: "But it is even more tragic, it is even more ruinous and injurious to the individual who hates." Hatred has a way of distorting a person's ability to think and see clearly. King's account of *agape* corresponds to the adage "love is blind." Likewise, his understanding of hatred draws on the truism that we become "blind with rage." On the one hand, love is blind because we love others regardless of how they appear to us—ugly or beautiful, foolish or wise. On the other hand, hatred blinds us to the degree that we are unable to see the harm we ourselves are doing. King pointed out, "You can't see straight when you hate. . . . For the person who hates, the beautiful becomes ugly and the ugly becomes beautiful. For the person who hates, the good becomes bad and the bad becomes good." In the end, hate "destroys the very structure of the personality of the hater." In this way, hate increases the harm done to a person who has been a victim, but this time, the victim helps put the harm upon oneself.

King provided a third reason for forgiveness: love has within it a redemptive power, a power that eventually transforms individuals. He held that this is precisely why Jesus says, "Love your enemies": "Because if you hate your enemies, you have no way to redeem and to transform your enemies. But if you love your enemies, you will discover that at the very root of love is the power of redemption." Loving others is wanting their good. When loving others persistently, even in the face of mistreatment, there is power in this unwavering love, as King highlighted: People who hate "can't stand it too long. Oh, they react in many ways in the beginning. They react with bitterness because they're mad because you love them like that. They react with guilt feelings, and sometimes they'll hate you a little more at that transition period, but just keep loving them. And by the power of your love they will break down under the load." Because it is love, the hatred is broken down, but the one who hates is lifted up and redeemed. This is the power of love, a creative and life-giving power. In this way, love and forgiveness enable the one who is wronged to take control of a situation and direct it toward good.

We might add two other motivations to King's insights on love and forgiveness of enemies. First, in loving and forgiving our enemies, we imitate Jesus, who not only taught about forgiveness, but lived it on the cross. Second, in loving and forgiving our enemies, we become more "God-like" or more "holy" as God is holy. Why? The answer is because this is the essence of God, who continues to love and forgive us, no matter our response. God cannot do otherwise. God continues to love and forgive just as God continues to make the sun rise and shine on the evil and on the good, and sends rain on the righteous and on the unrighteous (Matt 5:45).

The Church as the Context for Forgiveness and Reconciliation

Dr. King provided some very challenging thoughts on the attitude shift that we need in order to go about forgiving and loving, as well as providing the grounds for why one should forgive and love. Perhaps the challenge in this particular chapter is to become more specific about the ways in which the church encourages people to actually do the work of forgiveness and reconciliation.

As the writings of Scripture and the church fathers have become more accessible since Vatican Council II (1962–65), people have learned of the many "ordinary ways" that sin could be forgiven, most especially through prayer, fasting, and almsgiving.[10] "Alongside the radical purification brought about by Baptism or martyrdom," other ways of obtaining forgiveness of sins include "efforts at reconciliation with one's neighbor, . . . the intercession of the saints, and the practice of charity 'which covers a multitude of sins'" (1 Pet 4:8; 1434). Ordinary ways of forgiveness are extended to include "gestures of reconciliation, concern for the poor, the exercise and defense of justice and right, by the admission of faults to one's brethren, fraternal correction, revision of life, examination of conscience, spiritual direction, acceptance of suffering, endurance of persecution for

---

[10] *Catechism of the Catholic Church*, 2nd ed. (United States Catholic Conference—Libreria Editrice Vaticana, 1997), 1434. Subsequent references will be noted in the text by paragraph number.

the sake of righteousness." The *Catechism* also specifies, "Taking up one's cross each day and following Jesus is the surest way of penance" (1435). Further, it is noted that reading Sacred Scripture, praying the Liturgy of the Hours, praying the Lord's Prayer ("forgive us our trespasses as we forgive those who trespass against us"), and undertaking any other act of worship or devotion "revives the spirit of conversion and repentance within us and contributes to the forgiveness of our sins" (1437). Finally, ordinary ways to enter into a framework of forgiveness include embracing the seasons and the days of penance in the course of the liturgical year—especially Lent and each Friday of the week in memory of the Lord's death. "These times are particularly appropriate for spiritual exercises, penitential liturgies, pilgrimages . . . , voluntary self-denial such as fasting and almsgiving, and fraternal sharing (charitable and missionary works)," which lead to a change of one's heart and a sorrow for sins (1438).

In addition to these ordinary ways of forgiveness, the church provides sacramental moments to deepen conversion so that Christians might be united more closely to Christ. Through baptism—especially when this is celebrated through immersion—we symbolically die to our old selves and come to new life in Christ. Early church baptismal fonts helped to shape people's imaginations in this way. They were often in the shape of a cross or an octagon (representing the day of the resurrection on the "eighth day"). The font had steps that people walked down into the water, were submerged into it, and then walked up another set of steps to exit the font. These actions symbolized that the "old" self was "drowned" and the "new" self had been "raised to new life" in Christ. As St. Paul wrote,

> Are you unaware that we who were baptized into Christ Jesus were baptized into his death? We were indeed buried with him through baptism into death, so that, just as Christ was raised from the dead by the glory of the Father, we too might live in newness of life.
>
> For if we have grown into union with him through a death like his, we shall also be united with him in the resurrection. (Rom 6:3-5)

Through baptism, Christians continue to recognize this pattern of living—suffering, death, and resurrection—and see this pattern as a way of imitating and conforming themselves to Christ in the actions of their daily lives.

Similarly, the Eucharist is the weekly (or, for some, the daily) manner that this action is repeated in the memorial of the Last Supper, where Jesus gives of himself in his suffering and death, trusting in God's faithfulness to raise Jesus to new life. The action of the Eucharist—breaking this bread and sharing this cup in memorial of Jesus whose body was broken and whose blood was poured out for us in service and sacrifice—reminds Christians that they are to imitate Jesus in their service and self-sacrifice for others, trusting that God will bring new life out of their suffering and dying to sinfulness and selfishness in service to others. These repeated actions—and reflection upon these actions through the prism of the suffering, death, and resurrection of Jesus—make the Christian, over time, more and more closely conformed to Christ.

In this light, the Eucharist is a repeatable sacrament that sustains us on our lifelong journey of conversion begun in baptism. Kathleen Hughes puts this point well:

> Each time the community assembles for the celebration of the Eucharist, it celebrates its own conversion journey as well, and it acknowledges the paradox of the Christian life: that we are saved sinners, liberated yet ever in need of deeper conversion. . . . At every celebration we acknowledge that God never ceases to call us to a new and more abundant life, that as sinners we are invited to trust in God's mercy, that the covenant of friendship with God is a bond that need never be broken, and that now, today—the always present *hodie* [today] of the liturgy—is the day to listen for God's voice, to return and to be renewed in Christ.[11]

Through the Eucharist, we witness the goodness and saving acts of God and "give praise and thanksgiving that we have been counted worthy to stand in God's presence and serve." Each celebration of the Eucharist is a new "today" of God's redemption.

Once the reformed liturgy of Vatican Council II was celebrated in the vernacular, the penitential aspects of the Eucharist became more evident to liturgical participants. At the beginning of the Eucharist, we pause to call to mind our sins. This is an extremely important moment in the liturgy, for we can go no further without naming our need of God's healing.[12] Other parts of the Eucharist are explicitly penitential, such as the sign of peace, where we pray that God will look not on our sins, but on the faith of God's church, granting us peace and unity in accordance with God's will. We approach those around us in a symbolic gesture acknowledging that we need to be in communion with each other if we authentically are to

---

[11] *Saying Amen: A Mystagogy of the Sacrament* (Chicago: Liturgy Training Publications, 1999), 180.

[12] Ibid., 189.

be in communion with God as we approach the table of the Lord. And as we approach the Lord's table we are invited as redeemed sinners: "Behold the Lamb of God, / behold him who takes away the sins of the world." Our response indicates our recognition that we are unworthy and that all that God does for us is a gift and a grace to bring us forgiveness, healing, and wholeness: "Lord, I am not worthy / that you should enter under my roof, but only say the word / and my soul shall be healed."

Finally, we might reflect upon the dismissal, which many think may be the most significant words of the Eucharist: "Go and announce the Gospel of the Lord" or "Go in peace, glorifying the Lord by your life." Loved, forgiven, and reconciled by the actions of the Eucharist, we are called to be Christ in the world, agents of his love, forgiveness, and reconciliation. In this light, while many parts of the Eucharist remind us of forgiveness, the Eucharist itself *is* the primary sacrament of reconciliation, for in the celebration of the Eucharist "the passion of Christ is again made present; his body given for us and his blood shed for the forgiveness of sins are offered to God again by the Church for the salvation of the world. For in the eucharist Christ is present and is offered as 'the sacrifice which has made our peace' with God and in order that 'we may be brought together in unity' by his Holy Spirit" (*Rite of Penance*, 2). The words of the *Catechism* repeat these thoughts: "Daily conversion and penance find their source and nourishment in the Eucharist, for in it is made present the sacrifice of Christ which has reconciled us with God. . . . 'It is a remedy to free us from our daily faults'" (1436).

The Sacrament of Penance

Interestingly, only after setting out this liturgical and ecclesial context of baptism and Eucharist does the Introduction to the *Rite of Penance* begin to speak specifically about the sacrament of penance. In baptism a person is "implanted in the paschal mystery of Christ,"[13] receiving a share of new life, becoming a son or daughter of God and a member of the church. It is through the Eucharist that Christians continue to meet and experience their ongoing incorporation into the reconciling Christ. The purpose of the sacrament of penance, in this context, is to forgive and reconcile those members who, since baptism, "have fallen into grave sin, and have thus

---

[13] *Sacrosanctum Concilium*, in Austin Flannery, ed., *Vatican Council II: Constitutions, Decrees, Declarations; The Basic Sixteen Documents* (Collegeville, MN: Liturgical Press, 2014), 6.

lost their baptismal grace and wounded ecclesial communion" (*Catechism*, 1446).[14] While many may think of their sins only in relation to God, the Introduction to the *Rite of Penance* maintains that this sacrament has a dual focus: reconciliation with God the Father "who 'first loved us' (1 John 4:19), to Christ who gave himself up for us [see Gal 2:20; Eph 5:25], and to the Holy Spirit who has been poured out on us abundantly [see Titus 3:6]," as well as "reconciliation with our brethren and sisters who remain harmed by our sins" (*Rite of Penance*, 5). What follows explains the three rites for penance and how each stands in relation to the social nature of sin and the communal dimensions of forgiveness and reconciliation in the church. These communal aspects are significant within any conversation concerning restorative justice, which encourages a person to take responsibility for his or her actions and to work to provide restitution or amends for wrongs committed, thus reconciling him- or herself with the community that has been harmed by these actions.

Rite A

The prominent use of Rite A: Rite for Reconciliation of Individual Penitents tends to downplay the ecclesial and communal aspects of the sacrament of penance in the everyday experience of penitents. These aspects are manifested more clearly in Rite B: Rite for Reconciliation for Several Penitents with Individual Confession and Absolution, and Rite C: Rite for Reconciliation of Several Penitents with General Confession and Absolution—rites that are not celebrated frequently or, in the case of Rite C, hardly at all. Having said this, there are elements within Rite A that help to amplify the community's role in the sacrament of penance. The priest presider represents the community (the Body of Christ), which contributes to and cooperates in the conversion of the penitent. The priest has been described in this role by commentators as the community's host, public minister, or presider of prayer.[15] The rubrics instruct, "When the penitent comes to confess his sins, the priest welcomes him warmly and greets him

---

[14] See also *Rite of Penance*, 2.

[15] Gerald T. Broccolo, "The Minister of Penance," in *The New Rite of Penance* (Pevely, MO: Federation of Diocesan Liturgical Commissions, 1974): 55, 61–62; Richard Gula, "Challenges of the New Rite of Penance," *New Catholic World* 227 (January/February 1984): 10; Charles W. Gusmer, "The Key to the Sacrament of Reconciliation," *New Catholic World* (January/February 1984): 40; Thomas J. Murphy, "Sin and Reconciliation in a Time of Confusion," *Chicago Studies* 17 (Fall 1978): 374; Martin Slattery, "The New Order of Penance," *The Furrow* 25 (May 1974): 258.

with kindness" (*Rite of Penance*, 41). The word of God, although optional, provides an important impetus to move the penitent beyond an individual and private sense of sin, conversion, and reconciliation (43). Listening to the word of God, which is a proclamation of God's love, one is properly disposed to turn toward God's grace and salvation and not inward within oneself. Thus, in the words of Francis Sottocornola, " 'Confession' or the final proclamation of the mercy of God is joined to the 'confession' of sins to give it a new significance."[16] Hence, the penitent's act is not an isolated and individual exercise, but becomes part of the church's prayer, liturgy, and praise.

The penitent's solidarity with others in sin and redemption is a pronounced feature of the suggested Scripture texts (*Rite of Penance*, 72–83). The penitent is reminded that he or she does not stand alone in sin, for "[w]e had all gone astray like sheep" (Isa 53:4-6) and "we [are] still sinners" (Rom 5:8-9). Further, the penitent, through the Scriptures, remembers that he or she has been redeemed as a member of a people, for God indicated that "they will be my people" (Ezek 11:19-20), and that they are "God's chosen ones" (Col 3:8-10, 12-17). Indeed, the Christian stands with others, for "Christ loved us" (Eph 5:1-2) and "[h]e delivered us" (Col 1:12-14). The social nature of sin and the Christian life are highlighted in the texts that stress forgiveness of others (Matt 6:14-15), right conduct toward others (Luke 6:31-38), and the importance of fellowship with others (1 John 1:6-7, 9). Even the reaction of the community over the conversion of the sinner is symbolized through the image of rejoicing friends and neighbors (Luke 15:1-7).

The suggestion made for the general formula of confession also calls to mind the social nature of sin and the importance of the intercession of the community for the penitent (*Rite of Penance*, 44). Similarly, the absolution formula reminds the penitent that he or she is reconciled through the ministry of the church, and the imposition of hands is a sign of the conferring of the Holy Spirit and of reconciliation with the church (46). Particular prayers on the part of the penitent underscore this aspect of reconciliation and unity with the church community:

---

[16] Francis Sottocornola, *"Commentatium: Il Nuovo 'Ordo Paenitentiae,'"* in *Notitiae* 10 (1974); reprinted and translated in *A Look at the New Rite of Penance*, trans. Thomas A. Krosnicki (Washington, DC: United States Catholic Conference, 1975), 9.

Listen to my prayer:
forgive all my sins,
renew your love in my heart,
help me to live in perfect unity with my fellow Christians
that I may proclaim your saving power to all the world. (89)

Rite B

The communal nature of Rite B provides a setting that more clearly identifies the community's role in the sacrament of penance. The faithful have assembled to pray, to sing, to reflect upon God's word, to continue a process of conversion, to ask for forgiveness, to be reconciled to God and to the church, and to praise God for all that has been done for them (*Rite of Penance*, 48). That the entire community is called to cooperate in this rite is witnessed by the frequent invitation for all to pray (50), for everyone to understand the word of God more deeply (51), for all to join in saying a general formula for confession and the Lord's Prayer (54), for all the faithful to pray for each other in the litany (54), and for all present to offer thanks to God (56).

The language within Rite B always addresses the assembled group of people, reminding the individual members that they are assembled as a community. Indeed, this assembled community is joined through its prayer with the whole church, as is evident from the suggested concluding prayer of thanksgiving:

We thank you for the wonders of your mercy,
and with heart and hand and voice
we join with the whole Church
in a new song of praise:
Glory to you
through Christ
in the Holy Spirit,
now and for ever.
Amen. (57)

The assembly's attention is drawn to the social impact of sin through many different ways. In one of the opening prayers, sin is portrayed as that which divides and scatters—a situation made clear when the community gathers together in the name of Jesus:

Almighty and merciful God,
you have brought us together in the name of your Son
to receive your mercy and grace in our time of need.

Open our eyes to see the evil we have done.
Touch our hearts and convert us to yourself.

Where sin has divided and scattered,
may your love make one again . . . (99)

The suggested Scripture texts remind the assembly that they have been
called together as a people with whom God has made a covenant (Deut
5:1-3, 6-7). As God's people, they are to walk in love, imitating the love
of Christ (Eph 5:1-14), which in a concrete way entails love of both God
and neighbor (Matt 22:34-40; John 13:34-35; 15:10-13) (51). The homily
that follows is based upon these texts and leads the assembly "to examine
their consciences and renew their lives" (52).

The suggested general formula for confession highlights the community's role as a witness to the conversion process and as an intercessor
for the penitents. In this prayer the community members confess to God
and to their brothers and sisters, asking for the intercession of Mary, the
angels and saints, and all their brothers and sisters (54). The communal
nature of forgiveness is further emphasized in the Lord's Prayer, where
the community members forgive the sins of each other as they ask God
for forgiveness (54). The significance of reconciliation with the church in
the absolution formula and the imposition of hands is present, as in Rite
A (55). The litany before individual confession and absolution clearly
reminds the assembly that reconciliation is with God, but also with the
church. One part of the litany reads, "Forgive your children who confess
their sins, and restore them to full communion with your Church" (54).
In another part of the litany, this full communion is stated in eucharistic
terms where the image presented is of the penitent once again being welcomed at the table, the fullest sign of the community's unity: "Welcome
them to your altar, and renew their spirit with the hope of eternal glory"
(54). The concluding prayer, before individual confession and absolution,
also focuses on the role of the community as witnesses to the conversion
process and as ministers of reconciliation:

Lord,
draw near to your servants
who in the presence of your Church
confess that they are sinners.
Through the ministry of the Church
free them from all sin
so that renewed in spirit
they may give you thankful praise. (54)

Rite C

Rite C: Rite for Reconciliation of Several Penitents with General Confession and Absolution closely follows Rite B, with only a few, though significant, changes (*Rite of Penance*, 60). Having dealt with the community's prominent role in Rite B, the focus now will be on the differences that Rite C introduces. The form of satisfaction proposed to all penitents (no. 60) and the common sign of the penitents' willingness to receive absolution (no. 61) suggest to the community its solidarity in sin, conversion, and forgiveness. The trinitarian formula for general absolution also contains an assertion that the forgiveness of sins comes through the ministry entrusted to the presider, who represents the community, which is the Body of Christ (62). The optional formula for general absolution also clearly states that God's pardon and peace comes to the penitents through the ministry of the church (62).

Evaluation

Commentators on Rite A have tried to point out other ways to enhance the community's role, its understanding of the social effects of sin, and the notion of reconciliation with the church. One recommendation is for the priest to suggest concrete penances that will highlight the ecclesial, social, and communal nature of sin and reconciliation.[17] Another suggestion advises ordained ministers to carefully select texts that will emphasize these dimensions. For instance, the prayer of the penitent for Rite A makes no mention of the social aspect of sin and reconciliation with one's neighbor or the church, but there are other options that make this clear (*Rite of Penance*, 45).[18] When all the suggestions have been made, however, Rite A still appears to be a private and isolated encounter between priest and penitent, divorced from the community. Richard Gula summarizes this state of affairs: "The individual rite as we know it strains to express clearly the corporate involvement in sin and reconciliation. It lacks clear signs of being a community's worship and of expressing the communal nature of sin and reconciliation."[19]

Gula goes further—when individual expression becomes the focal point the communal nature of penance tends to be obscured:

---

[17] Richard Gula, *To Walk Together Again: The Sacrament of Reconciliation* (New York: Paulist Press, 1984), 255.

[18] There are other options available that more clearly highlight the social aspect of sin and the notion of reconciliation with the church. See, for example, *Rite of Penance*, 89.

[19] Gula, "Confession and Communal Penance," *New Catholic World* 228 (November/December 1985): 269.

The community plays no significant role in this [the individual] rite. This individual rite does not express well either the rediscovered sense of liturgy as the activity of the Church gathered for worship nor the heightened social consciousness and experience which we are attaining in the Church today. The continued insistence on the individual rite as the ordinary means of forgiveness strains the Vatican Council's vision for reforming the sacraments and poses a great challenge to the priest to be a vibrant symbol of the community and of forgiveness rooted in the community itself.[20]

It should be noted that individual and communal aspects of penance are not necessarily set in opposition. The communal nature of penance includes and requires individual confession and reformation (while the inverse is not necessarily the case).

While some liturgical commentators submit that Rite B is the ideal version of the three options,[21] most recognize the substantial problems inherent in the rite for reconciliation of several penitents with individual confession and absolution. While this communal rite better expresses the communal, social, and ecclesial dimensions of sin, conversion, and reconciliation, in the context of this communally rich experience, the culminating moment is done in an individual manner. While this rite may be seen as a combination of Rite A and Rite C, it sacrifices the best of both. Gula puts it succinctly when he notes that Rite B is a mixed rite, inserting private confession into a communal celebration. However, individual confession involving large numbers of people does not guarantee that the individual penitent will be orientated toward the communal nature of reconciliation. Furthermore, this situation can too easily make the individual confession "a formalistic element that must be done, and done quickly."[22] Ralph Keifer notes that Rite B makes no mention of the significant role of the community's intercession nor of the community's role in encouraging and leading one another to repentance. He understands Rite B more as a series of individual acts done in common before and after the

---

[20] Ibid. Also see Ralph Keifer, "The *Ordo Poenitentiae*: Revised Doctrine and Unrevised Ritual," *Hosanna: A Journal of Pastoral Liturgy* 1 (1982): 521. Aelfred Tegels ("The New Order, or Rite, of Penance," *Worship* 48 [1974]: 244) recognizes that even the goals of the rite as a time for prayer and dialogue cannot be met if there are too many penitents. Robert Hovda ("Reconciliation of Penitents in the Church," *Living Worship* 10 [December 1974]: 2) notes that Rite A still attempts to collapse all the penitential movements into one tiny act.

[21] See, for instance, Charles E. Miller, "The Best of Three Rites," *Homiletic and Pastoral Review* 78 (December 1977): 57.

[22] Gula, *To Walk Together Again*, 258.

actual sacramental celebration, than as a full communal and corporate sacramental celebration.[23]

Rite C emerged as an official liturgical rite with the publication of the new *Rite of Penance*. In many ways, it responds best to the conciliar request for communal celebrations of the sacraments and for the full and active participation of all the faithful.[24] However, the incorporation of the Pastoral Norms of 1972 within the *Rite of Penance* has severely limited its use, both through the restriction of occasion and the requirement for a subsequent confession of serious sin. Some liturgical commentators interpret such restrictions as a fear that the sacrament will be abused, that people "will try to take the easy way out."[25] Others construe that Rite C is understood as a deviation from the norm of individual and integral confession and absolution and that the two different forms cannot exist together.[26] Unfortunately, the restrictions on the use of Rite C deprive the church community of an opportunity to grow in understanding the social, communal, and ecclesial dimensions of sin, conversion, and reconciliation. Rather than an "easy option," Rite C, in the words of Monika Hellwig, "vividly expresses individual responsibility for the sin of society at large and communal responsibility for the sins of individuals."[27] This is accomplished because the community "meditates on scripture readings together, prays together, acknowledges sin and sinfulness together, and receives a common and communal assurance of the possibility of conversion in complex matters involving social situations and multiple relationships."[28]

---

[23] Keifer, "The *Ordo Poenitentiae*," 19.

[24] See Constitution on the Sacred Liturgy (*Sacrosanctum Concilium*) where it states that, in the reform of the liturgy, preference is to be made for rites to have communal celebrations involving the presence and active participation of the faithful over liturgies that are individual or quasi-private (27).

[25] D. Joseph Finnerty, "The Role of General Absolution," *America* 134 (April 1976): 286; Monika Hellwig, "Theological Trends: Sin and Sacramental Reconciliation, II," *The Way* 24 (October 1984): 309. Adolfo Nicolas ("Reconciliation: The Courage to Create a New Future," *East Asian Pastoral Review* 19 [1982]: 319) suggests that the real abuse is the loss of the sense of the social effects of sin and the communal aspects of penance, which are better signified in Rite C.

[26] Edward Foley, "Communal Rites of Penance: Insights and Options," in *Reconciliation: The Continuing Agenda*, ed. Robert J. Kennedy, 148 (Collegeville, MN: Liturgical Press, 1987); Gula, *To Walk Together Again*, 271; Pierre-Marie Gy, "Le Sacrament de Pénitence," *La Maison-Dieu* 139 (1979): 135.

[27] Hellwig, "Theological Trends," 309.

[28] Ibid. Also see John Gallen, "A Pastoral-Liturgical View of Penance Today," *Worship* 45 (1971): 43; and Hovda, "Reconciliation of Penitents in the Church," 4.

If the values of the new *Rite of Penance*, especially the community's more prominent role relative to the liturgical form before Vatican Council II, are to become part of the church's lived understanding, then the tasks of renewal and reform are not finished. Most Catholics still think of this sacrament as a very private affair, and the sacramental rites themselves often treat the community's contributions as appendages, indicating that the community's role is neither well understood nor seriously stressed as an important part of the sacramental celebration. Unless this renewal is taken up, the church can continue to celebrate the myriad ways of forgiveness and reconciliation—through baptism and Eucharist, as well as in the many other ordinary ways—but most of its members will not celebrate this graced moment in the particular sacrament where they can encounter the forgiveness and love of God in the most significant and difficult moments of life. This experiential loss in the sacrament of penance means that many Catholics are hampered in their lived sense of the social nature of sin and the communal dimension of forgiveness and reconciliation with a community that has been wounded by their sins. A deeper lived experience among Catholics of what is at the heart of this sacrament would help them to better understand restorative justice. If this were the case, Catholics would privilege restorative justice because they are experiencing it "in their bones," rather than viewing it as just one of many ways to provide justice in the face of sin and evil.

The sacrament of penance embodies a Christian response to sin that is centered on redemption and restoration. This sacrament prepares us for facing suffering that can break the human spirit. Marietta Jaeger knew that only an increase in her faith could bring her to respond compassionately to her young daughter Susie's abductor when he began tormenting her with periodic phone calls. For this reason she prayed only a single prayer. Assuming this man had killed her Susie, she daily prayed that she might move beyond her rage and desire for revenge to reach a Christlike response to this man. She was as shocked as Susie's killer when during one call, she responded to him with genuine compassion and concern. Drawing on her faith, she kept focused on the recognition that this person, in the eyes of God, was as precious and worthy of love as her beloved Susie. Her genuine query, "What can I do for you?" evoked his own remorse and her realization that her prayer had been finally answered. Her patient, compassionate response also helped police identify his location and prevent his harming other children. Marietta has spoken at churches and universities across our country about her own spiritual journey and related work to reform our criminal justice system. Members of our campus community were deeply moved by her words when she visited our campus. She and many other Christians deeply committed to restorative justice call us to live our daily lives, especially in their most trying moments, more closely conformed to Christ. Such Christian witness deepens our understanding of the central meaning of the sacrament of penance, which is that we forgive and reconcile with persons who have acted sinfully in ways that wound persons. Such sacramental life deepens our own imitation of Christ, who in daily, concrete ways always manifests the love of both God and all our neighbors.

Review and Looking Forward

Editors

Jeanne Bishop, an attorney, is a public defender in Cook County, Illinois.[29] She is also an advocate for gun control and gun violence prevention; she works for the abolition of the death penalty and the exoneration of the innocent on death row. Faith is central to her life. She is the author of *Change of Heart*, about the healing and renewal that come through forgiveness, not merely a simple (or verbal) and passive forgiving of a wrong, but active efforts to see the good in the wrongdoer (to see the offender as good) and work for his or her betterment.[30] She is also the family member of murder victims. In 1990, her sister and her brother-in-law—Nancy and Richard Langert—were murdered. Nancy was twenty-five years old and pregnant at the time. She and Richard came home one evening to find that a young man had broken into their house. They were executed in their basement, and the murderer apparently left money behind and bragged about the murders to his friends.[31]

Through decades after the death of Nancy and Richard, Jeanne has taken a long journey of forgiveness. At the beginning, forgiveness was a means to separate and protect herself from the killer; she refused to be victimized by hate. In *Change of Heart*, she tells of a remarkable transition; she realizes that to truly forgive she needed to pray for the killer, for David Biro's good, and to hope for his redemption. "I'd always thought

---

[29] See Jeanne Bishop's biography on her website, www.jeannebishop.info/jeannebishop.info/Biography.html.

[30] Jeanne Bishop, *Change of Heart: Justice, Mercy, and Making Peace with My Sister's Killer* (Louisville, KY: Westminster John Knox Press, 2015).

[31] Morgan Lee, "Forgiving Her Sister's Murderer, Face to Face," *Christianity Today* 59, no. 4 (May 2015): 40.

that the only thing big enough to pay for the life of my sister was a life sentence for her killer. Now I understood: the only thing big enough to equal the loss of her life was for him to be found."[32] In 2012 (twenty-two years after the murders), Jeanne wrote a letter to David in prison; he wrote back expressing shame and guilt, sorrow and remorse. Jeanne visited him in prison and continues to do so. "We are talking. We ask questions of each other; we answer. We speak, we listen. It is challenging, and good. We are not done yet."[33] Jeanne describes this transition—from shutting out the hate to opening to the killer—as liberation and grace. The heart of the transition is that she was convinced (by others) that to forgive another is to be committed to work for reconciliation.

Jeanne's story and Fr. Jim's chapter on forgiveness form an apt transition to the next part of the book on "Becoming Agents of Restoration." In chapter 11, Kirk Blackard will discuss problems, issues, and pathways of prison reform. Chapters 12 and 13 bring to light a whole host of programs in local communities and parishes, programs that bring healing and restoration to victims, neighborhoods, and offenders—while revitalizing parish and community life. The final chapter of the book tells the story of Vicki Schieber, one of this book's editors—the story of Vicki's continuing journey of hope and restoration. For Vicki, the pathway of restoration is much like Jeanne's sense of her own journey (cited in the paragraph above): it is challenging, and good, and not yet done.

Questions for Discussion

1. Jeanne Bishop explains that her new, life-giving understanding of forgiveness came with a renewed and hard recognition that she has been forgiven by God, who—in Jesus—suffered and died, not only by our hand, but also for us. Father Jim draws out the same themes in his discussion of the unforgiving servant (Matt 18:21-35). Too often, when we are called to forgive another, we forget that we have been forgiven a great debt.

   Consider another and connected form of forgetfulness—or at least inattention. In this chapter, Fr. Jim notes that there are many ordinary ways of forgiveness and reconciliation: prayer, fasting, giving

---

[32] Bishop, *Change of Heart*, 97.

[33] Jeanne Bishop, "The Shock of True Forgiveness," in *Restorative Justice in Practice: A Holistic Approach*, ed. Sheila M. Murphy and Michael P. Seng (Lake Mary, FL: Vandeplas, 2015), 55.

to and drawing near to the poor, admitting wrongs, working for reconciliation in daily life, and endurance for the sake of the good and the right. If this is the case, then we are, perhaps, forgiven far more than we ever realize. If we pray daily ("forgive our sins as we forgive the sins of others"), try to become better people and form better relationships, and live in the sight of God, then forgiveness and reconciliation are the natural fabric of our lives. Consider how we can be inattentive to the pattern of forgiveness and grace that is a constant part of our lives. Consider what difference it will make if we constantly remember that we are forgiven (unlike the unforgiving servant).

2. Think about Fr. Jim's contrast between private and communal confession. In short, he notes that communal penance is the context for individual penance (rather than vice versa). Communal penance provides a context for penance to follow more fully into healing and reconciliation in the community of faith. Consider, as well, that in communal penance each member of a community takes responsibility for fractures and fragmentation within it. That is, each person plays a role in forgiveness and repair, whether or not one is wronged individually or whether one has done something wrong. Sin is considered a matter for everyone to confess and heal.

   Likewise, for many years, Jeanne Bishop thought of forgiveness as a way to avoid the evil perpetuated by the offender ("I wiped my hands of him, forgot about him and moved ahead with my life").[34] With her new understanding (and sense of new life), she sees forgiveness as directed toward—as taking responsibility for—reconciliation. When this responsibility was introduced to her, Jeanne certainly believed it unreasonable and unfair. But when she actually took a leap of faith and opened a relationship with her sister's killer, she found that she had received a great gift.

Reflect upon the typical reticence that people have for taking on reconciliation when the problem "is not my fault." Also, what barriers are there to greater communal responsibility?

---

[34] Ibid., 52.

Part III

Becoming Agents of Restoration

Chapter 11

The Prison System

Editors

Bridges To Life is an organization that works "to connect communities to prisons in an effort to reduce the recidivism rate (particularly that resulting from violent crimes), reduce the number of crime victims, and enhance public safety."[1] The organization was founded in 1998 by John Sage, whose sister, Marilyn, was brutally murdered (stabbed, bludgeoned, and suffocated) by two nineteen-year-olds (who were found guilty and sentenced to death). Bridges To Life emerged out of John's own quest to find healing. In the aftermath of the trial, John experienced continuing depression and despair. Following on a spiritual path, he first volunteered for a victim-offender dialogue in a local prison and then started a program where "victims of brutal crimes—murder, rape, assault, severe spousal abuse—[could go] into Texas prisons to meet with inmates who committed such crimes against others."[2] In short, the goal of Bridges To Life is to bring healing to victims of violent crime and to their families. But, in their own journey toward healing, victims and victims' families found that they were transforming violent offenders and offering positive and peaceful contributions to communities ridden with violence.

[1] "Mission and History," Bridges To Life, www.bridgestolife.org/index.php?option=com_content&view=article&id=3&Itemid=6.
[2] Kirk Blackard, *Restoring Peace: Using Lessons from Prisons to Mend Broken Relationships,* Bridges To Life Program Edition (Houston: Bridges To Life, 2010), 7.

Kirk Blackard, the author of this chapter, is the chair of the organization's board of directors. In *Love in a Cauldron of Misery*, Kirk catalogs the inhumanity of the prison system—always careful to criticize the "system" rather than correctional professionals and employees, the "honorable and caring people just trying to do the right thing in very difficult jobs."[3] The system is badly broken, and one fundamental problem is that it is an impersonal system, isolated as a separate world of suffering. In *Love in a Cauldron of Misery*, the problem of our social-political detachment and disengagement from the system is expressed cogently by the late Emmett Solomon, a longtime prison chaplain:[4]

> In a hospital there is suffering but everybody is aligned against it. In the criminal justice system, you have suffering and it is renewed everyday by the system itself. . . . It manufactures suffering. And the people who manage it don't want to touch that suffering any more than they have to . . . keep[ing] it at arm's length . . . making rules that govern it so they don't have to actually promote suffering. Judges, attorneys, all those associated with courts, police, and the correctional system manage agencies that bring great suffering to society. They do it mechanically. . . . Problem is, we have never known what to do with our deviants, and since we don't know what to do, we do what we do now.[5]

The task of the prison chaplain and prison ministry—as explained by both Emmett and Kirk—is not to change the system, but to restore and redeem prisoners from within the current system. However, through his experiences in prisons and the work of Bridges To Life, Kirk does "believe that society, through its secular leaders, should develop a new theory of corrections and transform the system from top to bottom." Although secular, the prison system—he is convinced—should "move in the direction of biblical teaching—in particular the personal and relational values expressed in Jesus' call to forgiveness and love of enemies."[6] The basis of Kirk's proposal for "transformative incarceration" is found in this chapter.

---

[3] *Love in a Cauldron of Misery: Perspectives on Christian Prison Ministry* (Eugene, OR: Wipf and Stock), xi.

[4] Emmett Solomon was the founder and executive director of the Restorative Justice Ministries Network of Texas (http://www.rjmntexas.net/). About his life, see Anita Parrish, "Tribute to Emmett Solomon," *R.J. News* 15, no. 2 (December 2014), www.rjmntexas.net/rjnewsdecember2014.pdf.

[5] Blackard's interview with Solomon, cited in *Love in a Cauldron of Misery*, 57.

[6] *Love in a Cauldron of Misery*, xv.

Transformative Incarceration

Kirk Blackard

In his groundbreaking 1990 book, *Changing Lenses*, Howard Zehr described two lenses through which criminal justice might be viewed. The first, "retributive justice," describes our current system, as follows:

> Crime is a violation of the state, defined by lawbreaking and guilt. Justice determines blame and administers pain in a contest between the offender and the state directed by systematic rules.[7]

Under our retributive justice system, fault is generally determined in an adversarial plea bargain or trial involving the state's prosecutor and an attorney for the alleged offender. Crime victims are usually relegated to the sideline. Those found guilty typically are punished by sentencing them to prison and then continuing the punishment after prison through practices such as certain parole requirements, felon exclusion laws, and cultural stigmatization. Under this system the United States has become the world's leader in incarceration, with 2.2 million people currently in prisons or jails. Nearly one in one hundred adults is incarcerated, a rate that is five to ten times higher than in Western Europe and the world's other democracies.[8]

Zehr also presented an alternative lens, "restorative justice," as a goal for responding to crime in a more constructive way:

> Crime is a violation of people and relationships. It creates obligations to make things right. Justice involves the victim, the offender, and the community in a search for solutions which promote repair, reconciliation, and reassurance.[9]

The main objective of restorative justice is to deal with crime when it occurs in ways that meet the needs of all those involved. Administering punishment to offenders is not an objective. Instead, offenders, victims, and the community are involved in collaborative processes aimed at fixing the problems by focusing on the causes and dealing with offenders in ways that hold them accountable, are less likely to stigmatize them, and tend to minimize further offending. Restorative justice processes are intended to be the initial response to crime and wrongdoing. If they work, use of prisons is minimized or avoided.

[7] *Changing Lenses: A New Focus for Crime and Justice* (Scottdale, PA: Herald Press, 1995), 181.

[8] The Sentencing Project, www.sentencingproject.org/template/page.cfm?id=107.

[9] *Changing Lenses*, 183.

Restorative justice is evolving and has expanded significantly since its informal beginnings in the US in the 1970s. Its primary focus has been on criminal justice, where restorative practices have sometimes been used among juveniles charged with minor offenses, in situations of nonviolent adult crimes, and as a form of peacemaking between crime victims and the persons who harmed them and were sentenced to prison by our retributive system. It also has seen some practice in other areas of conflict, including issues of justice for families, schools, neighborhoods, communities, and even countries.

Notwithstanding its growth, restorative justice has not attained a critical mass in our criminal justice system; it has been used, at best, to augment our retributive system. Prison use has expanded, fueled in recent decades by our country's get-tough-on-crime policies. Concurrently, most prisons have implemented various rehabilitation programs, and a few prisons have been converted entirely or in part to "faith-based" or "character-based" facilities or therapeutic communities. In addition, various outside groups, mainly faith-based ministries, have implemented largely sporadic activities, both in prisons and outside in early post-release situations, aiming to foster peace, rehabilitation, and change among offenders who were incarcerated by our fundamentally retributive system.

The term "restorative justice" is often applied to these programs, even though it is a term of art that contemplates a particular meaning and several generally accepted principles (such as addressing the causes of crime, offender accountability, and collaborative encounters between all stakeholders) that most of the programs do not include. Further, one can question the implication of aiming to "restore" incarcerated offenders to their former lives—often involving drugs, abuse, lack of education, criminality, unemployment, and poverty—that led them to crime in the first place.

This chapter suggests that a better objective is to foster the "transformation" of the entire beings of incarcerated offenders. Such transformation requires more than ad-hoc interventions that address some of their specific problems. Instead, it requires a range of practices, some that embody the principles of restorative justice and some that do not. Each is part of a broader, integrated system intended to address a number of issues and foster transformation of the whole persons of those who are incarcerated. The phrase "transformative incarceration" has been coined to cover such an integrated program of practices in prisons and among recently released offenders. While the focus is on the integrated whole, each practice has to be implemented individually. And each practice, or several of them, offers a possible answer to the question, What should we be doing in prisons?

The Transformative Incarceration System

Transformative incarceration has roots in restorative justice, but is significantly different. It takes over after retributive practices have been used, and offenders are convicted and incarcerated. Transformative incarceration can be described as follows:

> Crime is a violation of people, relationships, and the law. Where the criminal justice system results in violators being imprisoned, justice involves the stakeholders, including crime victims to the extent feasible, working with those who are or have been incarcerated to foster their personal transformation and thereby build a greater sense of community, safety, and peace for all involved.

Transformative incarceration embodies the overarching goal of helping individuals or groups of incarcerated offenders transform their whole beings, find a wholeness they probably never have experienced, and become peaceful, law-abiding, productive citizens. It has three basic objectives:

1. Recognize the basic "humanness" of individuals who are incarcerated and make their lives more positive and fulfilling.

2. Make prisons as safe and positive as feasible under the circumstances.

3. Make society safer by reducing recidivism among those released from prison.

Transformative incarceration integrates existing programs and approaches involving a number of stakeholders to accomplish these objectives on individual, prison, and societal levels. The challenge is huge. To meet it, one needs to think about the principles of systems and systems thinking.

A system is a group of component parts (often other, smaller subsystems) that are highly integrated and work together to form a unified whole and accomplish an overall goal. The human body is a good example. Its many parts—brain, blood, veins, muscles, etc.—work together to make a single entity that is able to function in the broader world. Systems thinking is a holistic approach that focuses on the way a system's parts work together over time, within the context of larger systems, to accomplish its goal. Each part of a system affects and is affected by the other parts. If a system isn't functioning properly, changing one part rarely fixes the entire system, because of the way each part is connected to other parts. A broader "transformation," or change of the entire system, is typically required.

Transformative incarceration requires integration of many systems. However, thinking about two—the human system and the transformative

system—is key to understanding the basic concept. Each incarcerated offender is a system comprised of his or her physical body (a physical system
itself), along with other social and cultural attributes that make each one
the unique, whole human being who he or she is. The following is an il-
lustrative list of some important components of the human system that
make offenders the persons they are:

- Physical and mental attributes
- Family influences
- Religious training and beliefs
- Spiritual inclinations
- Educational status
- Community and cultural influences   } WHOLE HUMAN BEING
- Genetic predispositions
- Moral and ethical standards
- Drug influences
- Financial status

Nearly all incarcerated offenders have a number of problems and issues.
Several components of their human system are missing or broken, and
improving one does not solve their problems. All the missing or broken
components need to be addressed. A good metaphor for this situation is
a boat (a system of many parts) that is sinking because it has several holes
in its hull. Plugging one doesn't stop the sinking. Fixing several may not
either. One has to stop the leaking in all the holes to stop the boat from
sinking. It works the same way with most offenders. They have many needs
to be met. Their entire lives need to change if they are to avoid sinking
even further into despair and continuing criminality.

Transforming "whole" offenders requires a broad, systemic perspective
that recognizes the linkages between seemingly unrelated parts of each person's being, and between seemingly unrelated activities that are intended
to foster personal change. Transformative incarceration recognizes that
various programs, practices, and people aiming to foster transformation
of incarcerated persons are closely connected and need to function as a
holistic system that addresses "whole" offenders and a range of offender
needs. Various stakeholders need to address many issues in a quest for
personal transformation of offenders and a greater sense of community,
safety, and peace for all involved. A transformative incarceration system

covers a range of relevant practices in prisons and among recently released offenders who are still suffering the burden of their incarceration. The range of practices is represented by three related, overlapping subsystems or groups of programs—rehabilitation programs, ministry programs, and restorative programs. Each has its own unique focus, but also is part of a broader strategy where every program affects and is affected by the other programs and the outside world.

This concept is depicted below as three overlapping circles within a larger circle. All the circles are drawn with dashed lines, indicating that the boundaries are permeable to external influences. The larger circle indicates that each is part of the larger transformative incarceration system. Each smaller circle represents one of the groups of programs with similar focus and change objectives. All overlap with each other, indicating their interconnectedness. The three overlapping in the center indicates that when the three subgroups function together, they form an integrated system that can address "whole" persons and lead to transformative incarceration.

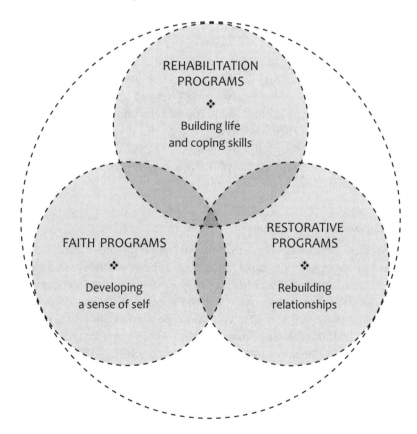

Programs in the three subsystems or groups work together to help offenders change their whole persons. For example, completing a high school education is of little value to an offender who does not live by an acceptable moral code, or getting a high school education and having a moral code may be of little value for an offender who is alienated from his family and its support. But an offender who gets a GED, adopts a strong moral code, and reestablishes family relationships has a chance.

"Whole" change moves toward the overarching objective of offenders' personal transformation that leads to safer, more positive prisons, helps offenders have better lives while incarcerated and after their release, and makes them less likely to commit more crimes and return to prison. Churches and individuals that are interested in fostering such change have myriad opportunities to participate in rehabilitation, ministry, or restorative programs.

Rehabilitation Programs

Rehabilitation programs focus on offenders' minds and bodies, aiming to provide offenders with the skills, abilities, and opportunities to succeed in the free world after release. Emphasis on rehabilitation has ebbed and flowed over the years. While the type and extent of such activities varies from institution to institution, essentially all offer some programs as an integral part of the prison experience, often with assistance of outside volunteers. They typically fall into one of four categories: education and training, substance abuse treatment, mental health treatment, and post-release programs.

Education and Training

Most prison facilities—more than fifteen hundred—provide some type of educational opportunities for inmates, with basic secondary and GED education and vocational training leading the way. Correctional education programs also often include remedial and special education to develop reading and math skills, GED preparation, postsecondary education or vocational training, literacy classes, English as a Second Language, parenting classes, wellness education, basic adult continuing education, and other such programs. Some prisons also offer postsecondary education in vocational and occupationally oriented areas, and over six hundred facilities provide college courses. An important component of training programs is on-the-job training, which offenders receive through institution job assignments and work in prison industries.

Substance Abuse Treatment

The connection between drug use, crime, and incarceration is well known. It's not surprising, then, that drug treatment programs are common in prisons. They include drug abuse education, typically involving classes that provide education regarding substance abuse and its effects; drug abuse treatment involving cognitive-behavioral therapy that addresses criminal lifestyles and provides skill-building opportunities; and more intensive programs involving various types of therapeutic community models where offenders experience living in a pro-social community that is separate from the general population. The programs are intended for incarcerated offenders with serious substance abuse, chemical dependency, or criminal ideology issues. Reentry programs often include various forms of drug interventions involving continuity of care after offenders are released.

Mental Health Treatment

Prisons and jails have become America's "new asylums," with the number of individuals with serious mental illness in prisons and jails now ten times the number in state psychiatric hospitals.[10] Many major mental disorders are accompanied by impaired functioning that affects a person's thoughts, emotions, behavior, and ability to adapt. Because treatment of mental illness is often not available behind bars, symptoms frequently get worse over time. The availability of psychiatric treatment for inmates with serious mental illness varies widely from state to state and also among prisons and jails within a state, although most provide significant mental health services. These include interventions such as screening inmates at intake, psychiatric assessments, therapy or counseling by mental health professionals, distributed psychotropic medications, and therapeutic or recreational programs. They tend to help offenders in coping with long incarcerations, dealing with separation from loved ones, and simply learning to survive in the prison environment.

---

[10] Treatment Advocacy Center, "The Treatment of Persons with Mental Illness in Prisons and Jails," www.tacreports.org/storage/documents/treatment-behind-bars /treatment-behind-bars.pdf.

Post-Release Programs

The need for rehabilitation doesn't stop at the prison gates. At least 95 percent of all prisoners will be released at some point: roughly 600,000 ex-offenders are released from prison every year and over 10,000 every week to return to the nation's communities. Approximately two-thirds will likely be rearrested within three years.[11] Released offenders face myriad problems. Some are very basic, like finding transportation to look for work or visit parole officers, or obtaining driver's licenses or other identification. Others seem larger, like breaking ties with gangs or others who fostered their bad choices, finding jobs and housing, dealing with continuing legal struggles and/or child support obligations, obtaining medical care, and reestablishing relationships with family and friends. These difficulties often lead to more problems and cause ex-offenders to get into trouble again. Numerous collateral consequences also are likely, including increases in child abuse, family violence, spread of infectious diseases, homelessness, and community disorganization.

Few systematic, comprehensive reentry programs are available to deal with the broad range of challenges people have after release. However, a number of specific programs exist, such as those that offer clothing, short-term housing, job assistance, bus passes, job placement, spiritual support, mental health assistance, mentoring, educational programs, and job training.

Faith Programs

Faith programs focus on offenders' spirituality, character, and religious life, aiming to establish or change offenders' relationships with God, restore their sense of self, and integrate them into supportive communities. Efforts such as chaplaincy programs, faith- and character-based prison dorms, and in-prison seminaries may be provided by the state, but faith programs often are provided by outside volunteer groups.

Faith programs in prisons have to recognize church-state separation issues and the First Amendment prohibition of any "law respecting an establishment of religion, or prohibiting the free exercise thereof." This amendment affords prisoners a right to practice their religion as long as

---

[11] Timothy Hughes and Doris James Wilson, "Reentry Trends in the U.S.," Bureau of Justice Statistics, www.bjs.gov/content/reentry/reentry.cfm.

doing so does not unduly burden the institution. As a general rule, correctional institutions must provide inmates with certain rights associated with the practice of their religion, such as the opportunity to assemble for religious services, attend different denominational services, receive visits from ministers, correspond with religious leaders, observe dietary laws, pursue name changes, and obtain, wear, and use religious paraphernalia. However, prison regulations may infringe upon an inmate's religious freedom if it is reasonably related to legitimate security and other prison interests. Prisons generally apply rules to prohibit activities such as disparaging certain religions, discriminating among religions, advocating violence or radicalization, or offering special perks on the basis of religious participation.

Most religious activities in prisons today are accomplished through the work of correctional chaplains, who serve a variety of functions. They administer religious programs, provide pastoral care to inmates and institutional staff, counsel troubled inmates, advise inmates of "bad news" from home or from correctional authorities; and often coordinate physical facilities, organize volunteers, facilitate religious furlough visits, contract for outside religious services, and train correctional administrators and staff about the basic tenets, rituals, and artifacts of nontraditional faith groups.

Volunteers from houses of worship or other external religious organizations help meet the spiritual needs of offenders, typically either as volunteer chaplains or when involved in ad-hoc programs. Volunteer chaplains perform many of the duties of staff correctional chaplains, under their supervision. Other volunteers may lead worship services or other religious rituals, lead religious education classes, run prayer or meditation groups, mentor offenders or their children, conduct letter writing campaigns, offer religious correspondence courses, disperse free Bibles and other religious communication, or do other tasks as requested by the staff chaplain. Volunteers are particularly important for the minority of inmates who belong to faiths that are not adequately represented among staff chaplains as compared to more traditional faiths.

Programs that involve faith and religion may serve either of two related but different purposes for offenders. Some aim to support a particular religious doctrine or foster religious and/or spiritual conversion, dealing mainly with matters of heaven and hell, the hereafter. Many prison ministries serve this purpose, which often involves evangelism through explicit preaching, teaching, and persuasion. Another approach is as part of a comprehensive strategy of change in offenders' lives in the here and now, a strategy that challenges offenders to examine their beliefs and then live up to them. It challenges offenders to learn, grow, and commit to regular spiritual practice that will reinforce their beliefs until they become second nature. It recognizes that offenders also need help, such as housing, transportation, counseling, life skills, and ongoing mentoring.

Available research shows that a conversion experience that happens as an isolated event and is not part of a larger effort is unlikely to transform an inmate's life or change his or her long-term behavior, and serious social problems such as those faced by incarcerated offenders rarely are solved through faith alone.[12] On the other hand, when faith and faith programs are allied with secular efforts provided by the prison system or community organizations, the reach and effectiveness of both are expanded.

Restorative Programs

Restorative programs focus on building or improving relationships. These relationships may be with persons that offenders have hurt (such as direct victims, family and loved ones, and others to whom offenders should be accountable); with self through focus on integrity, realness, and the recognition of how one's actions impact others; or with God.

Restorative programs are multidimensional, integrating the principles of restorative justice. They view justice—and prison—not just as punishment for wrongdoing, but also as an opportunity for responding to the legitimate needs of those who have committed crimes, those who have been hurt, and the community in general. They involve a number of different groups, relationships, and processes in collaborative encounters to address the causes of crimes and the harms done, for the mutual benefit of all who have been affected. Restorative programs might be offered by the state or by an outside group.

The People

The following groups of people should be involved in restorative programs that are part of a transformative incarceration system:

Offenders: Offenders have hurt people, and in order to transform their lives, they need to acknowledge what they have done to those they have hurt and deal with the consequences. Most of those who are incarcerated

---

[12] Byron R. Johnson, *More God, Less Crime: Why Faith Matters and How It Could Matter More* (West Conshohocken, PA: Templeton Press, 2011), 205.

live with broken relationships—with self, God, and others. They need help, including that which is offered by restorative programs. As a general rule, such programs, if available, are offered to any offenders who wish to participate and are not an unacceptable security risk. Restorative processes hold them responsible and accountable for their crimes and the harms done, and expect them to do what they can, either actually or symbolically, to make things right.

Victims: Restorative justice programs that respond to crime events typically involve people who have committed crimes and their actual victims working together to address specific, contemporary events and fashion remedies to the actual harm the offenders caused. Having incarcerated offenders and victims address actual cases in real time generally is not feasible in prisons. However, involvement in restorative programs in prison, perhaps as speakers or small-group participants or facilitators, can help victims gain a measure of peace with what has happened to them. Equally important, victims can help offenders realize the hurt they have caused, develop a measure of empathy, and be more likely to avoid crime and harm to others in the future.

Family: Family members who are not direct victims of crime need to be involved in restorative programs for two reasons: First, their behavior may have contributed to the offender's criminal lifestyle and needs to be included in a consideration of why the crime was committed. Second, in most cases family members have been badly hurt just by the fact of the offender's prosecution and incarceration and are in fact indirect victims of the offender's crime. Restorative programs need to help offenders deal with both situations. Direct involvement of family members in restorative programs inside prisons may be difficult, as they may not wish to participate or their participation may be prohibited by prison rules. However, family issues can be addressed in stories and dialogue, by offenders writing letters to family members—to be sent or perhaps not sent—or by establishing relationships with family members from whom they may be estranged through phone calls, writing, and visits.

Community: Officials and workers in corrections systems provide important community involvement in restorative programs through their efforts to foster programs generally and to lead or participate in specific efforts. People in the community at large can be part of a prison restorative process in a number of ways, such as organizing and managing programs, appearing on speaker panels, or serving as small-group leaders or facilitators. The greatest opportunity for contribution may be service as role models just by their voluntary participation and the act of showing up.

The Process

Restorative programs that are part of transformative incarceration aim to replicate the restorative justice process to the extent feasible. They typically should include five elements: time, small-group meetings, dialogue, stories, and faith.

Time: Transformative incarceration aims for more than a quick fix or jailhouse religion. Instead, it aims for transformation of the participating offenders. Such change does not happen easily or quickly. Offenders, most of whom have little or no experience with thinking deeply about their lives, have to first develop trust in the process and those involved in it— which takes time. Then they need to come clean about their pasts, make discriminating judgments, address the moral and spiritual implications of different situations, and discern God's will for their future. All this requires a process that includes looking back at what has been, envisioning what can be, praying for guidance, developing plans, taking the first actions in the right direction, and sticking with it. Such steps need to play out over time rather than in a single or a few sessions.

Small-group meetings: Collaborative processes in transformative incarceration take their essence from restorative justice processes involving small groups of affected people meeting together to address their mutual problems. Similarly, most prison restorative programs include small-group meetings of stakeholders, which often provide a framework for other restorative activities. The most commonly used group processes are offender conferencing (or victim-offender dialogue), circle processes (peacemaking circles, healing circles, etc.), family group conferencing, and small-group dialogue. Although they will vary depending on prison rules, number of people available, and objectives of the program, etc., the small-group meetings tend to be characterized in the following ways. They

- include at least five but not more than ten or twelve stakeholders,
- include offenders, victims, and community members,
- are led by trained facilitators,
- are absolutely confidential,
- are conducted in safe and structured environments,
- involve the same participants over a period of time.

Dialogue: Dialogue occurs in the small-group meetings, between victims, offenders, and often family and community members. In dialogue, people suspend their assumptions and preconceived notions and avoid judgment in a free exploration of issues of mutual interest. Its purpose is not to persuade or win, but to exchange information, ideas, opinions, or feelings, explore concerns, gain new insights and understandings, learn more about the other persons, and/or hold people accountable. For this to happen in a prison setting where relationships often are characterized by mistrust and bad behavior, and unpopular information can beget violence, confidentiality must be a top priority.

Stories: Restorative actions, such as accepting responsibility for a crime, or addressing the cause of a criminal life, or making things right for what one has done, often are contrary to the prevailing prison culture and are difficult at best for those inside prison walls. Offenders may need to do them symbolically or in their hearts rather than in actuality. This can be encouraged by having participants' confidential dialogue include telling the stories of their lives and hearing stories of others. The stories help them think about the themes of their lives, see the good as well as the bad, acknowledge the bad, and take responsibility for it before a group of peers and victims of crime.

Faith: The role of faith in transformative incarceration was discussed in some detail earlier. Restorative programs have a strong focus on morality and relationships. Therefore, while avoiding preaching and Bible study, small-group facilitators can include biblical stories and teaching in small-group dialogue in ways that challenge participants to think about their moral underpinnings, their relationship with God and others, and their need to change.

What Should We Be Doing?

Transformative incarceration is comprised of rehabilitation, faith, and transformative elements involving a disparate group of stakeholders brought together for the primary purpose of helping offenders transform their entire beings and return to free society as successful, contributing members. Offenders are at the core, and they need help. Many others need to be involved, in many different ways. This raises the simple question, What should the church be doing to foster transformative incarceration among those who are imprisoned?

The call of discipleship provides the context for the answer. This call challenges the church and its members to accept the grace of God and live a life that imitates Jesus. Two examples from the New Testament provide guidance. The first is Mark 10:42-45, where Jesus explains that discipleship is characterized by humble and loving service:

Jesus summoned them and said to them, "You know that those who are recognized as rulers over the Gentiles lord it over them, and their great ones make their authority over them felt. But it shall not be so among you. Rather, whoever wishes to be great among you will be your servant; whoever wishes to be first among you will be the slave of all. For the Son of Man did not come to be served but to serve and to give his life as a ransom for many."

The writer of Hebrews is more specific. He writes to restore faith and to expound on the lordship, supremacy, and sufficiency of Jesus Christ. His final exhortation begins,

Let mutual love continue. Do not neglect hospitality, for through it some have unknowingly entertained angels. Be mindful of prisoners as if sharing their imprisonment, and of the ill-treated as of yourselves, for you also are in the body. (Heb 13:1-3)

These Scriptures seem to say that we are to serve incarcerated offenders by treating them as though we were in prison with them. Catholic teaching is even more specific. It defines *such* charitable actions as *"works of mercy . . . by which we come to the aid of our neighbor in his spiritual and bodily necessities."*[13] The works of mercy are gleaned from Scripture, and have been divided according to the needs of the body (corporal works) and the needs of the soul (spiritual works). The traditional enumeration of the corporal works of mercy includes feeding the hungry, giving drink to the thirsty, clothing the naked, sheltering the homeless, visiting the sick, liberating the captive, and burying the dead. The spiritual works of mercy include instructing the ignorant, counseling the doubtful, admonishing sinners, bearing wrongs patiently, forgiving offenses willingly, comforting the afflicted, and praying for the living and the dead.[14]

Such corporal and spiritual works, which seem designed to meet the needs of most incarcerated offenders and to foster the aims of transformative incarceration, provide a checklist of what the church and its members should be doing for people who are imprisoned. But we live in a complicated world, where the ability to accomplish such acts may be limited by lack of expertise or resources, political and security constraints, and other such factors. Thus, churches and individuals generally need to carefully

---

[13] *Catechism of the Catholic Church*, 2nd ed. (United States Catholic Conference—Libreria Editrice Vaticana, 1997), 2447.

[14] "Corporal and Spiritual Works of Mercy," The New Advent, www.newadvent.org /cathen/10198d.htm.

consider what they should and can do, and choose the best fit from among the many opportunities to serve in the areas of rehabilitation, ministry, and restorative programs. Following are some things to consider in making such choices:

Support Catholic principles: The document *Responsibility, Rehabilitation, and Restoration: A Catholic Perspective on Crime and Criminal Justice* (treated in chap. 7) reflects the views of US Catholic bishops on matters of criminal justice—views entirely consistent with transformative incarceration.[15] It concludes, among other things, that both victims and offenders are important human beings, and their lives and dignity should be protected and respected. Society should seek justice and not vengeance. Punishment should have a clear purpose: protecting society and rehabilitating those who violate the law. Thinking about what the church and individuals should be doing for the incarcerated starts with support of the principles outlined in this document.

Teach and preach in support of restorative justice and transformative incarceration: The general public and most parishioners are largely ignorant of criminal justice issues and problems of the incarcerated. They need to be educated as part of an effort to create a critical mass of public support for such principles. Priests, deacons, and lay teachers can do this by preaching and teaching support for the principles of restorative justice and transformative incarceration. Such education should inform the public as to the value of restorative and transformative practices and the church's support of them, and encourage parishioners to carry out important tasks in furtherance of broader objectives.

Teach and preach the Gospel to those who are or have been incarcerated: As noted, faith in God is an integral part of transformative incarceration. It establishes a moral code for individuals accustomed to the code of the streets, outlines a process for change, offers hope, and demonstrates love. Teaching and preaching faith in God not only enhances offenders' spiritual lives, but also leverages rehabilitation and restorative programs to make them more effective in helping offenders transform their entire beings.

Advocate for smart justice: Most of the issues facing incarcerated persons are ultimately controlled by legal and political decisions. Making positive changes in the system suggests the need for the US Conference of Catholic

---

[15] United States Conference of Catholic Bishops, *Responsibility, Rehabilitation, and Restoration: A Catholic Perspective on Crime and Criminal Justice* (Washington, DC: USCCB, 2000), www.usccb.org/issues-and-action/human-life-and-dignity/criminal-justice-restorative -justice/crime-and-criminal-justice.cfm.

Bishops and other organizations, orders, and associations to engage in continuing advocacy of various political entities. Efforts should support criminal justice reform, restorative justice, a more rational incarceration policy, improved conditions in prisons, and more government support for transformative incarceration practices.

Sponsor transformative programs: The church and individuals can do much to organize and implement programs that go beyond teaching the Gospel to incarcerated or recently released offenders. Programs can involve ministries by priests, deacons, and laypeople working within the existing prison system to conduct activities that fit within the rehabilitation, ministry, or restorative categories. Programs might include activities such as visiting one-on-one with the incarcerated, teaching pre-GED, ESL, or basic skills programs, tutoring, and providing other such services to the incarcerated. Programs outside facilities can involve individuals and small groups conducting activities such as praying daily for offenders, creating parish-based aftercare teams, assisting ex-offenders in their transition to the community, and otherwise supporting those who have been recently released.

Fully utilize lay parishioners: The majority of church members are laypeople, and they should be expected to strive to embody the teachings of Christ and to share the gifts of their faith, whether spiritual or corporal. Church leadership needs to challenge, empower, and use them effectively. They can serve the incarcerated just as they can others, by acting as everyday ministers of the faith and assisting with transformative incarceration activities. They might take part in some of the sacred rituals of the church by being altar servers, lectors, and lay ministers who help distribute the Holy Eucharist during prison Mass services. They can also work individually or through church or secular programs to help provide the corporal needs of the incarcerated.

Support other efforts: Many good and effective secular or faith-based prison ministries and programs exist outside the church. Providing funding and other support to such programs that are consistent with the beliefs, practices, and objectives of the church, and meet the needs and objectives of offenders and the prison system, may often be an effective vehicle for accomplishing church objectives.

Conclusion

Transformative incarceration aims to use a broad, systemic approach to transform the entire beings of incarcerated offenders. It involves a broad array of people and processes working together to foster a greater sense of community, safety, and peace for all. But helping the incarcerated in today's prisons is not easy. Prisons exist to deal with—punish—people convicted under a retributive system. Their main purpose is to incarcerate, not to transform. Most prison facilities have elements that directly conflict with transformative programs: an offender focus, the need for security, restrictive rules, authoritarian decision making, and separation from community. Security, safety, and related issues take priority over transformative activities and often lead to inefficiencies and frustration on the part of those pursuing them.

Thus, a sponsoring church or other organization and those volunteering for work in prisons need the resources, a commitment to high levels of performance, resilience to deal with challenges, and a love for the unlovable that will foster consistency and persistence in difficult circumstances over the long haul. Volunteers, and the organizations supporting them, need to have a burning desire to help others, and also believe deeply in the causes of the effort they are involved in. Before implementing a program, an organization should be sure it has the resources and commitment necessary to navigate the criminal justice system and see its effort through, and not become just another disappointment to offenders with lives filled with unfulfilled promises.

Review and Looking Forward

Editors

After one of his sister Marilyn's killers was given the death sentence, John Sage expected to experience closure. "Finally, I could move on," he said to himself. He recollects, however, that he did not feel any sense of resolution. "I was no better off with the murderers on death row. It wouldn't bring my sister back. In a way, I'd become a prisoner too—of my own rage and depression." As noted in the introduction, John responded to this sense of despair by going deeper into a journey of faith. "I prayed daily, hourly. I joined a Bible study group, and it was there I learned what Jesus said to God in the Gospel of John: 'You sent me and have loved them even as you have loved me.'" Sometime later, he received a call from a reporter: "Your sister's killer has an execution date in a few months. . . . Are you excited? . . . You can watch her get the lethal injection. Won't it feel good?" John found himself saying, "No . . . No, it wouldn't feel good." The reporter was shocked. John was equally astounded; his hatred and depression seemed a lifetime away. "At that point I knew I had reached the place Marilyn would want me to be—where I could give God all my pain and He would give me the love I needed to take its place."[16] John marks this experience as a turning point, which eventually leads him to the founding of Bridges To Life.

Bob and Kathy Connell were group leaders and otherwise active members in Bridges To Life. Their introduction to the organization and its programs came through their own suffering—an unimaginable loss. Four of their children, Allen, Laurel, Lee, and Sara Jo (ages nineteen to twelve), were killed by a drunk driver, who struck them head-on, high on alcohol and drugs, driving seventy miles per hour down a country road. In the larger vehicle (pickup vs. economy car), he survived without lasting injury. Bob and Kathy went through much soul-searching and prayer. They decided that the drunk driver could never right terrible wrongs that he had inflicted; "he could, however, ever so slightly, reduce the chances of the same thing happening to other children and other parents."[17]

As far as the drunk driver, he received a short prison sentence after the district attorney consulted with Bob and Kathy. They were concerned, not only that he had four children to support and to raise, but also that he be called to responsibility. The short prison sentence required that the offender "provide a form of restitution for ten years." This included

- accepting a ten-year probated sentence,
- attending AA meetings regularly,
- maintaining four crosses at the location of the wreck,
- carrying pictures of the children he killed in his wallet,
- doing public service work at the high school the children had attended,
- making anti-drunk driving presentations to various groups as requested by the Connells.[18]

The Connells worked hard to bring goodness out of evil (it is really hard to fathom). Kathy explained, "The pain was more than we could stand. But there came a point when we had to decide if we were going to die along with them or if we were going to join the living. . . . [Our involvement in Bridges To Life] started off as a way to try to persuade people not to drive drunk, and it turned out to be a way to heal ourselves."[19]

---

[16] John Sage, "A Deeper Surrender," *Guideposts Magazine* (August 2000), www.bridges tolife.org/images/stories/john%20sage%20guidepost%20article.pdf.

[17] Blackard, *Restoring Peace*, 158.

[18] Ibid.

[19] Pamela Colloff, "Faces of Forgiveness," *Texas Monthly* (August 2007), www.texas monthly.com/articles/faces-of-forgiveness/.

Questions for Discussion

1. In this chapter, Kirk Blackard offers a list of things we can do. The first is to support Catholic principles as outlined by the US bishops (see chap. 7). Kirk notes a few: the "lives and dignity" of both victims and offenders should be "protected and respected"; "punishment should have a clear purpose: protecting society and rehabilitating those who violate the law"; and we should seek justice, not vengeance. Consider how our parishes and churches can teach and live out these principles—not in relationship to criminal justice only, but also in how we teach the Gospel and live out our call of discipleship day to day.

2. Faith has an obvious role in restoring victims of crime and in calling offenders to responsibility and transformation. In his *Restoring Peace*, Kirk discusses a profound passage from C. S. Lewis's *The Screwtape Letters*. In the letters, Screwtape, a demon master and expert, is advising a demon novice, Wormwood. In this particular passage Screwtape is instructing Wormwood on how to deal with a person who is repentant. "The great thing," Screwtape warns, "is to prevent his doing anything. As long as he does not convert it into action, it does not matter how much he thinks about this new repentance. . . . The more often he feels without acting, the less he will be able ever to act, and, in the long run, the less he will be able to feel."[20]

   Consider this point in terms of Kirk's proposal for transformative incarceration. Consider how our current retributive system inclines both victim and offender to inaction and how a transformative approach opens up pathways of action.

---

[20] C. S. Lewis, *The Screwtape Letters* (New York: HarperCollins, 1942), 66, cited in Blackard, *Restoring Peace*, 156.

Chapter 12

Restorative Justice Programs

Editors

We rarely think about what we take for granted because it is so obvious to us. The obvious is the way things readily present themselves, the commonplace way we see and conceive them. Yet it is interesting to look at the roots of the word "obvious." The word comes from the Latin root *obviam*, which means something that is "in the way" (*ob-viam*). So what strikes us as evident and plain to see may actually obstruct our view, as far as our thinking and seeing. By preventing us from considering what we just take for granted as being right and true, it may block and restrict our thinking.

In our current society the obvious way of thinking about and responding to wrongdoing is in terms of retributive justice. We three editors have spent years teaching and raising children. Except for Vicki Schieber's role as the parent of a crime victim, our responding to wrongdoing has focused mainly on responding to our children's and students' behavior. As parents, teachers, members of communities, and citizens, when wrongdoing occurs, we tend to think of retributive justice in terms of punishment. And when wrongdoing is repeated and especially if it escalates, we begin to think of stronger punishments. Retributive punishment tends to be our default way of thinking about wrongdoing.

This chapter's overview of restorative programming makes us rethink the obvious. It pushes us to think critically about how we view wrongdoing, wrongdoers, those affected by them, and our responses and their impact. There are communities in our society and across the world for whom the restorative response is the obvious way that sets the norm. Think of the immediate response of the Nickel Mines Amish community described in chapter 9. There was no debate about their response; they lived the Amish way, and thus knew they'd focus on restorative healing for everyone affected by the horrifically grievous wrongdoing. Their response surprised many of us, for it was at odds with what we expected.

This chapter gives readers an introductory overview of the most common forms of restorative justice programming. Many people, except for those familiar with prisons, have never heard of such programming. Exposure to it pushes us to become aware of and examine many of our unexamined assumptions about prisons, offenders, and victims. Kelsey Kierce's and Teressa Schuetz's chapter ends with a consideration of something we all know about and have spent years in—our school system. It is not surprising that they, as teachers, highlight restorative justice programs being introduced in American schools. They make a good point about fostering restorative justice, arguing that a paradigm shift toward restorative justice will only take place if our children begin to think and live restoratively at an early age. Creative restorative programming is being developed by administrators and teachers throughout our country. And when people learn about such programming, they in turn begin to envision creative possibilities for their own schools. This ripple effect pushes administrators, teachers, parents, and students to think beyond what previously had been obvious.

One such administrator is Yetunde Reeves, who decided to think beyond the commonplace when she became the principal at Ballou High School in Washington, DC, in 2014. The restorative justice programming she developed was so successful in such a short time that it caught the attention of a *Washington Post* writer.[1] Yetunde knew well the fights and other disruptive behaviors that erupt in high schools. These behaviors usually result in the students being sent to the principal's office and suspended for a period of time determined by the severity of the disruption. It is assumed that disciplining students means taking a punitive response, and that punishing must fit the wrongdoing. Teachers, administrators, and parents often wonder what good comes from banishing a student from school for a period of time, especially when missing classes negatively impacts a student's academic work. One suspension tends to lead to others, and serial suspensions often lead to students dropping out of school, which in turn has further negative effects impacting their future

---

[1] This account draws on Joe Heim's article "Restorative justice, positive change," which was published in the August 23, 2016, issue of *The Washington Post*.

prospects. Disciplinary measures that repeatedly push students out of schools (suspensions and expulsions) have been shown to increase the likelihood of students entering the criminal justice system, resulting in our speaking today of a school-to-prison pipeline.[2]

Yetunde did not want to just continue what had become the norm. She courageously set out to design an alternative way of responding to wrongdoing by students. She designed a program that encouraged students both to accept responsibility for their behavior and its effects on the school community and to begin to behave in ways that contributed positively to the community.

Restorative justice programs often have rippling effects. Prior to coming to Ballou, Yetunde had worked for ten years in the Oakland, California, public school system, where she learned about restorative justice programming for schools. She thought a restorative justice approach had the potential to address particular problems Ballou High School faced. The school sought to reduce the number of student suspensions and to avoid the kind of punishment system that led to a further spiraling of disciplinary problems. The punitive system was clearly not working, especially because it failed to address the contributing sources and root causes of problems. Yetunde was determined not to continue an ineffective, purely punitive disciplinary program. She set to work to build a restorative approach to discipline. The roots of the word "discipline" are interesting. The Middle English root is mortification by scourging, suggesting a purely punitive understanding. But the Latin root of *disciplina* ties discipline to knowledge and understanding. Our term *disciple* is associated with the latter understanding. Could discipline play a role in educating students and helping them to succeed?

The Ballou restorative program quickly began to produce positive results, showing it was effective in addressing problems. In the two years prior to Yetunde becoming principal, there were 1,018 suspensions/expulsions, which for a school of 816 students, meant that there were 125 suspensions per 100 students. Within two years of introducing the new restorative program, she saw the suspensions drop to 90 per 100 students and then to 51 per 100 students. The restorative justice programming was producing good results, and she is confident it will continue to bear better and better results.

[2] There are numerous studies of the impact of suspensions. Some of them are referenced in Advancement Project, *Test, Punish, and Push Out* (March 2010), http://www.umojacorporation.org/files/7213/5403/0728/Test_Punish_and_Push_Out_-_Advancement_Project_2010.pdf.

Donnell Honesty went through the Ballou restorative mediation process when he was involved in a fight with another student in the school cafeteria. As time passed, he could not even recall how and why the fight suddenly erupted. Rather than suspending the students in a way that would take a toll on their studies, Yetunde convened the students, their parents, and members of the school's restorative team for a mediation process, which resulted in the students accepting responsibility for their behavior, apologizing to each other and all the persons affected by their action, and then working to renew in positive ways their commitment to the school community. The process brought forth a number of positive things. It set up conversations that helped everyone understand what was going on with these students that had resulted in their disruptive behavior. It created a safe space in which the students could reflect on what they did, how it disrupted the activities of teachers and fellow students, and how they could act differently in the future. Very importantly, it also created supportive relationships among participants that would have an impact on the students' subsequent behaviors. Commenting on another student's situation, Yetunde explained, "Sending someone home for 10, 15, 20 days does not necessarily mean they are going to own the behavior, and actually do something different the next time around. So our goal is that our students will begin to accept responsibility for any wrongdoing, own it and move forward in a very different way."[3]

Yetunde stresses that these dialogues help students to understand the importance of their developing patience and a sense of responsibility for their behavior, and of being apologetic and capable of communicating with others. They also help students understand the meaning and goal of the punishments they are given, rather than just resenting them. Through the dialogues, students come to understand what they likely would not have understood if they had been just banished from the school for a period. The mediation process brought Donnell to understand why his behavior was harmful to himself and others and how disruptive it was to learning, the focus of the school community. Through it he began to explore for himself alternative ways of addressing conflicts so as to avoid the harm they cause. His restorative justice process did not end with the mediation sessions but continued with follow-up interactions through the program. The school recognizes that the behavior of teenagers plays a major role in shaping their adult lives. This was very true in Donnell's case. By the age of eighteen, he had gotten involved in fights at previous schools and already

---

[3] Matt Ackland, "Video shows Ballou High School student threatening his substitute teacher" (May 5, 2016), http://www.fox5dc.com/news/137478837-story.

had been arrested. The restorative justice programming made possible a timely intervention that had a positive effect on his development.

Andre Ford, Ballou's assistant dean of students, sees the effects of Ballou's restorative justice programming. He sees student participants applying what they learned to other encounters that might have gone differently and gotten them into more trouble. With suspensions, administrators at times don't know the out-of-school situation these students may face while suspended. For this reason he prefers in-school interventions that can be shaped in positive ways, attentive to the students' situations. Most importantly, the programming conveys to students a clear message: "We have not given up on you." For many kids this is the most important message they can hear. They know the school believes in their potential to do something more positive as they move forward. Yetunde Reeves views her school in terms of a network of relationships, and her "goal is that every kid feels welcomed and loved in the building. And even if they make a horrible mistake, that we welcome them back with open arms."[4] So far this message seems to be getting through. Embeddedness in relationships is at the center of each of the programs discussed in the chapter. Since restorative justice has its foundation in relationships, its focus always remains repairing relations when harm has been done to persons.

Models of Restorative Justice

Kelsey Kierce and Teressa Schuetz

"If crime is injury, what is justice?"[5] Members of our society believe that when a crime is committed, a wrong has been done. This wrong must be addressed in some way, and so we turn to the demands of justice. The overarching approach to criminal justice in our society is retributive. Retributive justice operates on the assumption that crime is a wrong done against the state by an offender who is found guilty of breaking the law. It is then the job of justice, as administered by officials of the state, to bring consequences to bear on the offender according to legal procedures set by the law. The problem with this approach lies not in viewing crime as a wrong done, but in acting as if the wrong was done to the state, and not to persons. Here is where restorative justice changes the fundamental way

---

[4] Heim, "Restorative justice, positive change."

[5] Howard Zehr, *Changing Lenses: Restorative Justice for Our Times* (Harrisonburg, VA: Herald Press, 2015), 188.

in which we view crime. As Howard Zehr emphasizes, restorative justice sees crime fundamentally as a violation of people and relationships. With this understanding of crime comes a different understanding of justice, embedded in a restorative response to crime:

> Instead of defining justice as retribution, we will define justice as restoration. If crime is injury, justice will repair injuries and promote healing. Acts of restoration—not further harm—will counterbalance the harm of crime. We cannot guarantee full recovery, of course, but true justice would aim to provide a context in which the process can begin.[6]

If justice is restoration, then the current state of our criminal justice system fails to enact true justice. Retribution is not restoration. Zehr's definition of justice sets the context in which restorative justice programs are developed. When looking at different programs addressing crime, one way to determine if they are operating according to restorative principles and practices is to compare how their missions align with this definition of justice. Do they recognize crime as an offense against persons? Do they attempt to repair injuries? Do they promote healing? If a program does these three things, it most likely is a restorative program. Most restorative justice programs involve all those who have been affected by the harm in question and are directed toward the goal of making things right. Programs that meet this definition can take many forms: victim-offender conferences, family group conferences and circles. Reentry programs can also be viewed as falling under restorative justice. Because of the many different types of programs that are spoken of as being restorative, it is helpful to reference Zehr's definition in determining whether in fact the programs in question align with that definition.

This chapter gives an overview of three different types of restorative justice programs. In writing it, we welcomed the opportunity to learn about and interview people in versions of these programs. We will first focus on accounts and examples of restorative conferences, circles, and reentry programs. These three types of restorative justice practices differ in their goals, but all seek to repair harm, restore relationships, and promote healing. Restorative justice programming in our country developed within the context of our criminal justice system but has since been introduced into school systems across the country. For this reason, this chapter will also consider restorative justice programming in schools. These programs

---

[6] Ibid.

are important since they assist in preventing harmful behaviors from continuing and formatively model for children and adolescents a restorative view of justice at a young age. After detailing these programs, the end of this chapter will suggest ways in which readers can begin or extend their involvement in a restorative justice approach to wrongdoing. It is hoped that this overview of programming will help readers better understand the possibilities of restorative justice programming and ways in which they can promote it in their own communities.

Victim-Offender Conferencing

Victim-offender conferencing is traced to Mennonite practices in Kitchener, Ontario, and Elkhart, Indiana, in the 1970s. Victim-offender conferencing brings together the victim and offender of a crime in a face-to-face meeting. Other members of the community, including family and friends, may be involved in this meeting. A trained facilitator leads the meeting. This face-to-face meeting allows victims to share their stories and express the ways in which they were harmed by the crime. It also gives offenders the opportunity to talk about their actions and to answer questions the victims have that are not typically addressed in the legal process. The meeting gives offenders the opportunity to take responsibility for the crime they committed and recognize the harmful effect their action had on the victim. A different version, referenced in Justice Janine Geske's chapter, brings offenders to meet with other victims who suffered crimes similar to the one they committed.

The process for victim-offender conferencing programs typically begins with a referral, perhaps by a judge, police officer, or the victim. All participants freely elect to participate in the meeting. A trained facilitator is then assigned to the case and has initial, separate meetings with the victim and the offender. These initial meetings explain the process, allow the participants to tell their story to the facilitator, and help prepare them for the victim-offender meeting. Support people, such as family members and friends, may be selected by each party to attend the meeting. At the conference, each party is given the opportunity to share their experience of the crime and how it impacted their lives. In most cases, a restitution agreement is made in an attempt to address and repair the harms done.[7]

---

[7] Howard Zehr and Allan MacRae, *The Big Book of Restorative Justice* (New York: Good Books, 2015), 126–28.

Victim-offender conferencing programs may vary to an extent depending on the organization that facilitates them.

The Victim-Offender Reconciliation program in Kitchener played an important role in shaping this form of restorative justice programming. This approach is traceable to the creative thinking of Mark Yantzi, a parole officer in the community who began to envision the possibility of offenders and victims interacting in ways that might lead to reconciliation and reparation.[8] Following a 1974 night of vandalism by intoxicated teenagers in the small town of Elmira, the teens pled guilty and awaited court sentencing. Mark was responsible for preparing their presentencing report for the judge. He began to mull over the usual functioning of the judicial system and to envision an alternative approach, focused on having these teens personally encounter the victims of their offenses.

This was influenced by his having volunteered for a year at a program directed by the Mennonite Central Committee (MCC), which had become involved in the local criminal justice system. Mark mentioned his idea to fellow committee members who were supportive, but never thought the presiding judge would be open to his recommendation. Dave Worth, another committee member, challenged him to move on his idea. When submitting his presentence report, Mark included a letter addressed to Judge Gordon McConnell, explaining his view that these young men might benefit from direct interactions with their victims.

On the sentencing day, the judge met with Mark and Dave in his chambers, and after listening to their plan of how they would proceed if the judge agreed, he explained that he did not think it was possible for him to ask the offenders to meet with the persons they had vandalized. But then, to everyone's utter surprise, at the sentencing that same day, the judge ordered a one-month remand so as to allow the two convicted offenders, accompanied by probation officer Mark and an MCC representative, to begin face-to-face meetings with their victims, on the basis of which damages would be calculated and reported. On the basis of this report, the judge specified a fine for their offenses, the length of their probation, and the restitution they would have to pay to each victim within a set period of time. Within three months, the teenagers had visited all the victims and paid them the required amount for their loss.

One of the offenders spoke of following through with the meetings and restitution as a way of maintaining his self-respect and his not having to

---

[8] Dean E. Peachey, "The Kitchener Experiment," in *Restorative Justice Reader*, ed. G. Johnstone, 178 ff. (Cullompton, Devon, UK: Willan, 2003).

look over his shoulder all the time because of what he had done. Victims' responses were varied, with some expressing their not wanting the teens to go to jail, others acknowledging that they had not been caught doing their own wrong actions in their youth, and some feeling surprised when they received the restitution, which prompted them to use the funds to do something to help others. Mark was clearly right in thinking this alternative approach might bear positive results. Mark and other MCC members went on to further refine the process they had created, eventually formulating what came to be called the Victim/Offender Reconciliation Project (VORP). Dean Peachey, who chronicles the project, emphasizes,

> Yantzi and Worth began to talk about how the state had "stolen" conflicts away from individuals and developed a monopoly on the criminal justice process. The innovators became reformers as they began to envision a fundamentally different approach to justice—one that placed the disputing parties at centre stage and defined justice primarily as psychological and material restoration rather than as retribution.[9]

Their efforts also led to other programs, such as MCC's Victim/Offender Services. Little did Mark Yantzi and Dave Worth know that in the 1970s such conferencing models were being shaped in other communities in Canada and the United States, based on the felt need to change the way of rectifying wrongs that have been done by persons to other persons. Janine Geske's chapter provides up-close examples of local conferencing practices used in a specific prison and community. The 1974 Kitchener experiment inspired ongoing creative variations of victim-offender conferencing in local communities that still continues decades later.

The Office of Victim Advocate of Pennsylvania is an example of an organization that facilitates such victim-offender conferencing. This victim-offender dialogue program began in 1998 after many victims contacted the office due to their interest in meeting with their offenders. The simply stated goal of this program is to address the articulated needs of the victims, that is, what the victims are looking for.[10] This mediation offers them the opportunity to ask questions about the crimes and to tell the offenders how it affected their lives.[11] It can also empower the victims by

---

[9] Ibid., 181.
[10] Karen Laird, personal interview (March 16, 2016).
[11] Jennifer R. Storm, "Dialogue Program for Victims of Violent Crime," Office of the Victim Advocate (2014), http://www.ova.pa.gov/Documents/Dialogue%20English.pdf.

giving them a sense of holding the offender directly accountable. This mediation can also be beneficial for offenders because it may bring them to accept responsibility and understand the ways in which their crime affected real persons. This mediation is always victim initiated, and the offender's participation is voluntary. The offender's participation has no effect on his or her institutional or parole status.

There is extensive prep work done prior to the mediation. Trained volunteer facilitators meet with both parties individually to prepare them for the face-to-face meeting, and these same facilitators provide follow-up after the face-to-face meeting. The mediation is held in the correctional institution that houses the offender or, if the offender is on parole, in a safe and private setting in the local community. At any point, either party can end or suspend the process. If the victim does not want to meet face-to-face, letter writing is another available option.[12] This program has been successful largely because it is voluntary on both sides; all participating parties want this mediation to occur.[13]

Conferencing Circles

Conferencing circles have their roots in indigenous traditions. Many draw on the Native American tradition of using a talking piece in the context of dialogue. The talking piece, which ensures that all voices are heard, is passed from person to person in the circle. Each person in a conferencing circle shares his or her story with the group; the reasoning underlying this process is that stories unite people through their affirming of a common humanity.[14] These conferencing circles are most commonly referred to as Peacemaking Circles. They are used in a wide variety of contexts: criminal justice systems, neighborhoods, workplaces, and schools. Peacemaking circles gather persons to discuss issues arising in their local community. These circles can have many different goals, including the promotion of understanding, healing, appropriate sentencing, support, conflict resolution, and reintegration into the community.[15]

While conferencing circles can have different specific goals, most share a common process. Traditional conferencing circles begin with a ceremony

---

[12] Ibid.
[13] Laird, personal interview.
[14] Zehr and MacRae, *The Big Book of Restorative Justice*, 286.
[15] Ibid., 296.

to set the tone and purpose of the circle. There is a facilitator for each circle who assures that each member of the group shares honestly and is respected. The facilitator keeps the conversation going by providing questions and suggested topics to be discussed. These circles feature consensus decision-making, meaning that participants come to accept and support the implementation of the decision that is made through the process.[16] Longmont Community Justice Partnership and Precious Blood Ministry of Reconciliation are two organizations that offer programs following a conferencing circle model.

Longmont Community Justice Partnership (LCJP) is a nonprofit organization in Longmont, Colorado, that provides restorative justice services to the local community and schools. In designing its programming, it focuses on the following guiding principles of restorative justice: (1) respecting all participants, as evidenced in respectful listening; (2) accepting responsibility for the harm done to persons; (3) repairing the harm as far as is possible; (4) restoring damaged relationships; and (5) reintegrating persons into the community. The Partnership seeks to create a safe community by bringing together persons in the local community who have been affected by conflict and crime so that they can be heard and their needs addressed. One of the programs through which it does this is called Community Restorative Justice, a program that facilitates conferencing circles or what they call community group conferences. Trained volunteer facilitators lead these programs. There are a select number of community members present who have been trained in the circle process and represent the voice of the Longmont Community in the conference. The crime victims can attend if they choose to participate. Some opt to participate, some choose to write a statement to be shared, and others choose not to be included in the conference. However, the conference only occurs if the victims approve it and if the offenders are ready to take responsibility for their offenses. Police officers decide if these requirements have been met.[17]

A conference occurs if the police determine that a restorative justice approach is an appropriate avenue for both the victim and the offender. The police check with the crime victim to determine if the victim is willing to participate. Then, if the offender is willing to take responsibility, the police refer the offender to this program. This is done before a charge is filed, and is done in place of going to court.[18] Most of the referred cases

---

[16] Ibid., 294–95.
[17] Jessica Goldberg, personal interview (February 17, 2016).
[18] Ibid.

would involve misdemeanor charges; however, felony-level offenses are also considered. These conferences are held so that all those present work together to arrive at what the offender can do to repair the harm. A contract is then developed. The police, community members, victims, offender, and their support people sign off on this contract. If the offender completes the contract, then he or she will not be summoned to court or serve jail time. LCJP stresses that all circle participants have an equal voice; the community or the offender do not function as authorities in the meeting.[19] The process is about coming together so that each participant can be heard and a resolution can be agreed upon with the aim of repairing the harm.

Precious Blood Ministry of Reconciliation (PBMR) is a center housed in Chicago that also offers a form of conferencing circles to its community. Missionaries of the Precious Blood and sisters from Precious Blood communities founded the center in 2000. PBMR seeks to provide programs that work to promote healing and reconciliation for those impacted by violent actions in the community and in the church.[20] Restorative justice is the very essence of what PBMR is and what its program does. PBMR seeks to create a space of hospitality and welcome, where relationships and trust can be built so that members of the community can be accompanied on their journey of healing.[21]

One of the ways that PBMR accomplishes this goal is through peacemaking circles. These circles are utilized whenever possible within the center and the community. Members of the PBMR staff who have been trained in facilitating peacemaking circles lead the circles. PBMR has used peacemaking circles to handle problems within the center (such as incidences of theft), to facilitate support and accountability for youth in the juvenile justice system, and to integrate suspended students back into the local high school.[22] PBMR also offers circle training sessions for community members that are hosted monthly in collaboration with the Community Justice for Youth Institute. This training has been given to lawyers, youth outreach staff members, probation officers, as well as various other community members. PBMR is a ministry that mediates between offenders and victims, and, through conferencing circles and training members of

---

[19] Ibid.

[20] Precious Blood Ministry of Reconciliation, "Ministries," http://www.pbmr.org /ministries/.

[21] Fr. Dave Kelly, personal interview (June 10, 2015).

[22] PBMR, "Restorative Justice," http://www.pbmr.org/ministries/restorative-justice -community/.

the community, assists in bringing all parties together to repair harms in a variety of settings.

Reentry Programming

Reentry programs are programs designed to help reintegrate offenders into society, given the complexities that arise on the journey from prison to the very different world of mainstream society. Offenders are often released from prison with no place to live, nothing to eat or drink, no possessions, and no way of working to meet their basic physical needs. On top of this, they often have lost contact with the people they knew in their pre-prison days and lack the social skills and resources needed to form new relationships or renew old ones in order to meet their basic social and emotional needs. Because many of their needs have been ignored or met in unhealthy ways during their stays in prison, men and women often emerge from prison more broken than before they entered. Even the most hopeful offenders, who genuinely intend to turn their lives around, often find, upon release, that the odds are stacked against them and that their basic survival is the most daunting challenge imaginable. For many, the overwhelming amount of unknowns and uncertainties resulting from freedom make the familiar regimented world of prison seem at times more inviting.

Given the fact that many criminals need to relearn the most basic skills needed for functioning in society, reentry programs are crucial for helping them to reenter society and avoid reentering the criminal justice system. Thus, reentry programs are at once restorative and preventative. Because they tend to focus less on the relationships and persons directly harmed by crime and more on the future of the offenders and their relationship with society, reentry programs generally fall on the less restorative end of the continuum proposed by Howard Zehr. But they are clearly important to furthering the overarching goal of restoration, and thus play a key role in restorative justice. Reentry programs can take many forms. However, at the heart of all truly restorative reentry programs is the hope for a fresh start and new life for the person who has been convicted of a crime. In this sense restorative justice has the power to be truly transformative, as has been emphasized in previous chapters. Reentry programs affirm and emphasize that persons who have committed crimes retain their dignity and worth as both individuals and members of the broader community and retain their capacity for renewal and transformation. Far too often our criminal justice program gives up on persons who are seen as broken beyond repair and not worthy of communal support and encouragement. Such attitudes contribute to the defeat and neglect of persons, whereas restorative justice offers hope and support for a new beginning.

One example of a reentry program is the Welcome Home Reentry Program of Maryland, which has locations in Montgomery County, Prince George's County, and Charles County.[23] The mission of this reentry program is to provide recently released offenders with a personal mentor who helps them with developing and exercising the basic skills needed to live in society, provides them with information about relevant community resources, and motivates them to become the best versions of themselves possible. The program was designed to reduce the recidivism rate within the member counties by providing released criminals with the necessary support they need for reintegration. Upon release from prison, program participants are matched with individual mentors who commit to them for at least one year (although many stay in touch with their mentees well beyond this minimum). The mentors and mentees meet for at least one hour per week. The mentors are trained to teach their mentees basic skills such as how to use the metro, open a bank account, save money, and access medical, rehabilitative, and mental health services. In addition, many mentors assist their mentees with finishing their education and with the application and interview process for jobs.[24]

Fr. Michael Bryant, the founder of the Welcome Home Reentry Program, calls attention to the fact that many participants who enter these programs are "institutionalized," meaning they have become dependent on the prison system for meeting their basic needs. Given the length of their prison sentences, for many it is often extremely difficult upon release to cope with all the changes that have taken place while they have been in prison, and many lack the resources needed to survive in such a changed world. Faced with the overwhelming task of such adaptation and survival, many of these offenders, who have already struggled with drug and/or alcohol abuse, look to these substances as a means of escape from their situation. Lacking support as they face these challenges on their own, the majority of newly released criminals reenter the prison system within thirty days of their release.[25] The Welcome Home Reentry Program is designed to address these challenges in ways that enhance the possibility of these individuals adjusting to and functioning well upon their reentry into the community.

---

[23] Welcome Home Reentry Program, Catholic Charities, Archdiocese of Washington, https://www.catholiccharitiesdc.org/welcomehome.

[24] Michael Bryant, personal interview (February 11, 2016).

[25] Ibid.

Hawai'i Friends of Restorative Justice is a nonprofit organization that works to improve the criminal justice system.[26] This organization offers Huikahi Restorative Circles, which are used in the reentry process, showing that various restorative justice models can overlap. These circles apply restorative justice and solution-focused brief therapy principles and practices, which make them goal-oriented and strength-based. The main purpose of these circles is to give individuals who are preparing to leave prison the opportunity to address their needs for transitioning successfully into the community. Such preparedness is seen as enhancing their chances for a positive reentry. The needs addressed through the circle include making amends for harms suffered by their loved ones, reconciliation, housing, transportation, continued learning, emotional and physical health, and any other needs identified by the imprisoned individuals.[27]

The prison staff participates in this process, as well as the loved ones of the imprisoned persons. There is a facilitator to guide the process, but the imprisoned persons ultimately drive the restorative process. The circle begins in a meaningful way designed to build within persons a sense of confidence and strength in meeting their reentry challenges. Participants then share what strengths they believe the imprisoned persons have. In the circle, these persons then relate their proudest accomplishments since being in prison, and identify their future goals to ensure that the future will be different from the past. Their reentry needs are explored and ways of addressing them are considered. Time is also allotted to discussing how their loved ones were harmed by their past behavior, and what can be done to repair this harm.[28] Written plans with concrete steps, timelines for reentry, and ways of addressing the discussed needs are prepared following the circle and are subsequently given to the circle participants. This process shows the importance of having a concrete plan of action in place before release so that reintegration is structured in ways that render it more successful. Hawai'i Friends of Restorative Justice has conducted 134 circles with 575 participants and has found that program participants measure increased optimism and stronger social bonds after having completed the

---

[26] Hawai'i Friends of Restorative Justice, http://hawaiifriends.org/.

[27] Lorenn Walker, "Modified Restorative Circles: A Reintegration Group Planning Process That Promotes Desistance," *Contemporary Justice Review* 12, no. 4 (December 2009): 419–31.

[28] Zehr, Walker, and Ian Crabbe, "Re-Entry Planning Circles: A Restorative and Solution-Focused Approach For Incarcerated Individuals and Their Loved Ones," webinar, Zehr Institute for Restorative Justice (October 14, 2015), http://zehr-institute.org /webinar/re-entry-planning-circles/.

circle. Preliminary research on the outcomes of the program indicate that these reentry circles help reduce recidivism.[29]

Shifting Society toward Restorative Justice

The three models of restorative justice detailed in this chapter are crucial to the reform of the criminal justice system. The goals of these programs are pivotal in creating a criminal justice system that addresses harms done to persons while respecting the human dignity of all those involved: victims, offenders, and community members. It is important to note that all the programs discussed thus far are reactive, in that they are utilized in response to crimes that have already been committed. Recognizing the reality of crime within our society, these programs have been put into place to address and mitigate the harmful consequences of crimes in the most restorative ways. However, the goal of society as a whole should be to reduce the need for such reactive measures, by addressing the societal factors that contribute to crime and reducing crime rates as much as possible. The only way to accomplish this goal is to invest in preventative measures within society.

Our society has come to recognize that the criminal justice system is in desperate need of reform and that a significant dimension of this rests on how we, as members of society, view and respond to crimes and offenders. However, a holistic societal shift toward restorative justice can only take place if there is a fundamental shift in the way we view and teach justice, beginning with the building blocks of society: our schools. By fostering a restorative justice approach within our schools, educators can begin to develop within students a restorative justice mind-set that accustoms them to constructive conflict resolution strategies and teaches them to view all members of the community as valued and redeemable. It is only through such a paradigm shift, focusing on the youngest members of our society and the future leaders of our communities and country, that a foundation can be built that creatively furthers the application of restorative justice principles and the development of restorative justice initiatives, which in turn build hope for the future.

While restorative justice practices began in response to the need for reform in the criminal justice system, school-based reform efforts based on

---

[29] Walker, "Modified Restorative Circles."

restorative justice models have begun to emerge in relatively concentrated pockets throughout the country. These efforts have been in response to the growing evidence of a school-to-prison pipeline, which reveals that disciplinary problems in school, coupled with a lack of resources and support systems, lead to offenses of increased severity as students enter adulthood with increasing risk of entering the criminal justice system. The school-to-prison pipeline shows a clear correlation between exclusionary (aka solely punitive) disciplinary practices and incarceration. In fact, students who are suspended from school are three times more likely to drop out of high school, and there is a correlation between drop-out rates and crime.[30] A purely retributive, rather than a restorative, approach to disciplinary offenses in our school system mirrors the approach we currently see in our criminal justice system. This realization reveals the depths of our society's deeply troubling retributive tendencies as well as our own need for self-reflection as to how we can counteract these tendencies in practical ways. Perhaps the most practical way we can do this is by providing our children with explicit instruction in restorative practices and fostering educational contexts in which they can be applied. This rationale is the basis of the following school-based restorative justice initiatives, which seek to change society's lens of justice one student and potential leader at a time.

One example of a school-based initiative is the work of Restorative Justice for Oakland Youth (RJOY). The initiative's focus is on responding to student conflicts in restorative rather than punitive ways and taking preventative measures to teach young adults how to channel their frustration and anger into productive conversations in safe spaces. The goal of their projects is to stop the cycle of violence, aggression, and incarceration before it begins and to teach students who have been in trouble in school or with the law how to channel their frustration, pain, and anger into productive conversations and personal growth. In this way, they can catalyze the disruption of the school-to-prison pipeline. RJOY staff members provide training to school personnel so that the schools in the Oakland School District have the skills needed to incorporate restorative principles and practices into their schools every day.[31]

The founder of RJOY, Fania Davis, began the initiative as a result of her realization that, much like the criminal justice system, exclusionary

---

[30] Fania Davis, "Discipline With Dignity: Oakland Classrooms Try Healing Instead of Punishment," *Yes! Magazine* (March 7, 2014), www.truth-out.org/news/item/22315 -discipline-with-dignity-oakland-classrooms-try-healing-instead-of-punishment.

[31] Jodie Geddes, personal interview (August 12, 2016).

disciplinary measures affect minority students at disproportionate rates.[32] These exclusionary measures take students who are seen as disrupting the cohesion of the classroom and put them on the streets, where they are more likely to get involved in serious criminal activity. Thus, these measures are perpetuating discrimination and oppression of minority students, rather than serving the purpose of schools, which is to assist *all* students in personal growth and provide them with the knowledge and skills they will need in life. In reality, exclusionary measures are alienating, detrimental, and ineffective, while restorative practices are integrating, productive, and effective.

RJOY, which has been a leader in the whole-systems approach to shifting school cultures toward restorative justice, has shown the very real benefits of a restorative approach to education. After only one year, 40 percent fewer African American students in the Oakland Unified School District were suspended for disruption/willful defiance. In schools that implemented restorative justice, there was a 24 percent decrease in absenteeism. This already impressive statistic becomes even more impressive when we consider that the schools in the area that are not implementing restorative justice saw a 62 percent increase in chronic absenteeism. In addition, a significant amount of staff members reported significant improvements to the school community, showing a real climate shift.[33]

One measure that the Oakland Unified School District has taken is its implementation of conferencing circles. Their circle model grew out of the concept of Circles of Support and Accountability (COSAs), which were originally used for sex offenders. However, currently they use primarily peer conferencing circles, which do not address a specific harm or predetermined topic for discussion. Rather, these peer conferencing circles are safe spaces for students to talk about their feelings, to share whatever is on their minds, to support each other, and to experience deep human connections. These circles serve a variety of purposes, depending on where they are used because RJOY currently trains staff at many different schools in the Oakland Unified School District. Some of these schools use circles as a way of instilling restorative principles in their students and building community, while some of them use these circles in response to specific harms or with students who have already entered the juvenile justice system. In the case of a circle that is practiced in response to a specific harm or break-

---

[32] Davis, "Discipline With Dignity."

[33] Oakland Unified School District, *Restorative Justice in Oakland Schools Implementation and Impacts* (September 2014), http://www.rjtica.org/wp-content/uploads/2015/04/OUSD-RJ-Report-full.pdf.

ing of the law, the restorative circle may also include other related persons, such as a trained facilitator, a person victimized by a similar action, family members, and appropriate members of the community (RJOY).

Northern Virginia Mediation Service (NVMS) has partnered with Fairfax County Public Schools to offer restorative justice conferences when specific disciplinary matters or ongoing conflicts occur. The school system contacts Bill Casey, an employee at NVMS, when there is a case. A person is then identified who has been trained to facilitate the conference or to mentor a school employee who will facilitate the conference. This conference is offered in lieu of other disciplinary actions. At most, a one-day suspension may occur prior to the conference to give the students a chance to cool off. After the case has been processed, a preconference is held separately with each party. The aim is to find out if the students have accepted sufficient responsibility for what they did, are willing to acknowledge it, and agree to participate in the conference with the aim of repairing the harm and restoring the relationship.[34]

When both parties are deemed ready, a joint conference occurs. A conversation is held about what happened during the conflict, what the consequences of that conflict were, and what opportunities there are to make appropriate repairs and restore the relationship. A school representative is present at this conference to speak on behalf of the school. Typically, the parties involved then generate a written agreement to repair any harm that has occurred. This might include the offer and acceptance of apologies, any restitution if damage had been done to property, and commitments to take action against triggers that may lead to subsequent similar episodes.[35]

One example of a broader school-based initiative is the Illinois Balanced and Restorative Justice Project.[36] The staff of this project does not provide direct services to students, but rather collaborates with school districts within Illinois to provide training to school personnel (including superintendents, teachers, and social workers) about restorative practices to be implemented within their school systems. The staff provides training in three types of restorative practices: circles, conferencing, and peer juries.[37] Sara Balgoyen, the executive director of the IBARJ Project, noted that each school district takes its own approach, but that all school districts in Illinois are now required to have programming in place to reduce the number of exclusionary disciplinary measures (i.e., suspensions and expulsions)

[34] Bill Casey, personal interview (June 4, 2015).
[35] Ibid.
[36] Illinois Balanced and Restorative Justice, http://www.ibarj.org/.
[37] Sara Balgoyen, personal interview (June 22, 2016).

due to Senate Bill 100, legislation passed in 2015.[38] With school districts now searching for alternative solutions to punitive discipline in order to be compliant with this new law, some have turned to using restorative practices in schools (although they are not required to use restorative practices) and are enlisting the help of the IBARJ Project. While this is certainly a step in the right direction, it may cause us to wonder why any school district in Illinois would *not* explore the implementation of restorative practices, given that all school districts now are required to reexamine their disciplinary measures.

Sara Balgoyen offered some insight into a few of the many challenges facing restorative justice efforts. She noted that, unfortunately, many people do not take restorative justice efforts seriously, precisely because funds for such programming are absent from budgets and such an approach has not been officially mandated by the government. She also interestingly noted that many people do not view working in the field of restorative justice as an official profession, which means that many of the efforts are run by volunteers. There are also many logistical barriers that make it hard for many social programs to remain open, let alone flourish. For example, in the case of the IBARJ Project, because at the time of our interview Illinois was at a financial impasse with no budget in place, social programs were severely underfunded. With only two paid staff members, the IBARJ Project is a very small project and, unfortunately, is not the only initiative mentioned in this chapter that is struggling to stay afloat. The challenge posed by such current lack of funding was voiced in almost every interview we conducted regarding restorative justice programming in schools. As Sara Balgoyen poignantly remarked, "It is clear to most people, including government officials, that restorative justice is the direction we should go, but states are not showing it through their funding." So our challenge becomes apparent: How do we, the people, assume an active role in changing the paradigm of justice from a solely retributive lens to a more restorative lens and resetting the understanding and practice of justice?

The Needed Call to Action

It would be difficult to identify one person working in or out of the criminal justice system who would not concede that the system, as it cur-

---

[38] Balgoyen, "Restorative Justice in Schools," Illinois Balanced and Restorative Justice, www.ibarj.org/schools.asp.

rently stands, is broken. Our "tough on crime" approach that many citizens so highly praise is not working. Clearly, with the highest rate of incarceration in the world, a serious overrepresentation of minority people in our system, a highly problematic recidivism rate, and a costly system that drains other needed social services, there needs to be a change. By no means is that to say that our society should get rid of prisons altogether or let offenders off easy without holding them accountable for their offenses. In fact, restorative justice recognizes that punishment may play a role within a restorative justice system. However, maintaining a form of justice based solely on retribution, with no regard for the restoration of the persons affected by crime (victims, offenders, and the community), is at best insufficient and at worst harmful to society.

As young children, we are taught that "two wrongs do not make a right." However, many persons have come to believe that the right and necessary way to respond to a harm is to inflict harm on the person who caused the harm. This mind-set risks both multiplying the amount of harm done to persons and failing to take effective measures to address the effects and sources of such harm-doing. Tim Wolfe argues persuasively in chapter 3 that we need to shift from being "tough on crime" to being "smart on crime," and that our society can no longer sustain the debilitating costs of our current criminal justice system.

The Catholic approach to criminal justice articulated by the US bishops, as outlined by William Collinge in chapter 7, calls for a holistic and comprehensive response to crime, grounded in Christian respect for the worth of each and every person. Such an account refuses to meet harm with more harm. A Catholic approach to crime meets harm with love—the love modeled by Christ in response to human wrongdoing. The Catholic approach to crime, grounded in Christian love, is naturally directed toward restoration and redemption and provides a powerful way for us to begin to reconceive the reform that is so needed in our criminal justice system.

So how can we get involved?

It is important to note that all the specific programs mentioned in this chapter were started by individuals who believed that a societal shift toward restorative justice was possible and that this shift begins with each of us. There are so many ways to get involved in the restorative justice movement no matter where we are and who we are. If there is a restorative justice program near us and we feel called to get involved, we can reach out and contact the program. However, obviously not everyone will be called to work directly in a restorative justice program and that is a *good thing*. We need doctors, social workers, teachers, lawyers, businesspeople, all dedicated to restorative justice. A societal shift cannot occur when only people in a specific field or occupation subscribe to and work to promote the idea of restorative justice. Rather, people in every walk of life must come to understand and promote restorative justice in their own lives and communities. So to people in all walks and seasons of life: there is always something we can do. We can advocate for restorative efforts within our state, our local community, and our schools. We can donate to the numerous restorative justice programs, such as the ones mentioned throughout this book. We can continue to learn more and talk openly about restorative justice—with friends, family, fellow parishioners, local school boards, elected officials, and anyone who will listen. We can hold book discussions about restorative justice in our parish or community center. And most importantly, we can consciously choose to practice restorative justice principles in our everyday life, serving as a living witness to the transformative power of restorative justice and mercy in action. The following is a list of some ways we can live restoratively, as proposed by Howard Zehr in his book *Changing Lenses*:

Ten ways to live restoratively

1. Take relationships seriously, envisioning yourself in an interconnected web of people, institutions and the environment.

2. Try to be aware of the impact—potential as well as actual—of your actions on others and the environment.

3. When your actions negatively impact others, take responsibility by acknowledging and seeking to repair the harm—even when you could probably get away with avoiding or denying it. . . .

4. Treat everyone respectfully, even those you don't expect to encounter again, even those you feel don't deserve it, even those who have harmed or offended you or others.

5. Involve those affected by a decision, as much as possible, in the decision-making process.

6. View the conflicts and harms in your life as opportunities.

7. Listen, deeply and compassionately, to others, seeking to understand even if you don't agree with them. (Think about who you want to be in the latter situation rather than just being right.)

8. Engage in dialogue with others, even when what is being said is difficult, remaining open to learning from them and the encounter.

9. Be cautious about imposing your "truths" and views on other people and situations.

10. Sensitively confront everyday injustices including sexism, racism, [homophobia,] and classism.[39]

Take some time to reflect on how *you*, our reader, are called to get involved. We need *you*. We need all that *you* have to offer your community, our society, and the world. Live intentionally. Live radically in Christ's love. Live restoratively.

Review and Looking Forward

Editors

This chapter ends by emphasizing that all the referenced restorative programs began with an individual who had the courage to think differently about justice—which in turn led to that person's work on programming that had an impact on institutions and communities. And these programs in turn seeded reflection by other persons who in turn influenced their institutions and communities. Restorative justice programming continues to have this ripple effect. After researching and discussing so many restorative justice programs, we now begin the work of designing one for Mount St. Mary's. The chapter shows us the transformative power of individual persons who think beyond the obvious. But in the end, restorative justice programming is not about the transformative power of creative individuals. Its focus is always persons in relationships. And the success of restorative justice programming is fundamentally about our willingness to be present to and see each other in new ways. All the programs described in this chapter are about face-to-face encounters between persons and the transformations that result from such encounters. Restorative justice is really about the courage of persons who are open to thinking differently about persons they encounter. In their book on restorative justice programming in schools, Lorraine Amstutz and Judy Mullet relate a story that illustrates this fundamental truth.

Five graduating seniors decided to pull a prank during their last year in high school. They originally planned to relocate five or six turkeys from a local farm to the school, setting up an unexpected morning event. They imagined the surprise of everyone the next day as they confronted the turkeys and their overnight mess. It seemed hilarious at the time. But

---

[39] Zehr, "10 ways to live restoratively," *Zehr Institute for Restorative Justice* (blog), Eastern Mennonite University (November 27, 2009), http://emu.edu/now/restorative-justice/2009/11/27/10-ways-to-live-restoratively/. Also in Zehr, *Changing Lenses*, 257–58.

growing excited as they executed the prank, they saw it go in unexpected directions. They tried to stuff turkeys in lockers so that students would face them flying out unexpectedly in the morning. Soon mayhem set in, as the disoriented turkeys started harming themselves as they thrashed about, producing a bloody mess throughout the school.

The case eventually moved its way through the legal system. As it came to an end, the judge recognized that the community had lingering wounds over this foolish prank. Hoping to address them, he referred the case to a local restorative justice program. The facilitators arranged restorative conferencing involving the students, their parents and community members, including members of the local faith community, who would represent the broader community. The superintendent, principals, a number of school board members and teachers, and the janitor were asked to participate. The total number of participants, including the six facilitators, was thirty-five persons. Pre-conferencing meetings were held with the seniors and their parents, and another one was held with the school community members, including the very angry janitor who bore the brunt of the prank. During the conferencing, the school representatives expressed their disappointment with the students, who were recognized to have positive traits; they also expressed their anger and feeling of betrayal to the students. The students explained how the prank got out of control in ways that filled them with shame and embarrassment. The students were visibly shaken as they apologized to their parents and the community. Toward the end one student explained how painful it was for him to walk through town because of the deep shame he felt. At the end of the conference, participants were invited to make final comments. The janitor's words powerfully captured the effect the restorative justice conferencing had on everyone. He rose to say that he accepted the students' apologies. He then turned to the last student who had spoken of his deep shame, saying, "The next time you see me on the street, you can look me in the eye because I will remember you for who you were tonight and not for what you did."[40] Restorative justice calls us to speak and listen to each other in ways that make healing possible. Righting the wrongs done to persons is only possible if we set up encounters between persons and open ourselves to the possibility of seeing each other anew.

---

[40] Lorraine S. Amstutz and Judy H. Mullet, *The Little Book of Restorative Discipline for Schools* (New York: Good Books, 2015), 5–6.

Questions for Discussion

1. Bill Pelke, a murder-victim family member who worked to establish Murder Victims' Families for Reconciliation and Murder Victims' Families for Human Rights, began his journey toward reconciliation with the teenager who killed his grandmother by reflecting on the gospels his grandmother taught in Bible studies. Bill said, "I am a Christian, and Jesus said, 'Whosoever has no sin, cast the first stone.' Under that criterion, none of us can cast the stone of death."[41] Discuss Bill's statement, which references the woman caught in adultery (John 8:1-11). Does Jesus just let the woman off the hook? Based on the account of this chapter, what do you think is the relationship between accountability and compassion?

2. Victims of crime often react negatively to talk about reaching "closure" and "moving on" following the harm done to them. Why does such talk annoy many of them? They know the crime and its harms can never be undone. Given this, what do you think they most desire? When you recall harms you have suffered, what might you desire, and what would likely help you heal?

3. Fr. David Kelly, who has worked at restorative justice ministry programs in Chicago (Kolbe House and Precious Blood Ministry of Reconciliation) for over thirty years, emphasizes that restorative justice is a way of life rather than a strategy. He says it is all about relationships, but repairing relationships requires that we create environments and spaces where we can encounter each other. Think about this in regard to relationships in your neighborhood, church, or workplace. Why is intentionally creating places of encounter and interaction so important? What tends to happen if they do not exist? How do the programs described in this chapter create such spaces? What challenges arise in doing this when persons have caused harm and hurt relationships?

---

[41] Journey of Hope, https://www.journeyofhope.org/who-we-are/murder-victim-family /bill-pelke/.

Chapter 13

Faith Communities

Editors

"Today this scripture passage is fulfilled in your hearing" (Luke 4:21). This declaration marks Jesus' ministry in the Gospel of Luke. It is the concluding point of his inaugural address, which he gives in his hometown of Nazareth. Beginning his ministry in Galilee, he celebrates the Sabbath in a Nazarene synagogue, where he reads from the prophet Isaiah (Isa 61:1-2):

> "The Spirit of the Lord is upon me,
> because he has anointed me
> to bring glad tidings to the poor.
> He has sent me to proclaim liberty to the captives
> and recovery of sight to the blind,
> to let the oppressed go free,
> and to proclaim a year acceptable to the Lord." (Luke 4:18-19)

In Jesus' declaration, the "year acceptable to the Lord" is happening through his words and actions. He is stating plainly that "the time is now." God's promises are fulfilled. It is a time of vindication and exhortation, a time of healing and wholeness, a time of God's restoration. In a word, Jesus proclaims that the peoples of the earth, through Israel, will be "gathered."[1] The poor and outcast will be invited to the feast; prisoners

---

[1] See the theme of gathering as it is traced through Scripture by Gerhard Lohfink in his *Does God Need the Church?: Toward a Theology of the People of God*, trans. Linda M. Maloney (Collegeville, MN: Liturgical Press, 1999).

and captives will be welcomed home; the blind will see the light of day. Jesus, in his person and ministry, is the way through which God will gather in imprisoned, ensnared, scattered, and fragmented humanity.

The theme of gathering is inextricably connected to the scene that follows—the Nazarene rejection of Jesus. After Jesus reads and declares the "today" of fulfillment, "all spoke highly of him and were amazed at [his] gracious words . . . They also asked, 'Isn't this the son of Joseph?'" (Luke 4:22). From this point on, Jesus seems intent on provoking the people of Nazareth. "Amen, I say to you, no prophet is accepted in his own native place" (v. 24). He harkens back to deeds of the prophets Elijah and Elisha, who gave care and succor to Gentiles (who lived outside the covenant with God). For instance, "there were many lepers in Israel during the time of Elisha the prophet; yet not one of them was cleansed, but only Naaman the Syrian" (v. 27). This allusion angers the people so much that they rise up as one in order to throw Jesus "headlong" from the crest of a hill and out of town. In effect, they seek to cast out the one who has announced the gathering in of the outcast.

There is no getting around the fact that Jesus provokes the hometown crowd. But why? Simple answer: Jesus knows where the barriers to their faith are situated. They will not share his hospitality for the stranger and the foreigner, the poor and unclean. This answer is consistent with Jesus' announcement of the Lord's "acceptance," and with his life, death, and ministry. Consider (in chap. 6) the hospitality that Jesus shows to Zacchaeus and that Zacchaeus then shares with those whom he has defrauded (Luke 19:1-10). From the time of Abraham, God calls out his people—the Hebrews in Egypt and at Mount Sinai, Israel from among the nations, Jews in their return from captivity in Babylon, and here the people of Nazareth—to be a kingdom of priests and a holy nation, a light to the world, and a city set on a hill. When Abraham is called by God (Gen 12:1-3), he is told that he and his descendants will be a blessing to the earth. The people of the covenant will be the ones through whom God calls and gathers all the peoples of the world. In the synagogue at Nazareth, Jesus announces that this time of gathering has come. It is today. But he knows that the response of the Nazarenes (and faithful people in general) is going to be less than hospitable. They will say to Jesus, "Do here in your native place the things that we heard were done in Capernaum" (Luke 4:23). They will want the power of God on their side. They will worry about their own place in the kingdom (Luke 9:46-48).

The event in Nazareth comes down to a simple contrast between Jesus' hospitality and our inclination (and what we think are good reasons) to be unreceptive to the disruptive presence of strangers and to the burdensome presence of those who carry with them torments and suffering that we do not share. The contrast is between our inclination to keep God for ourselves and God's call for us to be communities where sinners, outcasts, and victims are gathered in and restored. This call is the central theme of the chapter. Lydia Cocom and Karen Clifton show that efforts of our parishes to play a role in restorative justice offer us a way to respond to God's grace and gift of redemption.

The Role of Parishes in a Restorative Justice Movement

Lydia Cocom and Karen Clifton

In our work on the death penalty and criminal justice reform from the Catholic perspective, we have encountered countless individuals and families whose lives have been impacted, often tragically, by crime and our criminal justice system. Some are survivors and families of victims who struggle to come to terms with the trauma of crime in ways that, in some cases, have drastically shaken the foundation of their lives. Others are individuals who are currently or formerly incarcerated offenders and their family members who struggle to adjust to the impact of imprisonment on their lives and communities.

Many of these individuals draw great strength from their faith. Some have received impressive support from their faith communities in ways that have been integral to their adjusting and healing following experiences shaped by crime. Unfortunately, however, a common thread running through many of their stories is the experience of their church community struggling to figure out how to support them in their time of need. At times parish members feel uncertain and inadequate in responding to these fellow parishioners, resulting in these individuals being left on their own. Ironically those who commit and are victims of crime as well as their families are at times bound together by this common experience.

One family of an exonerated death row inmate felt the need to leave their parish following their painful journey tied to this wrongful conviction. Another individual, returning after serving a prison sentence, found old acquaintances avoiding her as she approached them following services. A grieving family of a murdered young man did not anticipate the lack of the support they so needed from their local church and community. A parish priest declined the suggestion to form a prison ministry program since the crime issue "doesn't affect us here," unaware that multiple parishioners were simply hesitant to share their stories. Far too often we tend to abandon those suffering the impact of crime due to our unawareness or sense of inadequacy.

Pope Francis has called on our churches to be oases of mercy in response to human suffering, but so frequently we fall short. Rarely is this done intentionally, out of malice, or from indifference. In regard to our response to offenders, the Catholic Bishops' Conference of England and Wales wrote, "[M]uch of our society's response to crime and punishment issues is not based in the hope of redemption but in the experience of fear."[2] There are deep stigmas, fears, and anxieties associated with crime and criminal justice, and this influences how we respond to both offenders and victims. In many cases, as in the words of one formerly incarcerated parishioner, "People may just not know what to say to you." What is playing out in many of our parishes is a reflection of a larger national reality. To meet the needs of all those who have been harmed by crime—victims, offenders, and their communities—and to build a true culture of mercy, we need to fundamentally change our society's approach to crime. And our local parish communities can play an important role in such change, if we accept this challenge.

Reorienting our criminal justice system and our personal and communal responses to persons affected by crime is no simple task. Starting with our parish communities and each of us as individuals, how can we begin to address the debilitating effects of a criminal justice system that in many ways works contrary to the tenets of our faith? Previous chapters have analyzed the problematic aspects of this system and the ways in which they stand in tension with the Catholic approach to criminal justice. Too often our responses fall desperately short of meeting the needs of victims, offenders, and communities harmed by crime. Too often victims of crime and their families face the trauma of crime without the support and assistance they need. Too often our prisons have become catch-all institutions for grappling with a range of problems our society has failed elsewhere to address adequately, such as poverty, homelessness, domestic abuse, mental illness, unemployment, and addiction. In this sense criminal justice reform requires wider social reforms that address both the sources and effects of crime. As William Collinge's chapter on Catholic social teaching emphasizes, the Catholic approach does not separate criminal justice from the range of inextricably related other social issues. This holistic approach offers a way of understanding that enables us to begin to address the complexity of such reform. Given this, how can we, as parishioners, come to

---

[2] *A Place of Redemption: A Christian Approach to Punishment and Prison* (London: Burn and Oates, 2004), 53.

better understand this Catholic approach and play a role in fostering a culture of mercy and criminal justice reform?

As we seek to meet our fellow brothers and sisters where they are in their diverse journeys of recovery following crimes, a restorative justice approach provides a helpful framework and set of practices. By becoming part of the national restorative movement, our parishes can be an integral part of the wider cultural change we seek. This chapter will look at two different ways parishes are currently engaging in restorative practices in order to bring about faith-based change. First, it will review the use of restorative practices as a tool for enriching parish life, which includes situations in which parishes are not directly focused on criminal justice issues per se. Second, it will look at how parishes can actively participate in restorative programming in ways that directly address criminal justice concerns and contribute to building the wider restorative movement through education and advocacy.

A Restorative Approach to Parish Life

The link between restorative justice and faith is a natural one. From penitentiary to parole movements, faith-based leadership and inspiration have played a central role in historical criminal justice reform in the United States. Restorative justice, both as an academic field and a social movement, has drawn significantly from religious traditions and sources, especially Christian ones. In considering these links, this section will explore the application of restorative justice approaches beyond the strictly criminal justice arena and then examine more specifically the potential fruits of using restorative practices within parishes, both to enrich parish life and to promote broad cultural and social change. Finally, this section will review suggestions from practitioners for parishes that are considering adopting restorative practices.

Developments over time in the field of restorative justice have set the stage for applying restorative justice practices within parishes. In its US development in the 1970s and through the 1990s, the scope of restorative justice was limited almost exclusively to the criminal justice arena. As Fernanda Rosenblatt writes, "Until about a decade ago, the predominant focus of restorative justice advocates was on crime and on the ways in which the aftermath of a criminal act should be handled."[3] More recently,

---

[3] *The Role of Community in Restorative Justice* (New York: Routledge, 2015), 7.

starting in the early 2000s, scholars and practitioners have challenged this narrow scope, redefining the applications for restorative justice, if not the very meaning of the word itself. John Braithwaite, for example, writes that restorative justice "is not simply a way of reforming the criminal justice system, it is a way of transforming the entire legal system, our family lives, our conduct in the workplace, our practice of politics."[4] Increasingly, restorative approaches and practices have been used to address harm and build community in other settings, including schools, workplaces, and faith communities. The adoption of restorative justice, or restorative-inspired approaches, in schools has been particularly influential and is well documented.

While some practitioners and scholars have expanded the understanding of restorative justice so as to apply practices that address harm in other institutional and social settings, they also have begun to speak very broadly of a restorative way of living. With this emphasis, restorative principles and practices are seen as promoting a restorative way of living one's life. As Gerry Johnstone writes, "There is a tendency to move from the use for restorative justice as a discrete and fairly well-defined intervention into a specific situation (e.g. the arrangement of a restorative conference to deal with a case of workplace harassment) to initiatives designed to change everyday behavior and governance in the setting."[5] Fred Boehrer explores attempts "to live a restorative lifestyle," one that "counters modes of thought and behavior of social structural violence we encounter [by] emphasizing a needs-based approach."[6] Epitomizing this shift was the publication in 2009 of "10 Ways to Live Restoratively" by Howard Zehr, widely considered the father of restorative justice in this country. His work serves as a guide for those who wish to shift how they live their lives to a restorative approach.[7] Increasingly, this approach of applying a restorative perspective to one's way of living is seen not as an "optional extra," but

[4] John Braithwaite, "Principles of Restorative Justice," in *Restorative Justice and Criminal Justice: Competing or Reconcilable Paradigms*, ed. Andrew von Hirsch and others, 1 (Portland, OR: Hart, 2003).

[5] Gerry Johnstone, *Restorative Justice: Ideas, Values, Debates* (New York: Routledge, 2011), 145.

[6] Fred Boehrer, "The Good Samaritan or the Person in the Ditch? An Attempt to Live a Restorative Justice Lifestyle," in *Handbook of Restorative Justice*, ed. Dennis Sullivan and Larry Tifft, 497 (New York: Routledge, 2006).

[7] Howard Zehr, "10 Ways to Live Restoratively," Zehr Institute for Restorative Justice (November 27, 2009), http://emu.edu/now/restorative-justice/2009/11/27/10-ways-to-live-restoratively/.

as embodying a core emphasis of the wider restorative justice movement. As Johnstone observes,

> There is a fairly widespread view amongst campaigners for restorative justice that it would be contradictory and self-defeating to seek to "restorativise" the societal response to crime whilst behaving non-restoratively in the workplace and in our everyday lives. Trying to transform the pattern of thinking that guides society's response to crime is currently just one concern—albeit still an extremely important one—of a social movement which aims to propagate a new way of seeing the world and living in it.[8]

As the applications of restorative justice have expanded, so too has the definition of the term been extended. Even though many of the proponents of the application of a restorative justice approach beyond criminal justice settings are careful to use terms like a "restorative *approach*" or "restorative *practices*" rather than "restorative *justice*," the term, both in practice and in scholarship, has definitely moved beyond its initial more narrow scope. For example, a recent article on restorative justice in schools used a definition that differs quite significantly from the far more specific and precise definitions used by Zehr and his counterparts in earlier scholarship. The authors of the research on schools write, "RJ is a broad term that encompasses a growing social movement to institutionalize peaceful and non-punitive approaches for addressing harm, responding to violations of legal and human rights, and problem solving."[9]

The expansion of the scope of restorative justice has not occurred without debate. Critics argue that as the definition and application of restorative justice expand, its meaning becomes less clear. Inge Vanfraechem and Lode Walgrave maintain that such extended understanding of restorative justice risks losing its original conceptual meaning and "risks becoming empty of significance. It then becomes vulnerable to misconceptions and misuse, and loses credibility."[10] When considering these concerns, it is important to distinguish between restorative justice as an academic field of inquiry, in which such an analytical critique is more pertinent, and restorative

---

[8] Johnstone, *Restorative Justice*, 156.

[9] Trevor Fronius and others, "Restorative Justice in U.S. Schools: A Research Review," WestEd Justice & Prevention Research Center (February 2016), http://jprc.wested.org/wp-content/uploads/2016/02/RJ_Literature-Review_20160217.pdf.

[10] "In favour of a restricted European Forum for Restorative Justice," *European Forum for Restorative Justice* 10, no. 1 (April 2009), http://euforumrj.org/assets/upload/Vol._10,_issue_1-1.pdf.

justice as a social movement, in which precise delimiting of the term may be less necessary. Even critics of the expanded use of the term are quick to admit that a larger social movement is indeed underway. As Rosenblatt writes, "No one can deny that there is an ongoing and very welcome wider social or ideological movement that, guided and inspired by the same participatory and peace-promoting philosophy of restorative justice . . . is aimed at promoting better socio-ethical attitudes in schools and in other non-criminal contexts."[11]

Given these developments, it is not surprising that restorative justice approaches have found a place in the life of parishes. Grassroots change makers at the parish level may have little concern for scholarly debates about the naming of the ministry in which they are engaged. Nevertheless, awareness of this context of debate can be helpful if parish-based practitioners are challenged on whether their work truly should be labeled as restorative justice initiatives. Of more pertinent concern are questions about the effects of an expanded range of application of restorative justice principles and practices. For example, Dana Greene, as interpreted by Rosenblatt, suggests that "by 'using' restorative justice to deal with both criminalisable and *non-criminalisable matters* (such as misbehavior or antisocial behavior in school), we may well run the risk of criminalizing extra-legal conflicts, and thus of expanding the network of penal control."[12] School systems must be attentive to this concern as they introduce concepts and practices that have their origin in our criminal justice system. But this concern does not appear to bear on the role of restorative justice in parish contexts.

Catholic parishes from California to Washington, DC, are increasingly seeking to apply restorative approaches to enrich parish life. From dealing with conflict surrounding a change in the Lectionary to addressing grief after the passing of a loved one, restorative practices, particularly the use of restorative circles, are already being used to meet a diverse set of parish needs. Parishes are already applying restorative practices to address the effects of crime and the criminal justice system within their communities and are developing restorative approaches to respond to a range of needs, including responding to harm and grief experienced by parishioners, promoting more inclusive discernment regarding matters of parish concern, and building community within parishes.

California is a center for Catholic restorative justice work and a worthwhile resource for parishes eager to adopt restorative practices. Each Cali-

[11] *The Role of Community in Restorative Justice*, 10.
[12] Ibid.

fornia diocese has its own restorative justice director, and many parishes are using restorative practices, especially to meet the needs of victims of crime, the incarcerated, and families of both groups. Julio Escobar, director of restorative justice for the Archdiocese of San Francisco, has worked with parishes for decades in this area. His ministry goals are to assist parishes in setting up service programs for parishioners who are homicide victim family members, including prayer vigils at the homicide site, accompaniment of families at funerals, home visits, a parish group for families who have suffered loss, an annual Mass, and a yearly retreat. Family members are then invited to participate in a three-day crime survivor assistant support training program that educates them on restorative justice community organizing and advocacy. Similar support exists for families of incarcerated persons, including accompaniment of families at court sessions, guidance in writing to incarcerated persons, home visits, an annual Mass, and a one-day retreat. Returning offenders are invited to a one-day retreat and a reentry conference at which information is available regarding education, housing, employment, counseling, and spiritual resources. Escobar says the programs have had a positive impact on the wider religious and nonreligious community as a whole, explaining that "the ripple effects have to do with healing services we offer. Every year it adds up and we see families come out of a wounded situation to be better healed."[13]

Many parishes have introduced restorative circle programming and other restorative justice practices to deal with issues unrelated to crime in ways that have produced encouraging results. For example, at Holy Trinity Parish in Washington, DC, parishioners gathered in a restorative circle to explore grief and loss during the holiday season. One participant observed that the circle process "gave comfort to those who had experienced a loss" and noted that "in the process of addressing someone else's grief, other circle members experienced healing and a new perspective on their own anger and loss." Mary Hallinan, a restorative-justice practitioner who works within the parish context, has experience with using restorative peacemaking circles to build community and deal with conflict within parishes. Her parish has used such circles to respond to everything from managing conflict over a change in the Lectionary to providing community building support regarding specific areas of concern, including grief and gender issues. Hallinan observes that these restorative practices "fostered greater respect and efforts to see the other points of view" within the parish

---

[13] Archdiocese of San Francisco, "Restorative Justice," https://sfarchdiocese.org /home/ministries/social-justice-life/peace-justice/restorative-justice.

community. Speaking of the parish she works with, she commented that the "community is becoming very attentive to everyone" and the implementation of restorative approaches has "led to a lot of caring within and without."[14]

Catholic parishes are joining a trend that also encompasses other faith traditions. As David Brubaker, a consultant for religious congregations seeking to apply restorative approaches, writes, "In the last decade, many religious congregations have also appropriated the principles and practices of restorative justice. Even when no 'offense' has taken place, the introduction of a talking piece and several simple ground rules can transform conversations about sensitive issues." According to Brubaker, churches, parishes, and faith communities can become the setting for persons to learn, practice, and experience the healthy community-creating benefits of RJ. "The impact on members and the broader community of such a commitment are profound. Congregational members report an increased love and respect for each other and the faith community of which they are a part. Community members sense that something has changed within the local congregation, and the reputation of the congregation in its own community can shift dramatically."[15] Beyond the immediate benefits to parish life, building a restorative approach within parishes is an important step in promoting wider restorative cultural change. As Ron Rolheiser explains, "Our prayer is honest only when our lives back it up."[16] If parishes seek to be genuine, active participants in positive cultural change, they cannot do so simply by fostering restorative ministries, prayer, and advocacy. These communities and their members must live on a daily basis the change they wish to see. As practitioner Mary Hallinan succinctly states, "This starts with ourselves becoming restorative."

Parishes across the country are becoming more engaged in understanding and practicing restorative justice. What makes the incorporating of restorative principles and practices successful in parishes? What pitfalls can be avoided in fostering these principles and practices in this context? Successful parish practitioners offer helpful suggestions:

1. *Start where the energy is.* Introducing restorative practices will not be successful in a parish without top-down cooperation from the pastor.

---

[14] Interview with Mary Hallinan (June 8, 2016).

[15] "Developing a Restorative Congregation," Congregational Consulting Group (June 8, 2015), www.congregationalconsulting.org/developing-a-restorative-congregation/.

[16] *Sacred Fire: A Vision for a Deeper Human and Christian Maturity* (New York: Random House, 2014), 47.

However, this is only the first step because restorative justice depends on grassroots community participation. A good way to introduce parishes to restorative practices is to start with an issue around which there is energy, then learn about how restorative circles can be introduced, and then pilot this process to give parishioners an experience of addressing an issue within such a context. If there is interest within the community, restorative tools can be increasingly applied to other areas of need over time. Some parishes have circles that regularly meet to address the needs of particular groups. Others have circle practitioners on standby so that as issues arise, restorative practices can be applied under their guidance.

2. *It is crucial that practitioners are well trained and supported.* Practitioners must have quality training and experience in implementing restorative practices. Given this, it is important to not rely on interested volunteers who have simply read about and been exposed to restorative practices. Becoming a restorative practitioner is a guided process. Therefore parishes interested in introducing these practices should tap into the rich available network of experienced restorative practitioners and mentors to guide and support them.[17]

3. *Take it slow; do it right.* Restorative practices such as the circle process and restorative conferencing operate differently than traditional resolution methods. Participants need to clearly understand how the process functions and why. Extensive preparation is needed to address challenges that might arise within circles. For this reason, the introducing of these practices cannot be hurried. Consensus discernment, central to restorative circles, at times leaves participants achieving something short of their ideally envisioned resolutions. Those who are accustomed to more top-down, nonconsensus-building means of resolving issues may find it challenging to resist the temptation to have themselves or others step in and take over the process. Coming to understand and effectively be engaged in restorative practices takes time and patience.

---

[17] Catholic Mobilizing Network has developed a comprehensive parish program to educate and initiate restorative practices in the parish setting. Please visit https://catholics mobilizing.org/resource/parish-educational-modules-restorative-justice-restorative -living-lens-learning-and-action. Some additional resources are International Institute for Restorative Practices, www.iirp.edu/; Kay Pranis's trainings, www.planningchange .com/restorative-justice-certification-program/; David Brubaker's restorative justice work as a consultant to faith communities, david.brubaker@emu.edu; Eastern Mennonite University's Zehr Institute, www.emu.edu/cjp/restorative-justice/about/; and the Restorative Justice Training Institute, http://www.rjtica.org/.

4. *Beware of replicating unhealthy relationship or power dynamics within the restorative space.* Creating a safe space in which participants can freely express themselves and encounter one another in a nonjudgmental and respectful setting is important, particularly when using peacemaking circles to address conflict and harm. Open, respectful discussion of shared values and problematic issues can help raise awareness about challenges that exist within a parish community and how they can be addressed effectively, collaboratively, and peacefully.

The Role Parishes Can Play in Furthering Criminal Justice Reform

"What is the future of RJ in the United States? Our crystal ball remains cloudy. . . . The RJ movement has some hard work ahead if it is to become central to contemporary criminal justice reform."[18] There is little doubt that the need for criminal justice reform has been recognized in the United States. A reform movement that would shift our criminal justice system from a heavily retributive to a more restorative approach is developing. As Dana Greene writes, "Both in the literature and in the field, there is a pervasive consensus that a restorative justice movement is underway."[19] We have briefly reviewed the use of restorative practices by parishes to enhance parish life and to promote wider cultural change. This section will explore how parishes can contribute in meaningful ways to reorienting our justice system in a restorative direction. In particular, exploring some of the weaknesses and needs of the wider movement can help clarify the potential contribution of parishes to this movement and identify strategic avenues for their participation.

Most observers agree that our country is ripe for criminal justice reform. As David Karp and Olivia Frank write, "For the first time since the 1970s, the political will for punishment appears to be declining."[20] They cite the conclusions of Christopher Muller and Daniel Schrage, who note that, in particular, "growing white dissatisfaction with criminal justice institu-

---

[18] David R. Karp and Olivia Frank, "Anxiously Awaiting the Future of Restorative Justice in the United States," *Victims & Offenders: An International Journal of Evidence-based Research, Policy, and Practice* 11, no. 1 (2016): 17.

[19] "Repeat performance: Is restorative justice another good reform gone bad?," *Contemporary Justice Review: Issues in Criminal, Social, and Restorative Justice* 16, no. 3 (2013): 366.

[20] "Anxiously Awaiting the Future of Restorative Justice," 2.

tions may increase the size of the political constituency opposing mass imprisonment."[21]

Calls for substantial criminal reform are increasingly bridging the political aisle and coalitions of unlikely partners have formed around the issue. One prominent example is the Coalition for Public Safety, which boasts such unlikely allies as the ACLU and the Koch brothers. At the national level, legislators from opposite ends of the political spectrum, such as Democratic Senator Dick Durbin of Illinois and Republican Senator Mike Lee of Utah, have joined together to spearhead sentencing reform. Significantly, a segment of conservative messaging about criminal justice issues appears to be shifting toward an approach increasingly oriented around issues of "cost, efficacy, and redemption" rather than fear and retribution.[22] It is hoped that this messaging continues and is even strengthened.

As support for current criminal justice paradigms wavers and willingness to engage in bipartisan reform grows, the restorative justice movement faces a unique opportunity. The movement's ability to effectively capitalize on this moment and steer messaging and reform will be key. Time will tell how these developments unfold over the next few years.

Unfortunately, this developing dynamic is not without its challenges and drawbacks. In "Repeat performance: Is restorative justice another good reform gone bad?" Greene provides one of the most provocative critiques of the current restorative movement so far. She argues, "This social change movement is not exhibiting creativity or sensitivity to the actual obstacles in its path. There is no talk of garnering wider public support, no efforts to reduce the use of current justice practices, no demands made on the system. The only groundwork being laid is for programming."[23] Her critique focuses around the movement's "insular and limited organizing by a relatively small, homogeneous group of actors,"[24] "overly grandiose claims" about potential of restorative justice "to 'cure crime and generate a more cohesive society' without mechanisms to address structural causes of crime and disorder,"[25] "overreliance on training volunteers to provide direct service to underfunded programs that receive negligible caseloads,[26]

---

[21] Ibid., 3.

[22] Ibid.

[23] Greene, "Repeat performance," 375.

[24] Ibid., 378.

[25] Karp and Frank, "Anxiously Awaiting the Future of Restorative Justice," 5. See Greene, "Repeat performance," 388.

[26] Greene, "Repeat performance," 381.

and a failure to educate and garner widespread public support or build the political coalitions necessary for anything more than marginal success."[27]

For Greene, these weaknesses do not simply risk jeopardizing the ability of the movement to have an impact, but in fact suggest that it may follow in the footsteps of previous so-called regressive penal reform movements that may superficially appear successful, "yet, in their wake, society is more attached to, and entrenched in the very ideals the movement set out to supplant."[28] Her concerns, which have since been explored by other scholars, can be broken down into a number of key areas, each of which presents opportunities for strategic parish engagement.

Education

Greene notes that the restorative movement has so far done little to develop a strategic information campaign to educate the public at large on restorative justice. It is difficult to find data on public awareness of the restorative justice approach, but analysis of media coverage of the term suggests there is still a strong need for an educational campaign. While a survey of RJ media coverage by Karp and Frank found a significant uptick in stories regarding restorative justice beginning in 2012, only 18 of the 505 stories from 2005 to 2014 "specifically linked RJ to criminal justice reform."[29] Their survey, significantly, did not track misuse of the term. For example, *The Washington Post*, touted by Frank and Karp as an example of a national newspaper that provides "substantial coverage" of restorative justice, has been known to print articles with misleading information. One glaring example is a 2016 article on the Stanford rape case that suggested the judge's decision to apply a light sentence to a defendant who clearly had not accepted accountability for his crime was an example of restorative justice.[30] Despite growing national energy for criminal justice reform at the legislative level, restorative justice, as applied to criminal justice, has

---

[27] Karp and Frank, "Anxiously Awaiting the Future of Restorative Justice," 5.

[28] Ibid., 4–5.

[29] Ibid., 10.

[30] According to *The Washington Post*, "Josh Marquis, an Oregon district attorney and sexual assault case veteran, said it's possible the California judge was embracing restorative justice, a philosophy that focuses on criminal rehabilitation. The approach, he said, best applies to young or first-time offenders who have damaged, say, property." Danielle Paquette, "What makes the Stanford sex offender's six month jail sentence so unusual," *The Washington Post* (June 6, 2016), www.washingtonpost.com/news/wonk/wp/2016/06/06/what-makes-the-stanford-sex-offenders-six-month-jail-sentence-so-unusual/.

only been mentioned six times on the House floor and five times in the Senate since 2011. This indicates that restorative justice still does not play a key role in shaping current discourse about criminal justice reform at the national legislative level.

An absence of broad public understanding and support of restorative justice is hardly conducive to a successfully growing social movement. Parishes, in collaboration with community partners, could play an important role in educating a wider audience about restorative justice as rooted in faith commitments. Churches are fertile resources for framing the discourse and message about restorative justice through a moral lens. The Catholic Mobilizing Network (CMN) is an influential source of Catholic messaging and educating that is actively working to engage parishes on this issue. Its website offers numerous restorative justice education, advocacy, and prayer resources for parishes (https://catholicsmobilizing.org). For some parishes, particularly those struggling with tight budgets and limited resources, such spiritual, educational, and community outreach may be a more feasible option than developing new parish-based restorative justice programming. Educating parishioners on the Catholic view of criminal justice, which so emphasizes restorative justice, may provide the greatest service parishes can provide to this movement.

Advocacy

Greene makes clear that more advocacy work is needed to ensure that restorative practices are *adopted by* rather than simply *promoted alongside* our current criminal justice system. She also argues that if the restorative movement focuses, as it has done so far, on promoting piecemeal restorative justice programming rather than linking this programming with state and national reform efforts to eliminate the elements of our criminal justice system that are anathema to restorative justice, systemic transformation will be impossible. Other scholars echo Greene's concerns. Karp and Frank write, "Federal mandates and state legislation are increasingly supporting RJ, but they have not led to widespread implementation."[31] Shannon Sliva and Carolyn Lambert assert, "While many states' criminal and juvenile codes contain references to restorative justice generally or specific restorative justice practices, few provide detailed support and structure to ensure

---

[31] Karp and Frank, "Anxiously Awaiting the Future of Restorative Justice," 10.

implementation. . . . Nationally, restorative justice remains a marginally supported justice practice at the level of state policy."[32]

Parishes can function as catalysts for such important reform. They can both advocate for the implementation of restorative justice practices and tie this advocacy into a wider narrative about the need for broad criminal justice and social reform. The Catholic tradition offers ample, rich insight that can inform the framing of this national discourse. The US bishops succinctly summarize the key moral insights of this tradition:

> A Catholic approach to criminal and restorative justice . . . recognizes that the dignity of the human person applies to both victims of crime and those who have committed harm. Justice includes more than punishment. It must include mercy and restoration. A simplistic punitive approach to justice can leave victims of crime with feelings of neglect, abandonment and anger making reconciliation and healing difficult. A restorative justice approach is more comprehensive and addresses the needs of victims, the community and those responsible for causing harm through healing, education, rehabilitation and community support.[33]

The United States Conference of Catholic Bishops provides ample resources for informing Catholics concerned about these issues.[34] In addition, the rich diversity of Catholic communities with diverse races, ethnicities, and social classes can broaden the perspectives brought to these discussions. Drawing Catholics into this discourse will broaden the inclusion of persons of color, especially African Americans and Latinos, and economic disadvantage who disproportionately suffer the inequities of our current criminal justice system. A current weakness of the restorative movement is the insularity of the core of their supporters who already understand and engage in restorative justice practices. Bringing Catholic communities into this discourse will enrich the discussion on the level of both moral insights and concrete social realities.

In summary, Catholic parishes can play important transformative roles in (1) implementing restorative programming in their parish communities,

---

[32] "Restorative Justice Legislation in the American States: A Statutory Analysis of Emerging Legal Doctrine," *Journal of Policy Practice* 14, no. 2 (2015): 88.

[33] "Background on Criminal Justice" (January 2016), www.usccb.org/issues -and-action/human-life-and-dignity/criminal-justice-restorative-justice/background-on -criminal-justice.cfm.

[34] "Criminal Justice—Restorative Justice," www.usccb.org/issues-and-action /human-life-and-dignity/criminal-justice-restorative-justice/.

(2) educating parishioners about the Catholic understanding of restorative justice, and (3) engaging Catholics in efforts to reform our criminal justice system on local, state, and federal levels. Catholics can be a powerful force for positive change within our society.

Conclusion

Restorative justice is an area of opportunity ripe for parish engagement. By educating parishioners about Catholic teachings on criminal justice, adopting restorative practices within parishes, and fostering support for reform efforts, Catholics can play an important role in bringing attention to our broken criminal justice system and reshaping our national discourse on crime.

Change comes slowly. To work to bring about change is to adopt a countercultural approach. Reorienting our culture away from using violence to achieve ends, responding to harm with retaliatory harm, and focusing narrowly on punishment as the way of justice is challenging, if not daunting. Ultimately, at the heart of this work is a radical commitment to cultural and spiritual renewal. Bringing a message of mercy, hope, and love that recognizes the dignity of all persons is radical work. To engage in it is to follow Pope Francis's call to all Catholics:

> I ask you, instead, to be revolutionaries, I ask you to swim against the tide; yes, I am asking you to rebel against this culture . . . that believes you are incapable of true love.[35]

In declaring a Jubilee Year of Mercy, Francis calls each Catholic, *each parishioner* to this restorative commitment—"to make compassion, love, mercy and solidarity a true way of life, a rule of conduct in our relationships with one another."[36] Our challenge is to work together through our parish communities to follow this calling and live this Christian commitment.

---

[35] "Pope Francis' Message for World Youth Day: 'Have the courage to be happy,'" *News.VA* (February 17, 2015), www.news.va/en/news/pope-francis-message-for-world -youth-day-have-the.

[36] Carol Glatz, "In Peace Day message, pope addresses death penalty, debt, migrants," *Catholic News Service* (December 15, 2015), www.catholicnews.com/services/englishnews /2015/in-peace-day-message-pope-addresses-death-penalty-debt-migrants.cfm.

Review and Looking Forward

Editors

Fr. David Kelly, CPPS, was introduced in chapter 2. He is a member of the religious community the Missionaries of the Precious Blood, and he has been living and working in poor neighborhoods of Chicago for over thirty years. He is the executive director of Precious Blood Ministry of Reconciliation. The mission of this ministry is:

> Sharing in Christ's mission of reconciliation, we work as agents of reconciliation and healing with those in our community and our Church who have been impacted by violence and conflict. Our ministries reach out to the victim, the wrongdoer, and the community to create a safe space where healing can begin and where people can find the support and encouragement needed to begin reconciliation. We strive to be a resource to the community to find restorative ways to heal and rebuild after violence and conflict.[37]

Fr. David has many stories to tell, stories "on the edge of hopelessness . . . where we must be willing to go."[38] For example, after a stabbing in the parish, he visited first the victim and his family in the hospital; then, from there, he went to see the offender in Cook County Jail. He knew both victim and attacker, encountering each after the stabbing, as though both were his children—in suffering and in guilt and despair.

Fr. David relates experiences like this to the events of Holy Saturday. For one young man, he prays for healing as he is literally on the edge of death. The other young man is on the edge of becoming "a throw away person," labeled as "a menace to society." He visits the victim in the hospital to offer support. He visits the offender to keep him alive (in a sense), even if only on the edge—knowing that accountability and responsibility are his only way to be restored to community with the victim. Holy Saturday represents a similar "edge." It is the time between Jesus' death on Good Friday and the celebration of Easter. "Perhaps the violence has ended; the killing is over; the crime has been done. But the resurrection's not here yet."

Along these lines—between death and new life—Fr. David indicates that restorative justice is at the center of the Christian faith:

---

[37] Precious Blood Ministry of Reconciliation, "Ministries," www.pbmr.org/ministries/.

[38] David Kelly, "Restorative Justice: Reconciliation and Righting Relationships," a paper given at the conference "Restore Justice! Encounter and Mercy," Washington, DC (November 21, 2014), 5.

Reconciliation and restorative justice are not strategies for achieving some other end. Restoration is not managed by series of mechanisms or techniques; rather, it is God's work, and we are workers within that field. We have to believe amid hopelessness and violence. We have to believe that if we are willing to be present, if we are willing to enter that muddled mess, if we are willing to go into Holy Saturday, God will bring forth new life.[39]

In effect, Fr. David shows why it is important for parishes—even in small and less dramatic ways—to promote habits and practices of restorative justice. Restorative justice is one way that we can live out our faith. By seeking restoration, we look forward to God's work of redemption. In small ways, we can join with God in gathering of the oppressed and persecuted, the outcast and the sinner—in hope and openness to the coming kingdom of God.

Questions for Discussion

1. Consider how your parish might be approaching its programs—from catechetical instruction to its ministry to the sick. For example, when youth receive instruction, do they experience hospitality? Do they experience an invitation to play a role in the church's role in the world? Are they brought into a process of restoration? Reflect on whether or not such programs could be improved or fostered in such a way that through them we might better experience the hospitality of God.

2. The authors, Lydia Cocom and Karen Clifton, note in the chapter that "a good way to introduce parishes to restorative practices is to start with an issue around which there is energy." This approach means starting within, with something that matters to a community. Consider issues of hospitality that are close to home. Sometimes these issues are difficult to see because we have developed habits of working around them rather than dealing with them directly. Can you think of any such problems or issues?

[39] Ibid.

Chapter 14

Conclusion

A Journey of Hope for Restorative Justice

Trudy D. Conway

> Today's world stands in great need of witnesses, not so much of teachers but rather of witnesses. It's not so much about speaking, but rather speaking with our whole lives. (Pope Francis, Address from St. Peter's Square, May 18, 2013)

These words of Pope Francis call all of us. And they may explain why so many persons—both Christians and non-Christians—are drawn to this man. Francis's whole life reveals his fundamental beliefs and commitments; his words and actions express them simply yet powerfully. So often people are moved by his revelatory facial expressions and gestures since they embody who he is. His daily living has a steady rhythm defined by engagement with and retreat from the world. Never aloof and ever open to both the joys and sufferings of the world, he remains attentive to persons, but most especially those who, as neglected, abandoned, or marginalized, often escape our notice or are quickly forgotten in the daily distractions of our lives. We can easily recall examples of Francis encountering these persons. He visited Libyan refugees in Lampedusa on his first papal visit, met with prisoners and their families in Philadelphia, expressed concern about immigrants after praying near the US border in Mexico, visited asylum seekers in a Lesbos detention center, and asked eight homeless men and women to join him for breakfast on his eightieth birthday. Before celebrating Holy Thursday Mass in Rome's Rebibbia prison, Francis washed the feet of twelve juvenile offenders. Then after gathering hundreds of inmates in the prison where Pope St. John Paul II forgave his assassin, Francis reminded them that "Jesus never tires of loving, forgiving and embracing us," recalling the gospel passage emphasizing that God remembers and loves even those forgotten by their own mothers. Francis's daily life centers on encountering persons in our world. But he also retreats from this world to prayer, meditation, and reflection, which further deepens his understanding of and engagement with the world. This daily rhythm of engagement with and retreat from the world imitates the way of Jesus, which centers his life. Pope Francis remains a witness, calling others to be witnesses with their whole lives.

Such witnessing is imbued with hope, for it shows us the possibility of change and the transformative power of lives, words, and actions. It tells us—do not be hesitant, weary of heart, or despairing; stay steadfast, uplifted by hope. A friend gave me framed words of the poet Emily Dickinson at a particular time in my life. I placed them at the center of our family's kitchen activities, for they lift my spirit, keeping me focused on what might be:

> "Hope" is the thing with feathers -
> That perches in the soul -
> And sings the tune without the words -
> And never stops - at all -
>
> And sweetest - in the Gale - is heard . . . [1]

Mount St. Mary's University has a curriculum rich in texts whose words definitely influence the lives of our students and faculty. But what affects our community most powerfully are speakers describing lives that fill us with hope. I recall a senior telling me, somewhat sarcastically, that he learned the most about ethics in hearing two of our alums, Bill and Kathy Magee (a surgeon and nurse), speak of their decades-long journey to underdeveloped countries, creating and expanding Operation Smile, which gathers medical teams to do facial surgeries that transform the lives of impoverished children born with cleft palates. The student was surprised that I agreed, while adding that the work of the Magees embodies so much of what we explore through the texts he studied. Our university knows the power of living witnesses. For this reason we have brought to campus many

---

[1] Emily Dickinson, "'Hope' is the thing with feathers," in *Dickinson: Selected Poems and Commentaries*, Helen Vendler, 118 (Cambridge, MA: Belknap Press, 2010).

speakers who have seen up close the need for criminal justice reform. I am grateful that our community was willing to dedicate funds and resources so we could learn about the work of so many people—murder-victim family members, exonerees, victims of crime, police officers and commissioners, legal experts, prison ministers, restorative justice advocates—dedicated to such reform. The interest they seeded helped build a community committed to restorative justice reform and sustained by the hope that such reform is possible.

Pivotal to this development was our initial inviting of parents of murder victims to discuss why they took a restorative, rather than a purely retributive, approach to the offenders who ended their children's lives. None of these parents had been previously exposed to our criminal justice system. Like so many of us, they knew little about how that system works and affects both victims and offenders, their families and communities. Many of them described being pulled into a system at odds with their fundamental, often faith-based, convictions. Encountering other persons who shared their convictions, they worked collaboratively to create organizations that helped reshape our society's assumptions about justice by fostering a more restorative approach to persons caught in the vortex of crime. Hearing these murder-victim family members led us to invite other persons who further educated us about the realities of our judicial system. These gatherings began a journey of dialogue, activism, and friendship within our community, which resulted in the work of two books, one on the death penalty and this book on restorative justice.[2]

One of our first speakers was Vicki Schieber, recommended by my daughter, who described the powerful effect of hearing her speak at another university. Our inviting Vicki was serendipitous, for sure. Vicki quickly morphed from an invited speaker to a community member cofacilitating our campus efforts to end the death penalty and promote restorative justice in affiliation with the Catholic Mobilizing Network (CMN).[3] Anyone who knows Vicki's magnetic personality can understand how she drew

---

[2] Our book *Where Justice and Mercy Meet: Catholic Opposition to the Death Penalty*, edited by Vicki Schieber, Trudy Conway, and David McCarthy, was published by Liturgical Press (Collegeville, MN) in 2013.

[3] The Catholic Mobilizing Network (www.catholicsmobilizing.com) is a Washington, DC-based organization founded by Catholics, including Sr. Helen Prejean, to educate Catholics and the general public on church teachings on criminal justice, specifically church support for the abolition of the death penalty and the promotion of restorative justice.

members of our community to care deeply about the issues to which she had dedicated decades of her life. Like Pope Francis, Vicki brought us to see that the issues, facts, statistics we debated at the university mattered—and mattered deeply—because they were about the lives of individual persons caught up in our criminal justice system. Her own journey showed us in concrete ways the transformative power of convictions and commitments. So it is fitting that our final chapter focuses on Vicki's own journey of hope for restorative justice.

Vicki's journey began in tragedy with the high-profile May 1998 rape and murder of her daughter, Shannon, as she ended her first year of doctoral studies at the Wharton School of the University of Pennsylvania in Philadelphia. Her family looked forward to celebrating this new milestone following her impressive studies at Duke University, where she graduated with honors in three years after triple majoring in economics, mathematics, and philosophy. All the hopes her parents and brother Sean had for Shannon were shattered that spring night. It took four long years before Shannon's assailant was finally captured in Colorado. Much continues to be written about the highly controversial two-state handling of the investigation and trial of Troy Graves, who was eventually sentenced in Colorado and Pennsylvania to two life sentences without parole plus 80–160 years. Of his known thirteen serial rape victims, Shannon alone was strangled to death while resisting his violent attack. The shocking death of their beloved and talented daughter was painful enough to bear, but this tragedy also pulled her parents into a criminal justice system in dire need of reform. The more they were drawn into this system, the more they understood all that is problematic about it.

Deeply grounded in their Catholic faith, the source of their ethical principles, the Schieber family never wavered in their conviction that Shannon's death could never be righted by taking another life in her name. They could not undo her assailant's actions, but they could choose their subsequent response to what he had done. Even before the assailant had been arrested, they knew their response to Shannon's killer would not be driven by all-consuming anger and vengeance. For them it was important that their response be shaped by the principles and beliefs by which they always had lived. So without any hesitation, they opposed the seeking of a death sentence by the district attorney in Philadelphia. And they stood firm even when their opposition subjected them to painful public criticism by those they presumed would be their family's advocates. It was clear to them that if they did not stand on their convictions in difficult times, then these were not truly their convictions. The Schiebers were spared the painful experience of an extended capital trial followed by decades of appeals when Troy Graves pleaded guilty and began serving a sentence that ensured he would spend his entire life in prison. As parents, the Schiebers were relieved that no other women would be subjected to his violent crimes. As Catholics, the Schiebers hoped that his life sentence might bring him to a state of penitent remorse for the harm he had done to victims, their families, and communities.

Over time Sylvester and Vicki Schieber took pleasure in seeing their family grow, as Sean married and began raising three delightful grandchildren. They both continued their dedication to demanding professional careers. But building on what both of them had learned, they each began to shape new commitments based on their experience of the criminal justice system. Both of them were deeply troubled by important aspects of the investigation and handling of the case. As an economist and well-published author, Syl began researching and analyzing data about what he identified as contributing factors in serial rape crimes. The deeper he delved, the more he learned of the national problematic handling of sex crimes, especially the mishandling of rape-kit evidence. His research eventually led to his becoming a passionate advocate for rape victims and critic of police practices that increase the likelihood that other victims will face the violence his daughter suffered. Fortunately, his advocacy, heard by lawyers similarly committed to such reform, resulted in significant improvements in the handling of rape cases throughout our criminal justice system. His efforts continue today since more reform is needed in the handling of rape victims and their judicial cases.

At the same time, drawing on her experience in social work and university-level teaching, Vicki sought out opportunities to speak at universities, churches, and conferences, gradually developing a reputation as a well-informed and passionate advocate of criminal justice reform on multiple levels. She soon emerged as a major national spokesperson for abolition of the death penalty. Working closely with other murder-victim family members, exonerated death row inmates, and relatives of executed persons, she helped develop a number of advocacy groups committed to abolishing the death penalty and promoting restorative justice, such as Murder Victims' Families for Reconciliation (MVFR) and Murder Victims' Families for Human Rights (MVFHR). She also became active in the Catholic Mobilizing Network (CMN) and other restorative initiatives. This in turn led to her reaching out to governors and state legislature representatives. Called to work on numerous state initiatives to repeal the death penalty, she testified before governing bodies and served on state commissions studying the death penalty in Maryland and Pennsylvania (the two states where Shannon lived). After serving on Maryland's Commission on the Death Penalty, she committed to working exhaustively to repeal Maryland's death penalty. A photograph of her joyful reaction to the 2013 Maryland legislature's repeal vote was shown in media coverage across the world. Her exuberance, captured in a single moment's gesture, manifests hope fulfilled through patient devotion to effecting change rooted in steadfast conviction and commitment. Soon after this victory, she was invited to work on Pennsylvania's Task Force and Advisory Committee on Capital Punishment, whose work continues today. All of us who came to know Vicki were amazed by both her passionate drive for criminal justice reform and the depth of her personal concern for individuals and families grappling with a system in dire need of reform. One sensed, as Vicki reached her seventies, that she was racing against a clock, pushing relentlessly with all her energy and buoyant hopes for the triumph of a Supreme Court ruling finally ending the death penalty and the successful reorientation of our criminal justice system from retribution toward restoration. For Vicki these two goals were inextricably linked—to commit to one is to commit to the other.

As with her husband Syl, the more Vicki learned of the lived experience of victims and offenders in our criminal justice system, the more she felt the urgency of the need for reform. Each personal encounter deepened her resolve. Collaboration with the CMN staff and the faculty of Mount St. Mary's University crystallized her insight that the repeal of the death penalty was one element—the key element—in the broader, deeper, and far more challenging project to shift our criminal justice system toward restorative justice. Vicki agreed with Pope Francis's video message sent to attendees of the 2016 6th World Congress Against the Death Penalty in which he stated that justice "does not mean seeking punishment for its own sake, but ensuring that the basic purpose of all punishment is the rehabilitation of the offender." He stressed, "There is no fitting punishment without hope! Punishment for its own sake, without room for hope, is a form of torture, not of punishment."[4] Our country's willingness to continue executing persons, especially through such a flawed, broken death penalty system, and to sentence so many persons to life sentences

---

[4] Video Message of His Holiness Pope Francis to the 6th World Congress Against the Death Penalty (June 21, 2016), https://w2.vatican.va/content/francesco/en/messages /pont-messages/2016/documents/papa-francesco_20160621_videomessaggio-vi -congresso-contro-pena-di-morte.html.

without the possibility of parole reveals how far we are from restorative principles and practices. Sentences of death and life without the possibility of parole (in contrast with life sentences) have to be seen in the context of our problematic understanding of justice.

Grounded in Catholic teaching on criminal justice, as succinctly stated in the US bishops' *Responsibility, Rehabilitation, and Restoration: A Catholic Perspective on Crime and Criminal Justice*, Vicki's work in recent years focused on two levels. In all of her public speaking and teaching, she encouraged broad awareness of restorative justice initiatives being undertaken across our country. Her message was clear: due to these growing initiatives, we have good reason to hope for reform and positive change. Her speaking incorporated these examples so as to inspire and build increased engagement in such efforts. At the same time, as she learned more and more about the positive effects of such programming in prisons, she began to hope for the possibility of her own participation in a guided restorative justice dialogue with Troy Graves, as he served his sentence in Colorado. Vicki knew all too well the bureaucratic hurdles and personal challenges such an encounter would entail. But she knew that facing them was well worth it. This encounter would be the culmination of all her efforts and the most powerful expression of her fundamental convictions and commitments, tested and sustained through tragic suffering and loss.

So often in our conversations about her hopes, it was evident that Vicki drew strength and delight from Pope Francis's words and actions. "I love that man!" she would often say. Chris Lowney's *Pope Francis: Why He Leads the Way He Leads* describes Francis's leadership in relation to that of Nelson Mandela and Martin Luther King Jr. Lowney references Mandela's description of his own fear in prison: "My greatest enemy was not those who put or kept me in prison. It was myself. I was afraid to be who I am."[5] The challenge for Mandela was to come through his decades-long imprisonment not broken by bitterness and anger, but strengthened by maintaining his deepest convictions. In a similar way Martin Luther King Jr. describes the choice he often had to make in response to the injustices he faced. King explains, "As my sufferings mounted, I soon realized that there were two ways that I could respond to my situation: either to react with bitterness or seek to transform the suffering into a creative force."[6] As

---

[5] Chris Lowney, *Pope Francis: Why He Leads the Way He Leads, Lessons from the First Jesuit Pope* (Chicago: Loyola Press, 2013).

[6] Martin Luther King Jr., *Strength to Love* (1963) (Philadelphia: Fortress Press, 1981), 152; as cited in Lowney, *Pope Francis*, 25.

I read these segments, my thoughts turned to Vicki and Syl Schieber. They faced these same options, and, after choosing, they too gained strength by living their convictions and transforming their suffering into creative forces, bringing good from evil.

Rooted in personal conviction strengthened through suffering, Vicki's commitment to restorative justice never wavered. If anything, her journey just increased the subtlety of her explanations of her commitment, which she knew furthered Shannon's deepest commitments. From a young age Shannon had a passion for social justice. She understood the concern for marginalized and neglected persons that Pope Francis expressed so often. Even as a youth she worked with low-income families needing home repairs through Rebuilding Together in Washington, DC, and years later became a volunteer teacher in Junior Achievement programs in the poorest sections of New York City and Philadelphia. She understood the importance of encouraging young people to commit to working to address the problems of poverty, discrimination, and unemployment evident in the inner-city neighborhoods she served. On the evening of the night she was murdered, her students in the West Philadelphia Catholic High School Junior Achievement program were busy planning a party to thank her for her supportive service. Amidst wide-ranging interests and preoccupations, social justice always held central place for Shannon. It is not surprising that social justice initiatives and prizes continue to be funded in her honor.

In her public speaking, Vicki often expressed her hope to have a murder-victim family member–offender meeting with Troy Graves. On her own initiative, she early on reached out to Troy's mother and brother in hope of understanding what brought this man to commit such acts of violence against women. Describing his horrific childhood with a violently abusive, drug-addicted father, his mother felt she too had lost a child to violence. As a social worker, Vicki already knew the spiraling of harm that results from unaddressed problems and human suffering in early childhood. Coming to understand how his family situation may have contributed to his violent behavior toward women and his difficulty in controlling anger helped her shape her response to him. Vicki refused to reduce Troy to a monster who should be eliminated by execution. Through their frequent recitation of the Lord's Prayer, Vicki and Syl knew that forgiving those who do us harm, even grave harm, is part of Christian living. They also knew how challenging this would be in response to Shannon's murder. Vicki had long reached the peace such forgiveness brings but wanted to express this peace and forgiveness directly to Troy in a face-to-face encounter. As with many other murder-victim family members, she also sought the answers to questions she had about Shannon's final moments and words, which only he could provide. Vicki desired this encounter with all her being, and her hope increased as the Colorado prison system slowly began introducing restorative justice programming.

Prison administrators at the Colorado State Penitentiary were making progress in establishing restorative justice programming at the time when Vicki met the interim executive director of the Colorado Department of Corrections, who very fortunately attended one of her public talks. Asking to privately speak with Vicki after the talk, he explained that he was willing to take steps to assist her in her efforts. He explained that neither he nor the Colorado Department of Corrections could make any promises, but agreed to put her in touch with system officials who would assist her, if they could. Vicki had been corresponding with and visiting a man on Maryland's death row for years, so she was very familiar with how maximum-security prisons operate. She also knew that this request for interaction that might open the possibility for restorative reconciliation with Troy was vastly different from getting permission to visit an inmate. Hope sustained Vicki during this period. Eventually, the prison warden gave permission for Vicki to begin corresponding with Troy, and soon after she started working with a victim advocate for the Colorado prison system to facilitate this exchange. Vicki's joy was obvious. She and Troy exchanged letters, and she secured his waiver of confidentiality so she could talk candidly with his court-appointed attorney. These developments brought her to finally know in detail what actually happened the night of Shannon's assault.

Prosecutors often speak of victims wanting closure. But murder-victim families know that the promised "closure," especially when brought by an execution, is an empty myth. But they do want to know about their loved one's last moments, hoping the restlessness of the unknown will end. In the end, I don't think what drove Vicki toward this restorative dialogue was primarily this desire for information about that tragic night. When I try to imagine her motivations, two paintings focused on transformative gestures come to mind. One is Rembrandt's *The Return of the Prodigal Son* and the other is Caravaggio's *The Calling of St. Matthew*.

When Pope Francis became a bishop and then pope, he chose the motto *Miserando atque eligendo,* which translates, "Having mercy, he called him." His words and Caravaggio's painting refer to the gospel account of Jesus calling the tax collector Matthew to be his apostle. Matthew is a man despised for supporting himself through the detested work of collecting taxes from the poor. Rejection and condemnation are expected in response to him. Being called by Christ to become his disciple is far from expected! Who would ever think a despised tax collector has the potential to become a disciple of Christ? So too Rembrandt's painting focuses on the radically unexpected. After the prodigal son requests and then squanders the inheritance that should be given to him only upon his father's death, the father joyfully welcomes his returning son, wishing only what is good for the son, whose ways caused suffering. The despised Matthew is called, and the squandering son is welcomed! We're baffled by these encounters, captured beautifully in paintings. In his chapter, Fr. Jim Donohue describes the disciples struggling to understand how Jesus could possibly be calling them to forgive the person who harmed them seven times in one day. He unlocks the meaning of the passage when he realizes that making sense of and *living* the Gospel requires an increase of faith. Fr. Jim's chapter ends with the journey of Marietta Jaeger, who prayed for an increase of faith so that she could respond to her daughter's killer in a Christlike way.

It is very hard for many of us to understand Vicki Schieber's desire to meet with her daughter's attacker, let alone to tell him of the peace she attained in forgiving him and the hope she has for his transforming his life into something good. Troy Graves's letters show her open, welcoming response to him is far from what he expected! And his response is what we would hope to hear. He expresses surprise, deep gratitude, remorse for all the suffering he has caused her family, and hope that he will continue to redeem himself by the good he tries to do in prison. Prison personnel had described the vast changes Troy has undergone over his long prison term with the help of counseling. He writes of his mother's deep admiration for Vicki, her gratitude for the conversations with Vicki, and his regret that she died before learning that Vicki sought this dialogue with him. He ends one letter with words from a text that he now associates with Vicki and her writing to him. He quotes a segment from Joseph Campbell's *The Power of Myth* that references Dante's *Divine Comedy* account of the love of God informing the whole universe, even down to the lowest pits of hell. The passage also speaks of the Buddhist Bodhisattva who embodies boundless compassion, the healing principle that makes continued living amidst suffering possible. Even though the Bodhisattvas have attained the peace and release from suffering all creatures desire, they choose to return to help those who still suffer. The two paintings, the gospel accounts they reference, and this Campbell passage all speak of a love and compassion that has no limits or boundaries. I think the three of these capture well what brought Vicki to this encounter.

It is obvious to anyone who knows Vicki what this correspondence meant to her. She is grateful to the prison officials who let it happen. But she viewed it as a step toward what she most desires—a direct personal encounter with this man who caused her journey to begin decades ago. This is seen by her as completing what she calls the "circle of life" following the loss of her beloved daughter.

The Colorado prison system has taken commendable steps to introduce restorative justice programming. Prison officials recognize they are in new territory, far from the common terrain of prison procedures and approaches. They rightly proceed cautiously and carefully. Heartbreaking was the brief letter Vicki received from the deputy executive director of the Colorado Department of Corrections. The letter praised the way in which Vicki had transformed tragedy into a commendable life's work of serving others and the extent to which the correspondence had been positive and rewarding for both of them. But then the director stated that, while Vicki's request for a face-to-face meeting was appreciated, she could not fulfill her request. The letter tersely explains that the Colorado Department of Corrections Restorative Justice/Victim Offender Program is relatively new, and they are in the process of establishing a strong foundation for safely managed and facilitated dialogues. She goes on to explain that "offenders convicted of sexual crimes are a very high-risk population in the arena of restorative justice, and especially in face-to-face dialogues with victims and survivors. We have made the decision to exclude sex offenders from our program based on the fact and the significant possibility of causing further harm to victims and survivors." After explaining this exclusion, she then goes on to add that Troy Graves's "extensive history of violent sexual crimes raises great concern for unintended, negative consequences of a personal meeting." She ends by thanking Vicki for her admirable work.

After reading the letter, I was confused and could understand why it threw Vicki back again into wrestling with unknowns. Was the door permanently closed on sex offenders participating in this restorative justice process? Was this exclusion solely for dialogues with victims/survivors or also with victim family members? Was the decision made solely because of administrative decision about exclusion or because of the particularities of Troy's current situation? Would the decision be revisited if he continues to make progress with counseling? The terse letter leaves the reader with all these unknowns. Perhaps their restorative programming has not advanced to this point yet; perhaps they are not confident that Troy is ready for this now, given the problems he has struggled with since childhood. Perhaps they have concerns about the uncertainty of how this particular encounter will unfold, even with the months of guided preparation by restorative justice facilitators it would entail. Perhaps they paternalistically fear it might cause Vicki more suffering (which is troubling for those who know the depth of her inner strength). The timing and ambiguity of the closing of this door were hard on Vicki. Having supported this book project, she envisioned the book ending with a positive description of the restorative encounter that defined the final segment of her journey.

But in some way, this ending to our book is more fitting. Through community and institutional efforts, our country has introduced restorative programming in our criminal justice system. And restorative justice momentum is building. More and more persons are learning about, supporting, and participating in restorative initiatives. Current support for reform is coming from unexpected sectors of society. We hear calls for reform from persons of very different political viewpoints who rarely can find common ground. We open our national newspapers daily to find stories and discussions of restorative justice. And these evidence that such programming is growing and flourishing across our country. Other societies are way ahead of us as far as such understanding, support, and practice. But for us this is a hopeful story grounded in evidence of increasing support and dynamic growth. But growth requires devoted attention, enduring support, and increased efforts if it is to be sustained and allowed to flourish. So in one way it is fitting that the story of Vicki's journey of hope ends exactly where we are today as a country.

Hope in things not yet seen is such an important moral and theological virtue. For thirteen years, I have been corresponding with and visiting a man who would have been the next death row inmate to be executed, if Maryland had not repealed the death penalty. He often speaks of his journey of transformation, from being a hardened criminal to a devout Christian committed to living a Christian life. Several things utterly amaze me about this man. I am amazed by his maintaining very close relations with his parents, sisters, children (and eventually his grandchildren) over thirty-four years of imprisonment in various parts of the country. I am most amazed by his unwavering hope and resilience, which are so hard to maintain in prisons today. I often wonder how he maintains them as he relates details of daily prison life. He once confided to me that he had prayed only one prayer—that God would let him experience what it feels like to be a good man.[7] I believe his faith in a God who loves him and would answer his prayer is the source of his hope and resilience in extremely trying prison conditions, especially during his thirty-two years on death row. I saw the

---

[7] I asked and obtained permission from him to include these details.

power of such hope as I spent time with him hours from his impending execution, the second time he faced an imminent execution. While I was certain the state would kill him shortly, never for a minute did he give up hope for the granting of a stay. Later, he joyfully explained his reasoning; given the progress he had made toward becoming a good man and all the good work he was doing to end the death penalty, improve our prison system, and be a positive force in others' lives, he *knew* God would never let his progress end prematurely! I joked that I only wished the state of Maryland similarly supported that progress! Hope sustained him and shaped his resilience—and his ability to be joyful!

My sharing in this man's and Vicki Schieber's journeys are among the most rewarding parts of my life so far. Both of them have brought me to believe in the transformative power of hope, sustained by conviction and commitment. Vicki confirms what this man now believes—that no person, including victims and offenders, should be judged as worthless or irredeemable. With good reason, Vicki's hopes are buoyed by the growth of restorative justice programming in our society. We three editors took pleasure in this book's research, which exposed us to so many creative restorative initiatives. It also brought us to envision new possibilities, even for our own campus community. But such growth requires ongoing, contagious commitment to the work of promoting restorative justice in our society and world. And this requires not just researching and reading, but each of us committing to doing the restorative work needed in our neighborhoods, parishes, communities, and states. In one of her books, Sr. Helen Prejean comments that she hopes reading this book will set its readers on fire. This book is written to fan those flames, to encourage you, our readers, to seek out opportunities to promote the understanding and practicing of restorative justice. And to do so with great hope and resilience!

To the utter amazement of so many of us, on her journey Vicki, like Sr. Helen Prejean, has shown indefatigable joy and unwavering hope. She has maintained her resolve through decades in the confidence that, in time, our work to end the death penalty and reorient our criminal justice system toward restorative justice *will* attain its goals. And all of her efforts were done always out of gratitude to her God and love of her daughter. Love and gratitude producing hope and joy! Henri Nouwen wisely warns us that joy and resentment cannot coexist. Vicki's exorbitant joy in response to suffering has taught us so much about the powerful resilience of the human spirit. A line from the popular play *Hamilton* speaks of an individual's legacy. It states that such legacy consists of planting seeds whose products *you will never get to see*. Vicki, in her endless hope and optimism, would tweak the wording to *"may* never get to see." Ever confident that these goals will be reached, she remains hopeful she *will* see them *for herself* in her lifetime. This hope is what keeps her going every day. Through Vicki, I've learned the power of hope—this thing that sings, and never stops. Dorothy Day wisely cautions those who work for justice not to give up hope when facing its demands and challenges. Her words and her life of witness help keep us going:

> We can to a certain extent change the world; we can work for the oasis, the little cell of joy and peace in a harried world. We can throw our pebble in the pond and be confident that its ever widening circle will reach around the world.[8]

> People say, What good can one person do? What is the sense of our small effort? They cannot see that we must lay one brick at a time, take one step at a time; we can be responsible only for the one action of the present moment. But we can beg for an increase of love in our hearts that will vitalize and transform all our individual actions, and know that God will take them and multiply them.[9]

And drawing on her words and witness as we end this book, we encourage you, our readers, sustained by hope, to seek out, step by step, opportunities to practice restorative justice, so that we may be "speaking [of it] with our whole lives," as Pope Francis advises. We wish you well on your own journeys!

---

[8] Dorothy Day, "Love Is the Measure," *The Catholic Worker* (June 1946), 2, http://www.catholicworker.org/dorothyday/articles/425.pdf.

[9] Day, *Loaves and Fishes* (New York: Harper & Row, 1963), 169.